What Wall Street
DOESN'T WANT
YOU TO KNOW

ALSO BY LARRY E. SWEDROE

*The Only Guide to a Winning
Investment Strategy You'll Ever Need*

What Wall Street DOESN'T WANT YOU TO KNOW

♦

How You Can Build Real Wealth
Investing in Index Funds

♦

LARRY E. SWEDROE

TᐧT

TRUMAN TALLEY BOOKS
ST. MARTIN'S PRESS
NEW YORK

www.stmartins.com

Library of Congress Cataloging-in-Publication Data

Swedroe, Larry E.
    What Wall Street doesn't want you to know / Larry E. Swedroe.
        p.   cm.
    ISBN 0-312-27260-X
    1. Index mutual funds.   2. Mutual funds.   I. Title.

HG45306.S896   2001
332.63'27—dc21   00-046699

First Edition: January 2001

10   9   8   7   6   5   4   3   2   1

*This book is dedicated to the most beautiful person I know, my wife, Mona
—walking through life with her has truly been a gracious experience
—and my daughters, the three Js: Jodi, Jennifer, and Jacquelyn—
no father could be more proud.*

It seems to me what is called for is an exquisite balance between two conflicting needs: the most skeptical scrutiny of all hypotheses that are served up to us and at the same time a great openness to new ideas. If you are only skeptical, then no new ideas may get through to you. You never learn anything new. You become a crotchety old person convinced that nonsense is ruling the world. (There is, of course, much data to support you.)

On the other hand, if you are open to the point of gullibility and have not an ounce of skeptical sense in you, then you cannot distinguish useful ideas from the worthless ones. If all ideas have equal validity, then you are lost, because then, it seems to me, no ideas have any validity at all.

—Carl Sagan, "The Burden of Skepticism,"
Pasadena lecture, 1987

Contents

Chapter 1
Past Performance of Fund Managers Is Not
a Predictor of Future Performance

Chapter 2
Markets Are Efficient and Active Managers Are Highly Unlikely to Add Value

Chapter 3
Increasingly Investors Are Shifting to Passive Management

Chapter 4
Neither Fund Managers nor Individuals
Can Consistently Identify Mispriced Securities

Chapter 5
Timing the Market
Is a Loser's Game

Chapter 6
Exposure to Risk Factors
Determines Investment Returns

Chapter 7
Investors Should Focus on the Long, Not the Short Term

Chapter 8
Active Management Imposes a Large Negative Impact on After-Tax Returns

Chapter 9
Understanding and Controlling Human Behavior Is an Important Determinant of Investment Performance

Chapter 10
Play the Winner's Game and Invest the Way "Really Smart Money" Invests Today

Contents

What Wall Street
DOESN'T WANT
YOU TO KNOW

Introduction

I am a principal of both the St. Louis–based investment advisory firm Buckingham Asset Management (Buckingham) and BAM Advisor Services (BAM), a provider of turnkey asset management services to financial advisory firms. Through Buckingham we provide investment advice to individuals, qualified retirement plans, and charitable endowments. Through BAM we provide administrative services, marketing materials, and investment advice and research on capital markets to other professional advisors throughout the United States. As director of research, I contribute to our firm's newsletter, the *Educated Investor*. One purpose of this newsletter is to expose the fairy tales, lies, myths, and legends created by the propaganda machines of Wall Street—what Jane Bryant Quinn calls investment pornography. In other words, the newsletter seeks to enlighten the reader as to *what Wall Street doesn't want investors to know.* John F. Kennedy stated it well: *"The great enemy of truth is very often not the lie—deliberate, contrived, and dishonest—but the myth—persistent, persuasive, and unrealistic."* An equally important function is to familiarize our readers with the Nobel Prize–winning investment strategy known as Modern Portfolio Theory (MPT). The fundamental tenets of MPT can be summed up as follows:

- Current market prices reflect the total knowledge and expectations of all investors, and no investor can consistently know more than the market does collectively.
- New information is incorporated into prices so *efficiently* (quickly) that prices instantly adjust to new data. This is why the Efficient Markets Theory (EMT) is an integral part of MPT.
- The competition among investment professionals is intense, making it very difficult to obtain a competitive advantage.
- If an investor gains a competitive advantage by discovering a market anomaly, competition will rapidly copy the strategy, thereby eliminating the anomaly.
- Risk and return are related, and riskier assets must therefore provide higher *expected* returns as compensation for the extra risk. Those higher returns are, of course, not guaranteed, or there would not be any risk. However, the longer the investment horizon, the more likely it is that the expected will occur.
- Portfolios can be constructed that are expected to deliver the greatest expected return for any given level of expected risk.
- Active management, the art of picking stocks and timing the market, is a *loser's* game because of the hurdle of the costs of research, trading, and taxes.
- Passive management is the *winners'* game, since that strategy is most likely to achieve the desired results.

This book is divided into 10 chapters. The first 9 cover *what Wall Street doesn't want investors to know*. In these chapters you will learn:

- Why past performance of active managers should not be used to predict future performance.
- How over the long term, the efficiency of the market, combined with the costs of research, trading, and taxes, creates virtually an insurmountable hurdle for active managers.
- Why certain asset classes provide higher *expected* returns (as compensation for greater risk) and how you can put this knowledge to work.
- Equity markets are far riskier than thought by the average investor, and, therefore, a very long investment horizon and the discipline to stay the course are key ingredients of the winner's game.
- Why institutional investors have been rapidly adopting MPT and passive asset class investing, and why individual investors are joining the bandwagon.
- How investment performance can be impacted by the emotional side of investing.

The last chapter provides the very specific knowledge and tools you need to implement the winning, prudent strategy. On the basis of feedback from readers of my first book, I have greatly expanded this section. You will learn, for example:

- How individuals can develop an individually tailored Investment Policy Statement that reflects their unique ability to accept risk (investment horizon), willingness to accept risk (risk tolerance), and need to take risk (financial goals).
- How investors can build a globally diverse portfolio of pas-

sive asset class funds that provides them the greatest likelihood of achieving their goals with the least amount of risk.

- How to determine the size of the investment portfolio you will need to retire, and how much you can withdraw each year for living expenses while having a high degree of confidence that you will not outlive your assets.

Each chapter concludes with a brief list of investment insights—or lessons to be remembered—to which you can easily refer. While each of the chapters and component sections can stand alone, I hope that taken as a body of work they will convince you that:

- Wall Street does not have the best interests of investors at heart.
- Wall Street wants to keep individual investors in the dark about both the academic evidence on how markets really work and the dismal track record of the vast majority of active managers.
- MPT best explains how markets really work.
- By applying the principles of MPT, investors are most likely to achieve their financial objectives, higher *expected* returns at lower costs, and greater tax efficiency.

It is important to understand that MPT deals with decision making involving outcomes that cannot be predicted—it deals with risk. Investing is not a science that provides us with certainty. The theory allows us to deal with the real world by constructing a model of how to address the uncertainties (risks) we face. My goal is to demonstrate that MPT does the best job of explaining how markets really work, and thus provides the understanding necessary to make wise investment choices. The end result will be that you will have the specific knowledge needed to build a portfolio that meets your unique situation.

As Thomas Paine said, "I offer nothing more than simple facts, plain arguments and common sense." No secrets or magic formulas are revealed. Investing is about risk and reward, and choosing the strategy that is *most likely* (not guaranteed) to deliver the *expected* (not assured) results over time. If I had any knowledge of how to create certain outcomes with high returns, I certainly wouldn't be writing about it. Instead, I would be exploiting it. My goal is to put the odds of success greatly in your favor.

To assist with the process, the summary at the end of the book contains 7 easy steps to follow. They cover both what to do prior to beginning your journey and what procedures to follow along the way. The 7 steps are followed by one of my favorite tales. The tale and the analogy together summarize what the book is all about, playing the winner's game in both investing and, more important, in life.

Hopefully, having read the book, you will have become a more knowledgeable and disciplined investor. If I have succeeded, you will change forever both the way you think about how markets work and the way you make investment decisions. I hope that you enjoy reading the book as much as I enjoyed writing it. Exposing fairy tales, lies, myths, and legends is a lot of fun.

The following section is meant as an introduction to the book and to provide you with insight into why I thought it important to write it.

Whose Interests Do They Have at Heart?

An out-of-town visitor was being shown the wonders of the New York financial district. When the party arrived at the Battery, one of his guides indicated some handsome ships riding at anchor. He said, "Look, those are the bankers' and brokers' yachts." The naïve customer asked: "Where are the customers' yachts?"
—Fred Schwed, Jr., "Where Are the Customers' Yachts?"

For decades individual investors have been trying to beat the market by either actively managing their own portfolios or investing in actively managed mutual funds. The vast majority has done so with about the same disappointing results that the Chicago Cubs have had in making it to the World Series. Active managers who fail to outperform their benchmarks because "it wasn't a stock picker's kind of year" have adopted the rallying cry of Cub fans: "Wait till next year." The problem for both the Cub fans and active managers is that "next year" has rarely delivered their hearts' desire.

Mark Carhart conducted the most comprehensive study ever done on the mutual fund industry. He found that once you account for style factors (small-cap vs. large-cap and value vs. growth) the average actively managed fund underperformed its benchmark by almost 2% per annum. Since he found no persistency of performance, Carhart concluded that when it comes to the performance of active managers, past is not prologue.[1] Carhart's study would have revealed even worse performance figures if the tax effect of the turnover of active managers was taken into account. The increased trading activity of active managers generally leads to increased fund distributions on which taxes must be paid.

One well-known Wall Street advisor, Robert Stovall, appearing on ABC News' *20/20* on November 27, 1992, was asked about Wall Street's underperformance. He responded: "It's just not true that you can't beat the market. Every year about one-third of the fund managers do it." He then quickly added, "Of course, each year it is a different group." Amazing! How is the average investor to know which group of fund managers will succeed? Five years later Mr. Stovall provided the following interesting quotation: "One thing the market has given us is some humility. Many of the old rules no longer apply."[2] Unfortunately, there is no evidence that his "old rules" ever applied.

The poor performance of active managers has not gone unnoticed by institutional investors. It is now estimated that about 40% of all institutional funds are invested using either index or passively managed asset class funds. On the other hand, individual investors have dedicated only a small fraction of their investments to a passive strategy. Why?

Despite the superior returns generated by passively managed funds, financial publications are dominated by forecasts from so-called gurus and the latest hot fund managers. I believe that there is a simple explanation for the *mis*information: it's just not in the interests of the Wall Street establishment or the financial press to inform investors of the failure of active managers. First, it is clearly in the interests of Wall Street to charge you 1.5% for an underperforming actively managed fund rather than 0.25% to 0.5% for a passively managed fund with superior performance. Also, unfortunately, it is not in the interests of the trade magazines that tout "The Best 10 Funds" to inform investors of what is in their best interests. The following two quotations are good examples. The first is from the August 1995 edition of *Money* magazine. "Bogle [of the Vanguard group of funds, the largest provider of retail index funds] wins: Index funds should be the core of most portfolios today." The headline

7

for the cover story read: "The New Way to Make Money in Funds." The second is from the February 1996 edition of *Worth* magazine. "The index fund is a truly awesome invention. A cheap S&P 500 or a Wilshire 5000 Index fund ought to constitute at least half of your portfolio." The irony in these two statements is that neither magazine will give passive management a wholehearted endorsement. If passively managed funds (i.e., index funds) are so good, why shouldn't they be the only ones an investor should use? These magazines withhold such wholehearted endorsement because if the magazine's readers believed in passive management, who would buy magazines touting which stocks and mutual funds to buy? Remember that the primary objective of most financial publications is not to make their readers wealthy, but is instead to get readers to buy more of what they are selling—their magazines. In addition, these magazines carry a large amount of advertising from actively managed mutual funds. The publishers do not want to risk losing valuable advertising revenue.

As John Merrill, author of *Outperforming the Market*, points out, investors need to be aware of the bias of the financial press. They must remember that the job of the media is to maintain and increase readership. They do so by getting listeners and readers "hooked" on the daily drug of financial information. In order to be successful the media must have investors believe that all the daily information has value and isn't really just noise. Contrast headlines such as "Sell Stocks Now" with their own advice that the road to success lies in a buy-and-hold strategy!

Merton Miller, a Nobel laureate, in an interview with *Barron's*, was asked what advice he would give the average investor. His response: "Don't quote me on this, but I'd say don't read *Barron's*." He continued, "because it will only tease you about investment opportunities that you'd best avoid."[3]

Jean Baptiste Colbert, finance minister to Louis XIV, described the act of generating revenue in this colorful way: "The art of taxation consists in so plucking the goose as to obtain the largest possible amount of feathers with the least possible amount of hissing." The same can be said of active managers—they want to keep plucking those large management fees from the pockets of individual investors with the least possible amount of hissing. In order to continue doing so, they must keep alive the myth that active management works. Frank Knight, a professor of economics at the University of Chicago from 1928 until his death in 1972 at the age of 87, said it best when he claimed that economic theory was not at all obscure or complicated, but that most people had a vested interest in refusing to recognize what was "insultingly obvious."[4] As Charles Ellis, author of *Winning the Losers Game*, points out, "Investment advice doesn't have to be complicated to be good. [For example,] there is no better advice on how to live longer than to quit smoking and buckle up when driving."

Perhaps most revealing about the question of whether Wall Street firms have your interests at heart is the following quotation: "It has been a problem since the dawn of the retail brokerage business. Brokers have a strong incentive to get customers to trade when it might be in clients' interests to do nothing."[5]

I believe that the financial press has an obligation to inform investors of the poor performance of active managers. They should also make far greater efforts to present the public with the results of the ongoing academic research on financial markets. For example, I am sure that most investors do not know that in 1990 the Nobel Prize in economics was awarded to three economists for their contributions to MPT. Building on their work, financial economists have demonstrated that efforts to beat the market are not only nonproductive but counterproductive because of the expenses and taxes that are generated. The only winners in the game of active management are the Wall Street firms that generate commissions, the publications that offer "expert" advice, and Uncle Sam, who collects more taxes.

If the media did a better job of presenting the public with the facts about investing, investors would get much better investment returns—mainly because Wall Street and Uncle Sam would be taking a smaller cut out of their investment pie. On the other hand, if they had been doing their job well, there would have been no need for me to write this book.

CHAPTER 1

◆

Past Performance of Fund Managers Is Not a Predictor of Future Performance

Even if you identify the managers who have good past performance, there's no guarantee that they'll have good future performance.
>   —George Sauter, Vanguard Group,
>   *Wall Street Journal*, June 17, 1997

Yesterday's masters of the universe are today's cosmic dust.
>   —Alan Abelson and Rhonda Brammer,
>   *Barron's*, October 5, 1998

In investment performance, the past is not prologue.
>   —Charles Ellis, *Winning the Loser's Game*

The biggest investment mistake people make is focusing on last year's mutual fund performance and not on what really drives returns.
>   —Barbara Raasch, partner at Ernst and Young,
>   *Business Week*, February 22, 1999

I do not believe that they (investment advisors) can identify, in advance, *the top-performing managers—no one can!— and I'd avoid those who claim they can do so.*
>   —John Bogle, *Common Sense on Mutual Funds*

11

One of the most popularly held beliefs is that past performance is a predictor of future performance. For example, when a business seeks to hire a new CEO it will look at candidates who have been successful at similar positions. When a baseball team looks to add a cleanup hitter to its lineup, it will try to trade for, or sign as a free agent, someone who has previously performed well in that role. In both cases the rationale is that the person being sought has clearly demonstrated the skills necessary to do the job. While there is no certainty of success, the rationale is sound.

Using the same logic, investors choose active mutual fund managers based on past success. Financial trade publications know that in order to create a best-selling magazine all they have to do is place on the cover a lead like "The Ten Hot Funds to Include in Your Portfolio." Unfortunately for investors, the logic used to hire the next CEO or to find the next cleanup batter doesn't apply to identifying the active managers that will outperform the market in the future. For example, you would think that if anyone could beat the market, it would be the pension funds of the largest U.S. companies. They have access to the best and brightest portfolio managers, all of whom are clamoring to manage the billions of dollars in these plans. Presumably, these pension funds rely on the excellent track records of the "experts" they eventually choose to manage their portfolios.

Piscataqua Research, in a study covering the period 1987 through 1996, found that only 10 (7%) out of 145 major pension funds outperformed a portfolio consisting of a simple 60%/40%

mix of the S&P 500 Index and the Lehman Bond Index, respectively. A 60% equity/40% fixed income allocation was used, since that is estimated to be the average allocation of all pension plans. The Piscataqua Research study provides evidence against not only the strategy of choosing managers based on past performance, but also the use of active managers in general.

In 1998, fewer than 20% of all equity funds outperformed the S&P 500 Index. That figure drops to 11% over the previous 10 years and to just 4% over the previous 15 years. And, as *Fortune* magazine put it: "Despite the solemn import that fund companies attribute to past performance, there is no evidence that the 4% who beat the index over the 15-year period owe their record to anything other than random statistical variation." (Given the number of players in the "game," the number that do succeed is far less than would be randomly expected.) "The whole industry is built up around a certain degree of black magic." *Fortune* concluded: "Despite volumes of research attesting to the meaninglessness of past returns, most investors (and personal finance magazines) seek tomorrow's winners among yesterday's. Forget it. . . . The truth is, much as you wish you could know which funds will be hot, you can't—and neither can the legions of advisers and publications that claim they can."[1] Despite being the very same magazine that glorifies the latest hot fund manager, they added: "We have learned that past investment records make lousy crystal balls."[2]

As H.L. Mencken said: "The most costly of follies is to believe in the palpably not true."

Investors simply have no way of identifying ahead of time the few active managers that ultimately turn out to outperform the market over the long term. Jonathan Clements, columnist for the *Wall Street Journal*, stated: "I believe the search for top-performing stock funds is an intellectually discredited exercise that will come to be viewed as one of the great financial follies of the late 20th century."[3] One example of this is a study that found that over two consecutive decades a remarkable 99% of top quartile funds moved closer to, or even below, the market mean from the first decade to the second. In fact, there was only one exception—the Fidelity Magellan fund. Its performance since then is evidence of the folly of believing that past performance of an actively managed fund is a useful predictor of future performance. "Make no mistake about it, the record is clear that top performing funds inevitably lose their edge."[4]

Even Smith Barney, which heavily advertises its funds that have received five-star ratings on the basis of past performance, had this to say: "One of the most common investor mistakes is choosing an investment management firm or mutual fund based on recent top performance." This was the conclusion they drew from their own study covering 72 equity managers with at least 10-year track records. The managers studied covered the full spectrum of investment styles: large-cap to small-cap, value to growth, and domestic to international. In fact, the study found: "The investment returns of top quintile managers tended to plunge precipitously while the returns of bottom quintile managers tended to rise dramatically."[5]

Perhaps most revealing is what John Rekenthaler, research director of Morningstar, had to say when asked how to pick a winning equity mutual fund: "We should have more answers." He also added that there is "surprisingly little" that we can say for sure about how to find top-notch stock funds.[6] More recently Rekenthaler stated that actively managed funds are beginning to show up on his cultural radar as a *marketing scam for buy~~~* *ers.*"[7] This chapter documents the results of investment strategies that rely on past performance to choose actively managed funds. After reading this chapter I hope that you will never again want to read an article with a title like "The Ten Best Funds."

Investors Rely on False Premises When Choosing Mutual Funds

Periodically investors go through the ritual of evaluating their mutual fund holdings. The usual process results in selling the poor performers and purchasing shares of the latest hot funds. Let's examine the methodology and results of the various approaches based on this "buy winners strategy."

Perhaps the most popular approach is to rely on fund ratings by such services as Morningstar, which rates funds using a star system similar to the one used by film critics. Evidence of the popularity of this approach is that it is estimated that over 80% of inflows into mutual funds go to four- and five-star rated funds. Unfortunately for investors, this approach has consistently produced below-benchmark returns for both bond and equity funds. For example, a Financial Research study covering the period January 1, 1995 through September 30, 1998, revealed that two- and three-star funds outperformed their four- and five-star counterparts for the entire period. The study's conclusion: "the linkage between past performance and future realizations is tenuous if not nonexistent."[8] A similar study, by Christopher R. Blake, associate professor of finance at Fordham University's Graduate School of Business, and Matthew Morey, assistant professor of finance at Fordham, found that for the five-year period ending December 31, 1997, five-star funds underperformed the market by almost 4% per annum. The study also found that the differences between the performances of the three-, four-, and five-star funds are so small as to have very little statistical significance.[9] Morningstar even stated that there is no connection between past and future performance and stars, historic star ratings, or any raw data and that the stars should not be used to predict short-term returns or to time fund purchases.[10] Here is an interesting observation. Expenses play such an important role in determining returns that investors could have done a better job of predicting performance than did Morningstar's star system simply by ranking funds by their respective expense ratios. Morningstar itself conducted a survey of management fees and their effect on mutual fund returns. They found that mutual funds that charge the lowest fees also generate the highest returns over time. "The simple fact is costs take a bite from investor returns so the higher costs lower returns," said Russell Kinnel, head of equity research at Morningstar.[11]

Investors should ask themselves the following question: If Morningstar, with all of its resources, can't identify with any degree of success the future winners, is there any rational reason to believe that I can?

Another popular approach is to rely on the recommendations of trade publications such as *Forbes*. Unfortunately, this approach produces the same poor results as does following the star system. For example, a 1991 Yanni Bilkey Investment Company study of the *Forbes* "Hall of Fame" list of mutual funds, which recommends the funds individuals should buy, found that for the seven five-year periods beginning in 1980, only once, and by the smallest of margins, did the group beat the S&P 500 Index. However, they never once beat the average equity fund. Another study on this famous list covered the period 1985 through 1999 and found that a portfolio of the Hall of Fame funds would have returned 10.46%, versus 16.43% for the S&P 500 Index.[12] Following the recommendations of other popular financial magazines produced similar results. Here is another interesting point. If past performance had predictive value, then the "buy" lists of publications would contain the same names year after year. If the same funds don't repeat, how valuable is the list?

Another often-used approach is to buy the funds that have produced the best returns during the recent past. In his book *A Random Walk down Wall Street*, Burton G. Malkiel reported that he did extensive testing on whether an investor, by choosing the "hot" funds, could outperform the market. The results showed the ineffectiveness of a strategy that chose the top 10, 20, 30, or more funds on the basis of the performance of the previous 12 months and then one year later switched to the new top performers. Since 1980 this strategy produced results that were not only below the average mutual fund but also below that of the S&P 500 Index. Similar results were found when Malkiel tried ranking funds by their past 2-, 5-, and 10-year track records. Even more compelling evidence of the risk of buying yesterday's winners comes from Mark Carhart. Carhart, now cohead of quantitative research at Goldman Sachs Asset Management, studied the performance of mutual funds all the way back to 1962. He came to the amazing conclusion that the top 10% of performers in any one year are more likely to fall to the bottom 10% than repeat in the top 10%. In other words, investing in last year's top performers is a crap shoot.[13]

Investors also fall prey to what is known as the gambler's fallacy, the idea that winners ride "hot streaks." Of course, there is no factual basis for that idea, either in gambling or investing. As further proof that selecting mutual funds that have previously beat the market is a loser's game, witness the effort of Mark Hulbert, publisher of the *Hulbert Financial Digest*, a newsletter that tracks the performance of investment newsletters. He constructed a portfolio of "market beaters" by choosing managers who had outperformed the market in the preceding year. That portfolio earned a 99% return over the next 15 years. Not a bad return, except for the fact that a portfolio of "market losers," those funds that lagged the market in the previous year, returned 350% over the same period. In contrast to these seemingly impressive returns, the stock market as a whole rose about 600% over the same period.[14]

While the press ignores the poor and inconsistent performance of active managers, it has not gone unnoticed by large institutional investors. Philip Halpern, the chief investment officer of the Washington State Investment Board (a very large institutional investor), along with two of his coworkers, wrote an article on their investment experiences. They wrote the article because their experience with active management was less than satisfactory and they knew, through their attendance at professional associations, that many of their colleagues shared and verified their own experience. They quoted a Goldman Sachs publication: "Few managers consistently outperform the S&P 500. Thus, in the eyes of the plan sponsor, its plan is paying an excessive amount of the upside to the manager while still bearing substantial risk that its investments will achieve sub-par returns." The article concluded: "Slowly, over time, many large pension funds have shared our experience and have moved toward indexing more domestic equity assets."[15]

Meir Statman advised that investors would do well to heed the advice of noted economist Paul Samuelson. While having kind words for a few active investment managers such as Warren Buffett and John Templeton, Samuelson drew the following conclusion. "Ten thousand money managers all look equally good or bad. Each expects to do 3% better than the mob. Each has put together a convincing story. After the fact, hardly 10 out of 10,000 perform in a way that convinces an experienced student of inductive evidence that a long-term edge over indexing is likely. . . . It may be the better part of wisdom to forsake searching for needles that are so small in haystacks that are so very large."[16]

If after all the evidence just presented, you still believe that you can select the future winning mutual funds based on past performance, I suggest that you ask yourself the following question. "What different process to select these future winners will I be using from that of others who have tried to do the same thing, relying on the same paradigm—of whom all failed?" If you can't identify any differentiation, then what logic is there in believing you will succeed where so many others have failed?

Top-Performing Actively Managed Funds and Encores

While it may be a good way to predict which batters are the most likely to hit .300 in a given year, unfortunately, past performance is a very poor indicator of the future when it comes to mutual funds and their managers. A study done by NationsBank, using Lipper Analytical Services data, provided further powerful evidence that investors relying on past performance as a predictor of future performance are playing a loser's game.

NationsBank examined the performance of mutual funds in the three asset class groups of growth, growth and income, and small company, for 10 one-year periods beginning in 1986. They calculated the percentage of funds that were ranked in the top 25% that repeated in the following year. Keep in mind that we would randomly expect 25% of the previous winners to repeat.

If it were a winner's game, a majority would do so. For Lipper's growth category the highest percentage of repeat performers was just 12%, and the average number of repeaters was just 8.4%. For the growth and income category the figures were just 10.5% and 7.2%. For the small company category the figures were just 17% and 8.4%. With just an average of 8% of all top performers repeating the following year, how is an investor to know which of the previous winners will repeat?

A study published in the April 200 issue of the *Journal of Finance* shed further interesting light on the issue of encore performances. Have you ever seen an ad for a mutual fund that advertises its poor track record? Of course not. The ads are a form of selection bias—you only see ads for the winners, never the poor performers. Why do funds advertise their winning records? The presumption is that investors will extrapolate past success into the future—despite the warning/disclaimer that the SEC requires, that past performance is not an indicator of future performance.

Prem C. Jain of Tulane University, and Joanna Shuang Wu of the University of Rochester, examined the performance of 294 U.S. equity mutual funds that advertised in *Barron's* or *Money* magazine. They measured the performance of the mutual funds one year prior to the first advertisement date, and one year after. The authors looked at fund objectives when considering returns. They placed funds into the categories of aggressive growth, growth, growth and income, small, and other. Given the bias that funds would not advertise poor performance, not unexpectedly the advertised funds performed well above average prior to the advertisement date. The average one-year pre-advertised return of the 294 funds was almost 6% higher than the return of comparable funds during the period from July 18,

1994, to June 30, 1996. The returns of the advertised funds were also 1.8% above the return of the S&P 500.

In the post-advertisement period, however, the same funds returned 0.8% below the return of all comparable funds. The funds also underperformed the S&P 500 by almost 8% per annum. Not surprisingly, the study also found that advertised funds attracted significantly greater investments than similar funds in the post-advertisement period, despite the forward-looking results basically being a random event.

The study considered the possibility that the poor post-advertising performance might have been caused by manager turnover. During the period 246 funds had no manager turnover. The study found that there was no difference in performance between the funds that experienced turnover and the funds that did not. The authors concluded that there was no persistency in fund performance and that past performance cannot be attributed to the skills of the fund managers.

It is important to understand that it is true that given the vast numbers of funds trying, there will probably always be some that will outperform the market. However, it is also true that no formula has ever been found to identify these great managers before the fact—especially since, as we have seen, past performance cannot be relied on as an indicator of future performance. Good performance may be as likely to be the result of luck as skill.

University of Wisconsin finance professor Werner De Bondt estimated that more than 10% of equity mutual funds are likely to beat the average performance of the average equity fund 3 years in a row, *just as a matter of chance*.[17] This is very important knowledge for investors to understand. It means that even a strong performance over several years is likely to be the result of random luck. While I am sure that most investors wouldn't bet their retirement savings on luck, the record indicates that since most investors rely on past performance to choose mutual funds, that is exactly what they are doing.

Relying on past performance to choose funds has proven to be a losing strategy. The winning strategy is a simple one, available to every investor: buy a passively managed fund, such as an index fund, that represents the asset class in which you wish to invest. That is the only way in which you can reliably receive market rates of return.

Beware of Deceptive Performance Claims

Investors are constantly bombarded by direct mail promotions from investment newsletters. These promotions are almost always accompanied by claims of superior performance. While providing entertaining reading material, the claims are often misleading.

Investors need to remember that, with so many newsletters making market forecasts, randomly we would expect that a few would be likely to outperform the market over any short period. Unfortunately, the longer the time frame, the fewer the number that outperform. Of course, the marketing promotions only tell you about the performance over the brief period when they were successful in beating their benchmarks. The perfect example of short-term performance being misleading is the *Granville Market Letter*. Providing a return of 89.4% in 1997, it was the top performer of all the investment newsletters tracked by Mark Hulbert. In 1989, it was also a star performer, returning an amazing 367.9%. According to Hulbert, however, the 15-year return for the *Granville Market Letter* was a 24.6% annualized loss.[18] An impressive feat, indeed, during the greatest bull market in history.

There is a lesson to be learned: the next time you read a promotion for a newsletter that claims great performance, you know that the odds are great that the performance was produced over a very short term and it is highly likely to prove unsustainable over the long term.

Long-Term Funds Will Do Best over Time, or Will They?

Clint Willis is a freelance reporter for Reuters News Service whose columns are often filled with recommendations on which mutual funds to buy. In the articles I've read by Mr. Willis, he virtually always recommends individual stocks and/or actively managed funds. He reports on studies showing performance records of the "best" funds. Investors are then generally advised to buy the funds with the best track records. The October 5, 1998, edition of the *St. Louis Post-Dispatch* carried a typical "Willis" story. He reports on a Value Line study that identified growth funds that placed in the top 20% of their category over the preceding one-, 5-, and 10-year periods. He then suggests that investors buy the funds that were able to achieve this feat. The implication is that the superior performance of these "best" funds can be relied on in the future.

Investors who read the article carefully can easily determine the fallacy of Mr. Willis's conclusion. There are two major problems with Mr. Willis's logic. First, if past performance of actively managed funds were a predictor of future performance, then we would see the top performers repeating their appearance on the best buy lists. Mr. Willis himself points out that only a single fund repeated its appearance from the same top 20% of a 1-, 5-, and 10-year periods study that Value Line performed in 1991. Obviously, the 1991 list of top performers had no value as a predictor.

The second problem for Mr. Willis is that, as he himself points out, only 16 funds were able to achieve the top 20% target for all 3 periods. With 1,300 funds in the study, we know that there are 260 top 20% one-year performers. If past performance were a predictor of future performance, then most of the 260 would repeat in the top 20%. On the other hand, if past performance had no predictive value, we would randomly expect 20%, or 52, of them to repeat as top 20% 5-year performers. Finally, we would expect 20% of those 52, or 11, to repeat as top 10-year performers. The fact that the Value Line study produced only 16 of the 1,300 passing the screening process is pretty good evidence that their success was random. More important, how was an investor to know in advance which of the 16 out of 1,300 would succeed? Could you have looked at the one-year performance? Obviously not, as only 16 of the 250, or about 6%, succeeded. If we assume that about 52 made both the one-year and 5-year cuts, then waiting 5 years would still have left you with only about a 30% chance of picking a winner.

Despite the tremendous body of evidence suggesting that the odds of success are very low, much of the financial press continues to extol the virtues of active management. For example, using Morningstar data, for the past 3-, 5-, and 10-year periods ending May 2000, large-cap index funds beat *at least* 70% of actively managed domestic large-cap funds. On a tax-adjusted basis, however, the outperformance increased to *at least* 88%. While it is true that there will in all likelihood always be some actively managed funds that beat their benchmarks, it is important for investors to know that since past performance is not a good predictor of future performance, there doesn't seem to be a way to identify ahead of time the future winners.

Out of Focus

An often-heard excuse for the failure of active managers to outperform their benchmarks is that the typical fund is over-diversified. By owning so many stocks the value of the manager's best ideas are diluted. The solution (or sales pitch) is to create "focus" funds: funds that own just the manager's top 10 or 20 best ideas. There are even funds that hire several sub-managers for just their single best pick.

The June 1998 issue of *Money* provided at least some evidence that the overdiversification excuse doesn't hold water. *Money*, with assistance from Chicago consulting firm Performance Analytics, reviewed the performance of 22 private account managers whose performance placed them in the top 20% of their peer group. Each firm provided their *single* best idea. For the period beginning in May 1996 and ending in mid-June 1998, the average return of the 22 best picks was 53.5%, or a negative value added of 13.2% when compared to the return of 66.7% for the Wilshire 5000.

Perhaps of equal interest is that none of the managers from the original survey were included in the new contest beginning in June 1998. This contest is further evidence of the lack of value of "best stocks" or "best funds" to buy lists. It is also further evidence that relying on past performance of active managers is a loser's game.[19]

Buffettology or Mythology?

I think it safe to say that if individual investors were asked to name the one money manager they would want to manage their assets, the overwhelming majority would choose Warren Buffett. Buffett clearly has earned his reputation by delivering superior returns over a very long time frame. Whenever I discuss the superior performance of passive investing over active management, the question that I am most asked is: "If that is true, how do you account for Warren Buffett (and/or Peter Lynch)?" In fact, I happened to be asked that question during a phone call on the morning of March 1, 2000. In responding, I try to be very careful because even questioning the possibility that Buffett was lucky is almost sacrilegious. The following is a summary of my usual response.

- First: it is certainly possible, if not likely, that given the length of his superior performance, Buffett is fully deserving of his guru status.
- Second: we only know that Warren Buffett "won" after the fact. If skill is truly involved, with so many thousands of active managers trying to win, how come far fewer won than would be randomly expected? In mathematical terms, the following analogy is appropriate. If there were as many monkeys playing the game as there were active managers trying to outperform, how come we end up with more monkeys winning than active managers winning? In other words, the distribution of the performance of active managers falls to the left of what a random (bell curve) distribution looks like. Yes, some monkeys win, and some active managers win. But how do we know ahead of time which will be the winners? Just as important, how do we know

that the past performance of the winning active managers is a predictor of future performance? Certainly, we can agree that the monkeys' past performance would have no value as a predictor. In the case of active managers, all the evidence suggests that past performance is also a very poor predictor. Even Morningstar admits that their 4- and 5-star funds underperform, *after* they are designated as superior performers. So how do we know for sure if Buffett was lucky or a true guru? As you will see, it may be harder to tell than you thought, and you will have to decide for yourself.

• Third: another possible explanation for Buffett's superior performance may come from the fact that he is not like other money managers. Typically, Buffett does not just buy stock in a company and take a passive position. His more usual involvement is as an active investor. He often takes an influential management role, including a seat on the board of directors, in a company in which he invests. It is certainly possible that it is Buffett's superior business skills that account for the superior performance of his investment portfolio. The recognition of his superior business management skills may also account for why Berkshire Hathaway's stock (the vehicle investors have for investing the Buffett way) has often traded at a large premium to the underlying net asset value (NAV) of its portfolio. This would not be the case if Berkshire Hathaway were an open-ended mutual fund that would always trade at its NAV. Investors must believe that Buffett's influence in the company will enhance their performance and investment returns.

At the end of this explanation I typically offer my own conclusion, which is that I am somewhat of an agnostic on the issue.

Clearly you cannot ignore his superior track record. However, my own inclination is that the answer probably is some combination of all three possibilities. It is very hard to prove the guru or luck story. Mathematics might suggest luck, but logic might provide another answer. And I have learned you are not likely to ever convince people who have already come to a conclusion that they should change their mind. The best you can hope to do is to get them to consider another possibility.

After concluding my March 1 phone call, I remembered that whenever someone presents something as "generally accepted wisdom," it pays to check the facts, or, as I like to say: "go to the videotape." Out of pure curiosity I decided to check the performance of Berkshire Hathaway's stock. I made the random decision to check its performance from the beginning of the 1990s right through the previous night's close, February 29, 2000. That seemed to me to be a reasonable time frame for a couple of reasons. First, as I stated, you only "know" an active manager is great after he or she has delivered superior performance for some reasonable length of time. So we need to have some length of time to observe Berkshire's performance before choosing Buffett as our standard-bearer. Second, I think that most people would consider that a decade is a sufficiently long time to consider (although I might suggest that the longer the better). Finally, the vast majority of money that is invested in the market today has come in since 1990. The result is that very few investment dollars benefited from any experience prior to 1990. (This is not to suggest in any way that returns prior to that should be ignored.)

Given the "generally accepted wisdom," I fully expected that I would find that the performance of Berkshire's stock would have far outperformed the S&P 500 Index (a good benchmark, as most of Buffett's investments have been large-cap stocks).

Remember that we have chosen with *hindsight* not just a great investor but possibly the single greatest investor. The decade of the 1990s began with Berkshire's stock at 8,675. It closed on February 29, 2000, at 44,000, an incredible gain of 407%. The compound growth rate was 17.3%. To my surprise, however, while that performance did allow the Buffett "faithful" to out-perform the S&P 500 Index, it was just by 0.2% per annum. Certainly, 17.3% per annum returns were great, and he did beat the Index, although not by much. Again, this slight outperform-ance comes from the one manager who we know only with hindsight is considered by most to have been the single greatest investor. Most investors that placed their faith in other gurus fared far worse.

I tried some other time frames, admittedly performing a bit of intentional "data mining" (intentionally choosing specific data points to "prove" your point) in one case. It is important to note, however, that some investors in all likelihood actually experi-enced the returns shown in the following examples. We can certainly imagine the following scenario occurring. An individ-ual investor comes into a large sum of money in June 1998 (through an inheritance, sale of a company, exercise of stock options, etc.). Lured by the sirens of superior performance, the investor decides to choose the active management approach. One logical candidate is Berkshire Hathaway, which has gone from 8,675 at the beginning of the decade to hit its all-time high of 80,900 (June 19, 1998). An investor unlikely (and unlucky) enough to invest on that particular date would have seen the value of his or her portfolio fall 46% between then and February 29, 2000. During the same period, the S&P 500 ran up from 1101 to 1366, an increase of 24%, not counting dividends. That would have been a very painful experience, possibly testing the individual's faith in Buffett's guru status. Some might begin to wonder if he had lost his "touch" or even question now was it luck in the first place. If you decided that you don't want to invest with Buffett any longer, now what paradigm do you follow? Do you try again to find that great guru based on past performance, having just seen that "fail" miserably? Or do you switch to passive investing? If you decide to stay with Buffett and he continues to underperform, when do you know it is time to "throw in the towel"? What will your criteria be for making that decision? You can see the dilemma. Again, I admit, I created a carefully chosen example, but one probably experienced by some investors.

I went back for a somewhat longer and less biased look, again covering a period that was probably experienced by many investors. If you look at the four-year period from 1996 through 1999, Berkshire rose from 32,100 to 56,100. Every dollar invested grew by about 75%. The only problem was that every dollar invested in the S&P 500 Index grew by about 155%. Again, I want to make clear that neither this example, nor the other two, prove the Buffettology or Mythology case. It does, however, at least in my mind, open the issue to questioning. Only time can provide the answer. Even then we may very well be left to speculate.

Unfortunately for investors, we don't live in a world where we get to see the results *before* we have to decide on the strategy. We must choose before we know the outcome. Investors choosing the passive side have the following in their favor.

- They will earn the market rate of return, less costs. However, they do give up the hope of outperformance.
- They know that very few active managers will beat their passive benchmarks in any given year. And the longer the investment horizon, the smaller that number gets.

- Historical data strongly supports the view that past performance is a very poor predictor of the future performance of active managers. This is true even of Warren Buffett if we consider just the recent past.

Investors choosing the active side have the following in their favor.

- Based on the historical evidence, they gain the small hope of outperformance. However, they accept the much greater likelihood of underperformance.

When you look at both sides of the ledger, you can understand why Charles D. Ellis, a highly respected author of numerous investment books, called passive management the winner's game and active management the loser's game. It's not that passive management is guaranteed to prove to be the winning strategy; it's just that it puts the odds greatly in your favor. Conversely, active management is not guaranteed to prove to be a losing strategy; it's just that the odds are stacked against you. Each investor has to make that choice for him- or herself.

One final point. Many investors have chosen as the winning investment strategy the building and holding of a globally diversified portfolio of passive asset class funds. For the past two years they have clearly been disappointed in their returns, especially when compared to the spectacular results of the S&P 500 and the NASDAQ indices. Particularly disappointing have been the returns of the asset classes of U.S. large value and U.S. small value. The lesson from the "Buffett experience" is that choosing active managers, even perhaps the greatest one of all time, is no guarantee of better results. Just as there will always be some periods when the S&P 500 will outperform all other asset classes, there will almost certainly be periods when it will be an underperformer. That, however, is what diversification is all about. Unless you can predict which asset class will do well when (and Buffett's recent experience may shed some light on the ability to do so), diversification is the winner's game, just as is passive management.

Investment Insights

- When it comes to the performance of active managers, past is unfortunately not prologue.
- While a relatively small number of active managers will generally outperform the market over short time frames, that number decreases as the investment horizon increases.
- Even choosing managers with long records of superior performance is a losing strategy.
- When examining claims of outperformance, make sure an apples-to-apples comparison is being made (e.g., comparing growth stocks to a growth stock benchmark).
- If past performance had predictive value, then the buy lists of publications would contain the same names year after year.
- Chasing yesterday's winning funds is a losing strategy.
- Choosing "focus" or concentrated funds is also a losing strategy.
- The fact that Peter Lynch and Warren Buffett beat the market isn't evidence that markets are inefficient. Turn the question around: How come with so many managers trying to beat the market far fewer succeed than would be randomly expected? Even choosing the greatest managers of all time is no guarantee of future outperformance.

- If you read a promotion for a newsletter that claims great performance, remember that the odds are great that the performance was produced over a very short term and is unsustainable over the long term.
- If institutions such as Morningstar and major pension plans, with all of their time and resources, are unable to identify future winners, is there a logical reason to believe that you are endowed with such skills?

CHAPTER 2

♦

Markets Are Efficient and Active Managers Are Highly Unlikely to Add Value

Index funds should outperform most other stock-market investors. After all, investors, as a group, can do no better than the market, because collectively we are the market. Most investors, in fact, are destined to trail the market because we are burdened by investment costs such as brokerage commissions and fund expenses.

—Jonathan Clements,
Wall Street Journal, June 17, 1997

Even in Japan, academic researchers and consulting firms have provided consistent evidence that the majority of actively managed funds fail to earn as good a rate of return as the index fund.

—Mamoru Aoyama, professor of finance,
Yokohama University,
Journal of Portfolio Management, fall, 1994

Experience is a dear teacher.

—Benjamin Franklin

When you are looking at companies like Microsoft, IBM, Merck and Coca-Cola, the ability to capture incremental insight is so damn challenging because so many people are looking at those stocks and it takes so long to get through the body of knowledge.

—Binkley Shorts, Wellington Management,
Wall Street Journal, July 14, 1997

The foundation of MPT is that markets are efficient. Believers in efficient markets argue that current market prices reflect the total knowledge and expectations of all investors and that no one investor can know more than the market does collectively. If this is true, active management becomes a losing strategy. For the EMT to hold true, one condition must be met: any new information must be disseminated to the public rapidly and completely so that prices instantly adjust to new data. If this is the case, an investor can consistently beat the market only with either the best of luck or with inside information (on which it is illegal to trade). Practitioners of active management, on the other hand, must believe that they have some insights into security prices that the market does not *yet* possess. Hopefully, after reading this chapter you will find compelling evidence that active managers rely on a false premise.

This chapter also addresses other myths created by Wall Street and the financial press regarding market efficiency. You will learn how the Wall Street press puts "spin" on data to create the illusion that markets are inefficient and that active management works. As Benjamin Disraeli said: "There are lies, damned lies, and statistics."

Just How Efficient Are the Markets?

Probably the most controversial and most debated hypothesis in financial economics is the EMT. In its simplest form, EMT states that markets are efficient when prices fully incorporate all available information. Given this condition, price changes are not forecastable. Any new information will be random (hence the term "random walk") as to whether it will be better or worse than the market expects. Believers in efficient markets argue that markets are made efficient by the participation of many active investors, each of them attempting to gain a sustainable competitive advantage. The competition among all the highly skilled competitors makes it very difficult to gain such an advantage.

The following analogy is insightful when thinking about the efficiency of markets. Imagine an art auction where you are the only expert among a group of amateurs. In that circumstance, it might be possible to find a bargain. On the other hand, if you are one of a group of mostly experts it is far less likely that you will find bargain prices. The same is true of stocks. The competition among all the professional active managers insures that the market price is highly likely to be the correct price.

In addition to the high level of competition making it difficult to gain an advantage, the speed with which today's markets incorporate new information is so great that the market quickly eliminates any profit opportunities. Does the existence of an efficient market make it impossible to gain a competitive advantage and be able to temporarily outperform the markets? That is not a likely proposition. However, it does mean that any competitive advantage is likely to be very short-lived. In other words, "an occasional free lunch is permitted, but free lunch plans are ruled out."[1] Let's explain.

The revolution in computer technology has made possible the testing of various strategies on the basis of computation-intensive research that would not have been possible until recently. Given the computing and intellectual power being applied to the task (given the size of the potential rewards), it is not logical to believe that strategies could never be uncovered that could exploit market inefficiencies. For example, intensive research analysis may reveal anomalies between security prices that can be exploited. There is also a whole new field, behavioral finance, which is attempting to understand how human behavior may lead to investment opportunities. One example is that behavioral economists believe that investors may only gradually incorporate earnings surprises—causing a momentum effect in stock prices. The result would be that a stock with a positive (negative) surprise would tend to continue to rise (fall) in price as the market gradually incorporates the good (bad) news, and vice versa. This knowledge, if correct, could lead to profitable trading strategies.

It is important for investors to understand that while the rewards for uncovering "anomalies" are great, it is also true that the anomalies are not likely to last very long. First, the barriers to entry are very low in the financial arena. Second, large profits will quickly attract competition that will "reverse engineer" the process to understand how the excess profits were derived. Thus it is likely that competition will quickly restore the market's efficiency and eliminate the "anomaly." Joseph Schumpeter called this process creative destruction. A great example is the recent demise of Long Term Capital Management. The firm was built upon solid academic research that discovered anomalies between certain securities prices. These anomalies could be exploited to gain profits far in excess of what appeared to be the risks involved. The company generated tremendous profits in its early years. Those profits attracted lots of competition, and the profit opportunities began to shrink. In order for the firm to continue to generate the same types of returns, large amounts of leverage were now required. Now risk and reward were related—the anomaly having disappeared or at least greatly diminished in size. The firm ultimately lost billions of dollars as the risk side of the equation overtook the reward side.

The reward for uncovering an "anomaly" is the economic profits that can be reaped. In the capital markets arena, opportunities for great rewards attract great amounts of competition. Economics professors Dwight Lee and James Verbrugge of the University of Georgia explain the power of the EMT in the following manner.

> The EMT is practically alone among theories in that it becomes more powerful when people discover serious inconsistencies between it and the real world. If a clear efficient market anomaly is discovered, the behavior (or lack of behavior) that gives rise to it will tend to be eliminated by competition among investors for higher returns. . . . [For example] if stock prices are found to follow predictable seasonable patterns . . . this knowledge will elicit responses that have the effect of eliminating the very patterns that they were designed to exploit. . . . The implication is striking. The more the empirical flaws that are discovered in the EMT, the more robust the theory becomes. [In effect] those who do the most to ensure that the EMT remains fundamental to our understanding of financial economics are not its intellectual defenders, but those mounting the most serious empirical assault against it.[2]

Understanding how efficiently markets incorporate new strategies designed to exploit anomalies is an important part of determining the winning investment strategy. If a fund manager has outperformed an appropriate benchmark, investors need to determine if that performance has any predictive value as to future performance. In order to make such a determination, we need to understand the source of the outperformance. There really are four possibilities: first, the performance was random luck; second, the performance was due to stock selection and market timing skills; third, the manager gained a competitive advantage by uncovering an anomaly; finally, the manager took greater risk—and was appropriately rewarded.

As to the first two possibilities, the academic evidence is overwhelming that past performance is a very poor predictor of future performance and that managers show very little if any skill in stock selection or market timing. Over the long term, far fewer managers outperform their benchmarks than would be randomly expected. And those that do manage to outperform rarely repeat. The reasons are:

- Gaining a competitive advantage over fierce competition is very difficult.
- Any competitive advantage is likely to be quickly copied and therefore reduced and eventually eliminated.
- While the markets are very efficient, they need not be perfectly efficient for a passive strategy to be the winning one. The reason is that while it is possible for active managers to gain an information advantage, there is no evidence that they can gain enough of an advantage to consistently beat the market, after accounting for research and trading costs.

Turning to the ability to exploit a discovered anomaly, Charles Albers, who uses quantitative techniques to screen his stock selections for Oppenheimer's Main Street Growth and Income Fund, points out two examples of "creative destruction." Monitoring the buys and sells of insider trading worked well until the mid-1980s. "Then, everybody was looking at it, and the information was worthless." Albers later discovered that companies that were doing secondary share offerings started to do poorly shortly after the offering. He incorporated that information into his screening process. Shortly thereafter academics started publishing research on the phenomenon and it became less effective. Excess profits breed competition, rapidly eliminating the excess profits.[3]

The fourth possibility is that the manager took on extra risk for which he or she was compensated with higher returns. One way to increase risk and expected returns is to borrow money and use the funds to buy stocks (this is called using leverage). Another way to increase returns is to buy riskier stocks.

The conclusion for investors is that if you uncover an investment manager with superior investment performance, you should carefully examine the source of that outperformance. Was it random luck, or perhaps the taking of extra risk? Another explanation may be that a real competitive advantage may have been gained by uncovering a strategy that others have not yet discovered. If it is the latter, how long is that advantage likely to last? By the time the manager has demonstrated, through superior performance over time, that a competitive advantage has been gained, the odds are probably very good that any advantage won't last very much longer.

The Impact of News Events on Market Prices

Two of the basic tenets of the EMT are:

1. Current market prices reflect the total knowledge and expectations of all investors.
2. Any new information must be disseminated to the public rapidly and completely so that prices instantly adjust to new data.

A study by Robert Butman, president of TQA Investors LLC, a New York hedge fund, looked at how thousands of stocks reacted to both positive and negative earnings surprises for the period 1995 through 1998. He then compared his results to those from a similar study for the period 1983 through 1989. Butman found that for both periods, in relation to the market, stocks fell about 8% on negative news and rose a similar amount on positive news. However, while that 8% move occurred over a 3-to-4-week period during the 1980s, it now takes only 2 days. There are several reasons for the more rapid response. The most obvious reason is improved technology. Mr. Butman's conclusion: "The impact of news events is being absorbed by the market almost instantaneously."[4]

Other studies confirm Butman's conclusions. A study on how quickly the fixed income markets incorporate new information found that a considerable portion of the changes in interest rates can be attributed to scheduled macroeconomic announcements such as employment reports and inflation data. The major adjustment to the information release (and the window for trading profits) lasts about *40 seconds*.[5] The speed of the stock market's response to new information is almost as startling. A recent study on the after-trading-hours quarterly earnings announcements of 100 NYSE and 100 NASDAQ firms found that the majority of the price response is realized during the *opening trade*. Earnings announcements that occurred during trading hours caused adjustments to occur very quickly; for NYSE stocks the price adjustment occurred during the first several post-announcement trades; for NASDAQ stocks the price adjustment was concentrated in the first postannouncement trade.[6] One can only conclude that the U.S. markets are very efficient at processing information and incorporating that information into valuations.

Another study looked at the efficiency of the U.K. markets. The study examined the impact of 9 major economic announcements (such as inflation data, retail sales, etc.) on stocks of the FTSE 100 (Financial Times Stock Exchange 100, a U.K. equivalent of the S&P 500). The study also examined the impact on fixed income instruments. The authors concluded that the U.K. equities markets took 75 to 90 seconds, or about 7 trades, to adjust to the new data. The fixed income markets took about the same amount of time.[7] It seems like the U.K. markets are just about as efficient as the U.S. markets.

Investors should draw this conclusion: since current market prices already incorporate all that is knowable, the next piece of news is random in terms of whether it is better or worse than the market expects. Since the market adjusts almost instantly to that news, active managers are highly unlikely to be able to add value through research and trading activities. This makes passive management the winning strategy.

Market Efficiency and the Value of Forecasts

Gary Brinson is one of the copublishers of the now famous study "Determinants of Portfolio Performance" (*Financial Analysts Journal*, July–August, 1986), which demonstrated that approximately 94% of a portfolio's return is a function of asset class selection and that market timing and stock selection accounts for about 2% and 4% of returns, respectively. In an interview in the July 1997 *Morningstar Investor*, Mr. Brinson commented on the ability of active managers to add value in the international arena by correctly forecasting country growth rates: "No study has ever found any correlation between economic growth and stock-market returns. . . . What matters are the expectations embedded in security prices. The future returns from securities are then a function of whether those economies—whether they be high growth, low growth, or declining growth—deliver results that are either consistent or inconsistent with those expectations. But growth rates, in and of themselves, are uncorrelated with stock-market returns."

Brinson's comments support the theory that markets move in a random manner. In other words, it is not whether the next piece of news is good or bad in an absolute sense for an individual stock, a stock market, or an economy in general. Instead what matters is whether or not the news is better or worse than the market expected. Few, if any, economic forecasters have proven the ability to provide forecasts that are consistently more accurate than the market expects. Therefore, active management of portfolios based on such forecasts is highly unlikely to add value beyond the costs of producing those forecasts and the costs of acting on them. The conclusions for investors are:

- Markets, both domestic and international, are efficient at incorporating economic forecasts into current evaluations.
- The strategy that is most likely to produce the highest expected return is a passive investment strategy.

Paul Samuelson, one of our most respected economists, concluded: "A respect for evidence compels me to the hypothesis that most portfolio managers should go out of business. Even if this advice to drop dead is good advice, it obviously will be not be eagerly followed. Few people will commit suicide without a push."[8]

Are Active Managers Likely to Add Value?

There are two hypotheses as to the winning investment strategy. The Wall Street wisdom is that active managers, through superior skills at stock selection and market timing, can add value by outperforming their appropriate benchmark, be it a large-cap, a small-cap, or a value index. The other hypothesis is that the competition between all of these very bright active managers and the costs incurred in their efforts makes it difficult to add value. In other words, the markets are efficient, and efforts to outperform the market over the long term are highly unlikely to succeed. Today's leading financial economists fall clearly in the camp of efficient markets theorists.

Professors Eugene F. Fama and Kenneth R. French have built a 3-factor model that they believe supports the EMT. At an October 1997 conference held at the University of Chicago, Fama presented a study covering 31 major pension plans representing $70 billion of total assets under management. The time period for each pension plan studied varied depending on data availability but ranged from as few as 6 years to as many as 12. Individual plan assets were benchmarked against the Fama-French 3-factor model. The 3-factors are the portfolio's degree of exposure to the risk factors of equities, size, and value. If active managers were able to add value, when the 3-factor model was applied to the portfolios of the pension plans, active managers would have what are called positive "alphas," or returns above those predicted by the model. In addition, the model would have poor predictive ability, as demonstrated by a low coefficient of correlation between the predicted returns and the actual returns of the active managers. On the other hand, if the economists were right, then the "alphas" (value added) would be zero or negative. In addition, if the 3-factor model's predictive value is high, then the coefficient of correlation between the returns predicted by the model and the actual returns of the pension plans would be very high.

The results of the study strongly support the view that active managers have a very difficult time outperforming their appropriate benchmark. First, the alpha, or value added beyond what the model predicted, before expenses, was only 0.02% per month. I think it is relatively safe to say that after expenses the alpha was zero or negative.

This news is doubly disheartening for individual investors. First, these returns are all pretax. Unfortunately, the turnover of actively managed funds results in realized gains on which current income taxes must be paid. Therefore, the "alphas" of active managers would be negatively impacted. While not 100% tax efficient, passively managed funds have lower turnover rates and therefore deliver higher after-tax returns, when pretax returns are similar. Second, the average expense ratio for actively managed funds is now about 1.5% per annum. When you subtract the 1.5% expense ratio from the returns actually received beyond what the model (the equivalent of a passive strategy) predicted, you clearly get substantial negative performance even before taxes are considered.

Finally, like the proverbial nail in the coffin, the coefficient of correlation between the returns predicted by the model and the actual returns was 97.2%. The combination of the zero alpha and the high coefficient of correlation is very strong support for the EMT and passive asset class investing as the winning investment strategy.

Value Line Advice Beats Market! Or Does It?

The Value Line Investment Survey has an incredible track record. Value Line touts its market-beating track record in advertisements hawking their services. Even Fischer Black, one of the fathers of the EMT, once stated that Value Line's results were a big exception. Black concluded: "almost all Wall Street firms would improve performance if they fired all but one of their security analysts, and then provided the remaining analyst with the Value Line Service."[9] Mark Hulbert, publisher of the *Hulbert Financial Digest*, found that the Value Line survey has been one of the very few that have beaten the market since he began monitoring the performance of investment letters in the mid-1980s.[10]

A logical conclusion would seem to be that if anyone could beat the market using Value Line's advice and strategy, it would be Value Line itself. To test this hypothesis an investor could compare the performance of Value Line's funds with the performance of comparable benchmarks in the form of Dimensional Fund Advisors' (DFA) passively managed asset class funds. The Value Line fund, classified as a large-cap growth fund by Morningstar, returned 17.14% per annum over the 15-year period ending June 30, 1999. Value Line also runs the Value Line Leveraged Growth fund, also a large-cap growth fund. It returned 18.47% per annum for the same period. The DFA Large Company Fund, an S & P 500 Index fund, outperformed both, returning 19.06% per annum. Value Line also runs the Value Line Special Situations Fund, a small-cap growth fund. Its return for the same 15-year period was 12.08% per annum. This compares to the returns of the two DFA small-cap funds of 12.52% per annum (DFA 6–10 fund) and 12.39% per annum (DFA 9–10 fund). The DFA 6–10 fund basically buys all the stocks that are ranked by market capitalization in the bottom half of all stocks (deciles 6–10). The 9–10 fund buys the smallest 20% (deciles 9 and 10). Value Line has a newer fund, the Value Line Small-Cap Growth Fund. Its 5-year performance for the period ending April 30, 1999, was 14.81% per annum. This compares to the returns of 15.81% (6–10 fund) and 15.71% (9–10) for the two DFA funds. In all cases the Value Line funds underperformed their proper benchmarks.

Investors should also consider that these return figures are all pretax. Since the Value Line funds are actively managed and the DFA funds are passively managed, for taxable accounts the underperformance of the Value Line funds would in all likelihood have looked even worse. The greater turnover of actively managed funds results in greater capital gains being realized and greater taxes having to be paid.

What accounts for the underperformance? First, a publication's recommendations carry none of the operating expenses of a mutual fund. Neither do they incur transaction costs in the form of commissions, bid/offer spreads, and market impact costs (a mutual fund buying or selling large blocks of stocks will likely drive the price against itself, increasing the transaction's cost). Another explanation is that the funds might not have exactly followed Value Line's own recommendations. And, of course, publications pay no taxes. It is worth noting that Hulbert estimated that if an investor followed Value Line's stock picks, buying only stocks rated 1 and selling any that were subsequently downgraded to 2 or lower, the investor would have experienced a turnover rate of about 200% per annum.[11] The implication for investors is that they would never have earned the returns implied by the recommendations and advertised by Value Line since the recommendations carry no transactions costs or taxes (200% turnover will generate substantial expenses and taxes).

The conclusion for investors is that it is often a long way from the theoretical results of a strategy to the actual results that can be obtained. Another way to think of this is that the market doesn't have to be efficient for active management to be the losing strategy (and passive to be the winning one). It only has to be relatively efficient. The reason is that active management incurs costs that must be subtracted from the gross returns of a strategy. Think of it this way: if the market consistently misprices securities by 2% (the market is inefficient), but it costs 4% to exploit the mispricing, then efforts to exploit inefficiencies are counterproductive. If one of the very few newsletters to beat the market can't deliver market-beating returns through an implementable strategy, it seems a logical conclusion that passive management is the winning strategy.

Foreign Market Efficiency

On July 1, 1998, at a conference sponsored by DFA, Rex Sinquefield presented a study that addressed the popular claim that foreign stock markets are inefficient and that they are especially inefficient for small-cap stocks. Of course, the corollary to that claim is that active managers can add value to portfolio returns.

To examine this claim, DFA studied the performance of Unit Trusts, the U.K. equivalent of U.S. mutual funds, for the period 1978 through 1996. They compared the performance of the trusts to the results predicted by the 3-factor (Fama-French) model. The 3-factor model is based on MPT: the belief that the vast majority (about 97%) of investment returns are determined by a portfolio's exposure to the 3 risk factors of equity, size (market cap), and value (book-to-market value). If the markets are efficient, then active management (stock selection and market timing) is likely to produce results that are not only nonproductive but counterproductive because of the expenses and taxes incurred in the effort. If the EMT hypothesis holds true, the 3-factor model would predict the performance of Unit Trusts with a high degree of accuracy (show high correlations or r-squareds) and the value added (alphas) of active managers would be zero or negative.

DFA studied the overall performance of the Unit Trusts. They also examined the issue of survivorship bias: the tendency of mutual fund performance to appear to improve with age as poor performers die off and their performance numbers magically disappear. For the time period studied, 249 (34%) Unit Trusts died, leaving 476 remaining at the end of 1996. In addition, DFA examined performance by sector (growth and income, growth, equity income, and smaller companies) and style (size and value). Finally, they examined the question of persistency: Do past winners repeat their performance?

During this time period the FTA Index (equivalent of the S&P 500) had an annual compound return of 18.1%, the HGSC Index (a small company index) produced an annual return of 18.5%, and the U.K. Large Value Index rose at a compound rate of 20.1%. The live Unit Trusts produced a compound growth rate of 17.4%, compared to the 18.1% return for the FTA Index. The correlation with the 3-factor model was over 98%. The alpha (value added) of active managers was a negative 0.05% per month. When the dead funds were added back in, the compound return earned by investors dropped to 16.82%, the alpha fell to a negative 0.09% per month, and the r-squared remained above 98%.

When we look at performance by sector and consider both live and dead funds, we find the following results:

Sector	Monthly Alpha (value added)	R-Squared
Growth and income	−0.07%	.981
Growth	−0.12%	.977
Equity income	−0.07%	.960
Smaller companies	−0.08%	.965

In every case the alphas were negative and the correlations were high. The negative alphas show negative value added by active managers. The high correlations demonstrate that asset class selection, not stock selection and market timing, determines the vast majority of returns.

The study then turned to the question of the alleged inefficiency of the asset class of small-cap stocks. DFA divided the Unit Trusts into size categories, ranking them by decile. What they found was that the Unit Trusts that had the most negative alphas (−0.18% per month or about 2% per annum) were those with the smallest average market cap. These figures demonstrate that active managers are generally unable to exploit any supposed information inefficiency; that is, the trading costs exceeded the possible gains.

The study then examined the question of whether past performance repeats itself. To a very limited degree the answer was yes. DFA studied whether a 3-year performance record was indicative of performance in the next period. What they found was that the worst performers tended to repeat their miserable performance. For example, the bottom decile performers produced monthly alphas of −0.26% (worse than −3% per annum). All but the top 2-decile performers produced negative alphas. The second decile's alpha was just barely above 0 at 0.02% per month. The top decile also produced a positive alpha of 0.07%

per month, or less than 1% per annum. It is worth noting that any ability to profit by switching to the recent winners would be difficult to exploit because of transaction costs (a 4% load is typical for U.K. Unit Trusts) and the taxes incurred by realizing gains in order to make the switch.

Another study covering the U.K. market for the 10-year period ending in 1995 found that only 2 of 79 growth and income mutual funds outperformed the market.[12] As W. Scott Simon points out in his book *Index Mutual Funds*, this means that less than 3% of these funds that employ money managers who take themselves seriously and pay themselves accordingly were able to achieve what they were paid to do. Since these figures did not take into account taxes, it could very well be that none of the managers were able to beat what they claim to be a "no-brainer: match the market on a tax-adjusted basis."

Taken as a body of work, these studies demonstrated that:

- International markets (at least in the U.K.) are just as efficient as U.S. markets.
- Active management is the losing strategy.
- Active management is just as much a losing game in international small-cap stocks as in U.S. small-cap stocks.
- Asset class allocation, not stock selection or market timing, determines the vast majority of returns.

Those Really "Inefficient" Emerging Markets

The inability of active managers in the large-cap asset class to outperform the S&P 500 Index funds, even before taxes, has led many practitioners to concede that active management in the large-cap asset class is a loser's game. The asset class for which the active management argument is made the strongest is the emerging markets. The logic is that this asset class is clearly "inefficient" and there is clearly less competition. Believers in active management have one problem—there isn't any evidence to support their claim. In fact, we now have substantial evidence supporting the opposite position.

The sharp drop in emerging markets equities in 1998 brought down the reputations of many emerging markets fund managers. As Richard Oppel Jr. of the *New York Times* put it: "Another casualty of the [emerging markets] sell-off: the widely held notion that emerging markets are fertile ground for active fund managers." 1998 was certainly a year when active managers had plenty of opportunity to add value, either by moving to cash or by choosing the winners (i.e., South Korea, +110%; Greece, +87%; Thailand, +27%; and Portugal, +26%) and avoiding the losers (i.e., Russia, −87%; Turkey, −51%; Indonesia, −45%; Mexico, −38%; and Brazil, −38%).[13] Let's look at the facts. The 164 actively managed emerging market funds tracked by Morningstar fell 26.9% in 1998, far more than the 18.2% loss by the Vanguard Emerging Markets Stock Index fund, the third largest emerging market fund.[14] That is an underperformance of almost 9%, and that is even before considering taxes on fund distributions. Let's examine the performance of some of the great active managers, the very ones who claim that they add value through stock and country selection and market timing. The following is the performance of the nine other largest emerging markets funds.

SSGA	−15.9%
Templeton	−18.7%
Sanford Bernstein	−21.1%
Lazard Institutional	−23.5%
MSDW Institutional	−25.4%

Fidelity	−26.6%
GMO III	−28.9%
SEI Institutional	−32.0%
Montgomery	−38.3%

Only 1 of the 10 largest funds, and a very small handful of all the emerging markets funds, outperformed an "easy to beat" index fund.[15]

We can also compare the performance of the active managers to the performance of the DFA emerging markets fund. While not an index fund, it is passively managed. This fund uses some common-sense screens to determine which country's securities are eligible for purchase, as follows.

- There exists a commitment to free markets.
- There is reasonable treatment of foreign ownership in terms of taxes and restrictions.
- The stock market is well organized and there is ample trading liquidity.
- There exists a good legal system in terms of property rights and contracts.
- There exists a strong payment and delivery system.

The fund then invested in 11 countries (as of 1999 it had been expanded to 13), each equally weighted to reduce country risk. For the year 1998, the passively managed DFA emerging markets fund was down only 9.4%, outperforming every single one of the leading active managers. This underperformance occurred during a period (a bear market) when active managers both begin with an advantage (holding more cash reserves) and claim that they can add the most value by anticipating the market's decline. If the active managers can't add value in the really inefficient emerging markets during a bear market, when and in what asset class can they be expected to do so?

To show that 1998's poor performance by active managers was not a fluke, using the Morningstar database I examined the performance of all emerging markets funds for the 5-year period 1995 through 1999. The Morningstar database provides us with a list of 43 emerging market funds with a 5-year track record (when multiple classes of the same fund were available, only the A class was considered). Even excluding survivorship bias (poor performing funds, and their poor results, being made to disappear by their sponsors or their investors), the DFA fund outperformed the vast majority of surviving funds on both a pretax and after-tax basis. The other fund classes (like B,C, etc.) generally have higher expenses and would negatively impact the returns of the actively managed funds. On a pretax basis, the DFA fund ranked ninth out of 43 funds, outperforming all but 19% of the active managers. On an after-tax basis DFA ranked seventh, outperforming all but 16% of active managers. Keep in mind that this poor performance is in the very asset class in which active managers claim it is easiest to win. It is worth pointing out that the DFA fund was over 93% tax efficient, losing less than 7% of its returns (about 0.5%) to taxes.

When I extended the period 1 more year, to cover the full 6-year life of the DFA emerging markets fund, here is what I found. There were just 17 actively managed funds in the Morningstar database that had survived the entire period. Only 2 beat the DFA fund, and the greatest pretax outperformance was just 0.08% per annum. On the other hand, the worst underperformance (Fidelity's fund) was by over 6% per annum.

For believers in active management this data strikes a double blow. First, the poor performance refutes their hypothesis on market inefficiency. The second blow is a strike at those believing that past performance of active managers is a predictor of future performance. Both of the legendary Templeton Emerging Market funds underperformed the DFA fund for both the 5- and 6-year periods. Other well-known underachievers included Van Kampen, Warburg Pincus, Lexington, Merrill Lynch, UAM, Paine Webber, Govett, J. P. Morgan, and Fidelity. In fact, Fidelity's performance ranked them dead last for both periods, underperforming the DFA fund for the 5-year period by about 12% per annum. I guess that explains why the television commercials in which Peter Lynch appears touting Fidelity's actively managed funds never mention their emerging markets fund, or their many other underperforming funds, for that matter.

Further evidence of the failure of active managers to exploit the "inefficient" emerging markets comes from a study by Micropal, a London-based research firm. The study looked at Global, Asian, and Latin American emerging market funds. The study covered the 3-year period ending June 30, 1996, and compared the performance of the actively managed funds to the Barings Index for those sectors. In not one case did the active managers come close to matching the performance of their benchmark indices.

Micropal Emerging Market Indices	Number of Funds	3-Year Sector Average Total Return	Barings Index
Global	95	+24.68%	+39.70%
Asia	169	+34.41%	+58.35%
Latin America	53	+22.21%	+31.71%

Source: Micropal

Even this poor performance is overshadowed by the fact that for the first half of the 1990s not a single actively managed fund outperformed the MSCI Emerging Markets Index.[16] The only conclusions one can draw from the data are:

1. The emerging markets are not as inefficient as the active managers claim.
2. The costs of operating an emerging market fund and the costs of trading in the less liquid markets of these countries are together so great that once costs, including taxes, are considered, active managers are unlikely to add value. According to Joshua Feuerman, manager of the State Street Global Advisors Emerging Markets, a round-trip purchase and sale of a block of stock in a typical emerging market costs about 4.5% of the value of the stock. "It's a disgustingly expensive asset class to trade in."[17] Because turnover is much greater in actively managed funds, trading costs hit them harder than passively managed funds. Maybe it is just a coincidence, but Feuerman's estimate of the cost of trading at about 4.5% is about equal to the percentage by which actively managed funds underperformed the passively managed DFA fund over the 5-year period.
3. Passive management is most likely to prove to be the winning strategy.

With the clear evidence in favor of passive management in the most efficient markets (U.S. large-cap stocks) and also in the least efficient market (emerging markets), it seems that active managers have very little left to try and hang their hats on.

Prophets and False Profits

Academic theory and the Wall Street establishment (including the financial media) are clearly at odds over the issue of the value of security analysis and stock selection. The active managers of Wall Street and the mutual fund industry must believe that they can add value or they would be committing economic suicide. Academics have no such biases. They study the historical evidence and report their findings.

Unfortunately for believers in active management, virtually all of the data has supported passive investing as the winning strategy. But wait! A recent study appeared, at least on first glance, to support the view that Wall Street's stock analysts are worth listening to. Let's examine the results of the study: *Can Investors Profit from the Prophets? Security Analysts Recommendations and Stock returns.*[18]

Covering the period 1986–1996, the study looked at over 360,000 analyst recommendations, from 269 brokerage firms, as reported by Zachs Investment Research. Recommendations were rated from 1 (strong buy) to 5 (strong sell). Among the strategies analyzed was one of buying the most favorably rated (highest average score) stocks and rebalancing the portfolio on a daily basis, as analysts ratings changed. Trades were based on the assumption of end-of-day prices (quick/same day investor reaction).

To the delight of the active management faithful, the analysts' best picks outperformed a value-weighted benchmark by 4.3% p.a. (18.8% p.a. to 14.5% p.a.). They also outperformed a portfolio controlled for risk (exposure to the size, value and momentum factors) by 4.13% p.a. Also worth noting was that the least favorite stocks (strong sells) provided returns of just 5.78% per annum.

At this point, however, we have only half the story. While providing positive alphas (above benchmark returns) may demonstrate that there are market inefficiencies, it is not sufficient to demonstrate that either relying on the stock selection skills of stock analysts is a winning strategy or that the market is inefficient. In order to make this point, the strategy must demonstrate positive net (after all costs) returns. The first return figures we looked at were gross, not net returns. Once trading costs were considered we saw a totally different picture—one that is perfectly in line with academic (the Efficient Markets) theory. The following summarizes the study's major findings:

- The strategy required a great deal of turnover—over 450% per annum. Thus trading costs were very high.
- For the few hundred largest market cap stocks there was no reliable difference in returns between the most highly rated and the least highly rated selections. This is consistent with the great amount of competition focused on analyzing the stocks of the largest companies. The intense level of competition makes it very difficult to gain a competitive information advantage. Thus while trading costs may be low in the largest cap stocks (the average bid/offer spread for the stocks in the first decile when ranked by market cap is only 0.65%),[19] it is very hard to gain any information advantage that can be exploited (despite the low trading costs).
- The large positive *gross* alphas were found in the smallest cap stocks. This too is consistent with academic theory. Since the smaller cap stocks attract fewer analysts, the lower level of competition may allow for anomalies (mispricings) to be discovered. Unfortunately, it is in these very small-cap stocks that the trading costs incurred in attempting to exploit inefficiencies are the greatest (the bid/offer

spread in the smallest cap stocks of tenth decile is 4.27%).[20] Keep in mind that the bid/offer spread is a good estimate of the cost of a *single* round-trip trade (buy and sell), and that annual turnover was in excess of 450%.

- The above estimates of trading costs are consistent with the estimate of trading costs from a study of institutional investors. The study estimated that trading costs were 0.73% for the largest cap stocks (70% of the sample), 1.94% for the medium cap stocks (20% of the sample), and 4.12% for the smallest cap stocks (10% of the sample).[21] Using these estimates of trading costs, combined with the 458% required turnover, results in an estimate of trading costs for the strategy of 6%, far more than the gross positive returns. Once trading costs were considered, the positive alphas turned negative.

- If in an attempt to reduce costs, turnover was reduced from daily to biweekly or monthly, the 4% positive alphas fell to just 2 and 1%, respectively. This was even before considering trading costs. Once trading costs were included, active trading strategies actually produced negative alphas.

- Breakeven for the strategy of buying the analyst's best picks would have required transactions costs of well below 0.5%, a highly unlikely proposition.

What conclusion should investors draw? While it may be possible for security analysts to uncover market inefficiencies, those inefficiencies are not likely to prove exploitable after expenses. This is exactly what the EMT states—information should he rewarded to the extent of the cost of obtaining it, but no more. Also keep in mind that this study did not consider the tax implications of generating all the ordinary income and other realized capital gains (from the high turnover) that are minimized by a passive strategy. Once again, the evidence clearly supports the view that a passive strategy is most likely to be the winning one.

The Value of Security Analysis

The basic premise of active management is that through diligence and hard work, security analysts can discover stocks that are mispriced by an inefficient market. In May 1999, at a conference of financial economists at UCLA's Anderson School of Business, Bradford Cornell presented a very interesting example that provides insights into the value of such efforts.

Mr. Cornell had assisted on a project at Intel. The company had accumulated $10 billion of cash and was trying to determine if it made sense to use the cash to repurchase stock. At the time of the project the stock was trading at about $120 per share. It would seem a reasonable assumption to make that Mr. Cornell and his team had access to far more information than any securities analyst would ever have. Yet even with detailed nonpublic information of projected cash flows, the best careful analysis could produce was a very wide range of reasonable valuations. The team concluded that Intel's stock was worth somewhere between $82 and $204 per share. If the stock was really worth just $82, Intel should have immediately issued more shares to take advantage of the market's overvaluation. On the other hand, if the stock was worth $204, the company should have immediately embarked on an aggressive repurchase plan.

If corporate insiders, with access to far more information than any security analyst is likely to possess, have such great difficulty in determining a "correct" valuation, it is easy to understand why the results of conventional stock-picking methods (active management) are so poor and inconsistent.

The "Benefit" of Inside Information

If any group of investors could beat the market, it would seem that corporate insiders (senior officers with access to nonpublic information), investing in their own stocks, would be the most likely to succeed. They certainly have the "benefit" of insider information. In fact, one of the most popular investment strategies is to track insider trades and then follow their lead. Corporate insiders are senior corporate officers with access to information that is not yet public. When insiders are buying, investors take this as a sign that the company's senior officers believe that the stock is undervalued and are acting on the belief that they have information that may not yet be accurately reflected in the company's stock price. Therefore, when insiders are buying their own stock, it is taken as a buying signal.

The April 1998 issue of the *Journal of Finance* provided some very interesting insights into the advisability of following insider trades. It also provided further evidence on the efficiency of markets. To test the value of insider information, the authors of the study examined the performance of insider trading on the Oslo Stock Exchange for the period 1985 through 1992. They chose this market because it was "a stock market with a reputation of being an insider's market." The specific period was chosen because it was a "period of lax enforcement of insider trading rules."

The study's conclusion: there was no evidence of abnormally high insider returns. In fact, the returns were zero or negative as compared to the market. And this excluded transaction costs and taxes. One conclusion is that possibly the market is more efficient than corporate insiders think. In other words, investors really knew what the insiders thought they didn't, and that knowledge was already reflected in the current stock price.

The authors also examined the performance of the 7 largest mutual funds on the Oslo Exchange. The study concluded that while the mutual funds managed to outperform the corporate insiders, there was little systematic evidence that the returns of the average mutual fund exceeded that of the market itself.

The results of this study strike another blow to the hearts of believers in active management. If corporate insiders, with knowledge that the market supposedly does not possess, can't outperform in an "inefficient" overseas market like Norway, how can individual investors or portfolio managers hope to do so in the more efficient U.S. markets?

There is another reason that knowledge of insider trading activity is not likely to prove of value. Access to information about corporate insider trading activity was once limited to institutional investors. Thanks to several Websites, this is no longer the case. Not only is this information readily available, but it can be had at little or no cost. Several sites not only list the trades but go so far as to massage the data to make it more useful. One such site, *www.insiderscores.com*, even analyzes the predictive value of each insider's trading activity, on the basis of past performance of the company's stock after similar previous trades.[22]

Because the information is so readily available it is very difficult, if not impossible, to gain any competitive advantage from it. The bottom line is that while the information may provide some insight, it is hard to see how that insight can be translated into a profitable trading strategy if you can't get it, and act on it, ahead of the rest of the market.

There is good news here for those investors who like to pick their own stocks, even if it is only for the entertainment value: since the market is efficient at processing information, investors don't have to worry when they trade that they might be unaware of any important information. The market has done the work for them by already incorporating the news into prices. Another way to think about this is that while diligent and hard-working investors are unlikely to gain any information advantage, less knowledgeable or less diligent investors don't have to worry about buying an "overvalued" or selling an "undervalued" stock. Both types of investors are trading at the price that is most likely the correct one!

In Search of the Holy Grail

Identifying mutual fund managers who have outperformed the market in the past is easy. Unfortunately, identifying the future winners is a lot more difficult. As we have seen, for the vast majority of investors this effort has resulted in inconsistent and below-market results. Academics argue that the EMT explains this loser's game. Simply put, EMT states that efforts to identify undervalued securities fail to produce returns in excess of the market's overall rate of return because everything knowable about a company is already incorporated into the stock price. Thus, the next piece of information will be random (nonforecastable) as to whether it will be better or worse than the market expects. However, knowledgeable investors know that the real question is not whether or not the markets are efficient. Instead, investors should ask whether active managers can exploit any inefficiency in the market that may exist and add value *beyond the costs incurred in the effort.*

Let's begin by looking at the overall record of active managers. For the 15-year period ending May 31, 2000, the annual return for all domestic equity funds that survived the period was 14.4% or just 87% of the 16.5% return of the Wilshire 5000

Index.[23] On the other hand, an index fund with operating expenses of about 0.2% would have provided close to 99% of the available returns. The difference in returns was due to the impact of costs. In addition, the difference in returns is actually understated because of both survivorship bias (poorly performing funds disappeared from the data) and the impact of taxes on fund distributions. Let's examine the impact of the various costs mutual fund investors bear in their search for that Holy Grail.

Operating Expenses

The financial press has made most investors aware that a fund's operating expenses should be considered prior to making any investment decision. The average operating expense for actively managed domestic funds as of May 31, 2000, was 1.43%.[24] For the typical domestic index or passive asset class fund, the expense ratio is between 0.2% and 0.5%. For their international counterparts the expense ratio might be slightly higher. Thus actively managed funds begin the game with a cost hurdle of 1% or more that they must clear in order to add value. This 1% hurdle does not include any 12b-1 expenses or load fees. If a fund imposes any such fees, the hurdle obviously increases.

The Cost of Cash

While operating expenses are important, unfortunately they are not the only expenses funds incur. A hidden (and therefore most likely ignored) but not insignificant cost is the "cost of cash." This cost is hidden in the sense that, unlike operating costs, it is not reported. Instead it shows up in reduced returns. Let's assume that the typical actively managed fund maintains an average cash position of about 10%. For the 15 years ending in 1999, the S&P 500 Index provided total returns of about 19%. During that same period, one-month Treasury bills (a good proxy for the return earned on invested cash) yielded about 6%. We can now calculate the "cost of cash" for actively managed funds to be 1.3% per annum ([19% − 6%] × 10%). For a passively managed fund, being generally 99% invested, the "cost of cash" is only 0.13%. The "cost of cash" hurdle for actively managed funds is thus in excess of 1%. When added to the operating expense hurdle, the value-added bar has now been raised to in excess of 2% per annum.

Trading Expenses

Investors should also consider another hidden cost, trading expenses. The average actively managed fund has turnover of about 90%, and the cost of trading (commissions and bid/offer spreads) is approximately 1% to buy and 1% to sell. (For very large-cap stocks the bid/offer spreads are somewhat lower, and for very small-cap stocks the spreads are much wider.) The result is that the average actively managed fund incurs trading costs of about 1.6% (1% × 2 × 0.9).[25] Depending on the index it is attempting to replicate, the typical passively managed fund will have turnover of between 3% and 25% (lower for passive large-cap funds and greater for passive small-cap funds). If we assume an average turnover of about 15%, then we can estimate the cost of trading at 0.3% (1% × 2 × 0.15). For active managers the hurdle of trading costs is therefore 1.5% (1.8% − 0.3%).

This estimate of the negative impact of the turnover of active managers is supported by the results of a Morningstar study. Morningstar divided mutual funds into two categories, those with an average holding period greater than 5 years (less than 20% turnover) and those with an average holding period of less than one year (turnover of greater than 100%). Over a 10-year period Morningstar found that low turnover funds rose an average of 12.87% per annum, while high turnover funds gained only 11.29% per annum on average. Trading costs and the impact on prices of trading activity reduced returns of the high turnover funds by 1.58% per annum—not much different from our estimate of 1.5%.[26]

When we include the costs of trading, the value-added bar has now been raised to well in excess of 3% (in excess of 1% each for operating expenses, "cost of cash," and trading costs). It is worth noting that for international actively managed funds the value-added hurdle is even greater, as the operational costs and trading costs differences (versus passively managed funds) are even greater than they are domestically. Commissions, custodial fees, and bid/offer spreads are generally much higher, and then you have to include costs such as stamp duties that are not incurred in the United States.

Market Impact Costs

Unfortunately for active managers, the costs of trading do not end with commissions and bid/offer spreads. Active managers incur "market impact" costs. Market impact is what occurs when a mutual fund wants to buy or sell a large block of stock. The fund's purchases or sales will cause the stock to move beyond its current bid (lower) or offer (higher) price, increasing the cost of trading. Barra, a research organization, recently completed a study on market impact costs. While the cost of market impact will vary depending on many factors (fund size, asset class, turnover, etc.), the cost can be quite substantial. Barra noted that a fairly typical case of a small- or mid-cap stock fund with $500 million in assets and an annual turnover rate of between 80% and 100% could lose 3 to 5% per annum to market impact costs—far more than the annual expenses of most funds. In another example, for the period studied the PBHG Emerging Growth Fund had the highest estimated market impact cost among small- or mid-cap funds at 5.73% per annum. Even large-cap funds can have large market impact costs, as illustrated by the 8.13% figure estimated for the Phoenix Engemann Aggressive Growth Fund.[27] For the sake of consistency and conservatism, let's assume that market impact costs add a further 1% hurdle for active managers to climb. That raises the total hurdle to at least 4% per annum.

Taxes

Unfortunately for investors, we have not come to the end of the road. In fact, for taxable accounts we have not yet covered what is often the greatest hurdle, the burden of taxes on IRS Form 1099 fund distributions. For the 15-year period ending June 30, 1998, the Vanguard S&P 500 Index fund provided pretax returns of 16.9% per annum. The fund lost 1.9% per annum to taxes. Its after-tax return of 15% meant that the fund's tax efficiency was 89%. The average actively managed fund provided pretax returns of 13.6% and after-tax returns of just 10.8%. Losing 2.8% per annum to taxes resulted in a tax efficiency of just 79%.[28] The hurdle of taxes for the average actively managed fund was almost 1% per annum (2.8% − 1.9%). While passively managed small-cap and value funds are not as tax efficient as an S&P 500 Index fund (because of their greater turnover), the tax hurdle for actively managed funds is still significant. It is important to note that investors now have available to them passively managed small-cap and value funds that are also tax-managed, making this example more applicable to other asset classes. Once taxes are included in our cost/hurdle equation, the value-added burden jumps to in excess of 5% per annum. This large hurdle is why so few active managers are able to outperform their benchmarks.

Closet Indexing

In addition to the 5 hurdles of operating expenses, cost of cash, trading costs, market impact costs, and taxes, there is a sixth hurdle that most investors have never even heard of, let alone thought about. It is the burden of closet indexing. A closet index fund looks like an actively managed fund, but the stocks it owns so closely resemble the holdings of an index fund that investors are unknowingly paying very large fees for minimal differentiation. The amount of differentiation from an index fund can be measured by the actively managed fund's correlation with its benchmark index (i.e., the S&P 500 Index). The higher the correlation—defined as a fund's r, or the correlation coefficient—the less the differentiation. The r-squared (r × r), or the correlation of determination, is commonly used to measure the degree of correlation compared to a benchmark. For example, a fund with an r-squared of 0.95 would have 95% of its returns explained by the performance of the S&P 500.

The following example will illustrate the extra hurdle that closet indexers bear. Let's assume that an investor places $100,000 in an actively managed fund with an operating expense of 1.2%. The average actively managed fund has an r-squared of more than 86%.[29] The impact of this r-squared on the investor in the average actively managed fund can be measured as follows. The investor is paying $1,200 (1.2% × $100,000). However, $86,000 of the actively managed fund's assets are the same as those of an index fund. The cost of managing that $86,000 if it were at Vanguard's S&P 500 Index (fee is 0.18%) would have been only $155. The result is that the investor is really paying $1,045 ($1,200 − $155) on the $14,000 of differentiated assets. The net is that the investor is really paying about 7.5% ($1,045 ÷ $14,000) on the differentiated portion of the portfolio. Add this large hurdle to the other expenses actively managed funds and their investors incur, and the hurdle becomes virtually insurmountable. Remember that the larger the fund, the more diversified it must become. The more it diversifies, the greater becomes its r-squared, and the greater the hurdle the manager must overcome in order to outperform. The problem is so great that 8 of Fidelity's largest 11 funds had 3-year r-squareds of over 94%.[30] That is less than 6% differentiation. The differentiation in fees between these funds and an index fund must be multiplied by almost 17 to calculate the true expense on the differentiated portion of the portfolio.

The following is evidence of the difficulty of overcoming a high r-squared, given the greater fees and the other expenses incurred by active managers. For the 3 years ending August 31, 1999, the 5 largest funds with r-squareds over 95 returned between 21% and 26.9%. After taxes an investor would have received between 18% and 24.6%. Vanguard's S&P 500 Index fund beat them all. It returned 28.5% pretax and 27.5% after tax. Of the 80 largest funds with r-squareds over 95, only 3 managed to beat the Vanguard Index fund and just barely did so. And none did so after taxes.[31] That's about $400 billion of underperforming assets and probably over $20 billion per annum that investors left on the table because of their belief in active management.

Summary

We can now return to the real question for investors being not whether or not the markets are inefficient but instead whether active managers add value in excess of the costs of their efforts. Mark Carhart conducted the most comprehensive study ever done on the mutual fund industry. He found that once you account for style factors (small-cap vs. large-cap and value vs. growth) the average actively managed fund underperformed its benchmark on a pretax basis by almost 2% per annum.[32] Considering the size of the hurdle that active managers have, it appears they were able to exploit market inefficiencies (since the hurdle before taxes was in excess of 4%). The only problem is that since they underperformed their benchmarks (the hurdle proved greater than the inefficiencies), active managers would have been better off if they had never pursued the Holy Grail of outperformance in the first place. They were playing the loser's game: The hope of outperformance was exceeded by the risk of underperformance.

The following analogy is a fitting conclusion for this tale. The long-term goal of investing is to multiply the eggs in our basket. Too many investors are focused on producing more eggs (getting high returns) but pay little attention to the fox (costs) that perpetually robs the hen house. If you ignore the fox, soon there will be nothing left to produce more eggs.[33]

The Efficiency of Fixed Income Markets

"Basically, we were guessing on interest rates. . . . What we've come to believe is that no one can guess interest rates." That is what Fred Henning, head of fixed income investing at

Fidelity Investments, said in an interview in the *Los Angeles Times*, July 7, 1997. Mr. Henning may be the only one to admit it, but there is plenty of evidence that the efforts of fixed income fund managers to guess the direction of rates are not only non-productive but counterproductive because of the expenses incurred in the effort.

As with equity markets, if fixed income markets are not efficient, then one should observe active managers outperforming their benchmarks. If, on the other hand, the markets are efficient, then active managers will be playing a loser's game and will fail to outperform their benchmarks.

A study covering as many as 361 bond funds showed that the average actively managed bond fund underperforms its index by 85 basis points a year. Furthermore, depending on the benchmark, between 65% and 80% of the funds generated excess returns (returns from their active trading) that were negative.[34] A 1994 study found that only 128 (16%) out of 800 fixed income funds beat their relevant benchmark over the 10-year period covered.[35] Finally, for the 10-year period ending 1998, the average actively managed bond fund returned 8.2%, underperforming the Lehman Brothers Aggregate Bond Index by 0.7% per annum.[36]

John Bogle of Vanguard studied the performance of bond funds and concluded that "although past absolute returns of bond funds are a flawed predictor of future returns, there is a fairly easy way to predict future relative returns." After he separated the bond funds into their major categories of quality and maturity, he analyzed returns in terms of their expense ratios. Bogle placed funds into 4 categories: those with expenses of less than 0.5%; those with expenses between 0.5 and 1%; those with expenses between 1 and 1.5%; and those with expenses of over 1.5%. Bogle found that "in every case, and in every category, the superior funds could have been systemically identified based solely on their lower expense ratios. At the extremes, the lower expense funds outpaced the higher expense funds by between 1% and 2.2% annually. The ability to predict interest rates played no part in the performance of the bond funds."[37]

William Reichenstein's study *Bond Fund Returns and Expenses: A Study of Bond Market Efficiency* confirmed the results of Bogle's study. Reichenstein studied the 5-year period 1994 through 1998. He sorted bond funds by investment quality (low, medium, high) and by maturity structure (short-term, intermediate, and long-term). His conclusion: fund expenses are dead weight to investors. He found that there was virtually a perfect inverse relationship between expenses and returns—increases in expenses lead to a direct proportional 1:1 reduction in returns.[38]

Another study focused on whether there was any persistency in the performance of actively managed bond funds. In other words, is past performance of actively managed bond funds predictive of future performance? The study examined the performance of all 27 actively managed bond funds that survived the period 1982 through 1993. The study acknowledged a survivorship bias in that there were 34 bond funds at the start of the period. A full 20% of the bond funds that existed at the start of the period disappeared, presumably because of poor performance. Even with this bias, the study concluded that bond funds' past performance doesn't predict future performance and that bond fund managers generally are ineffective at increasing risk adjusted returns.

The study found that statistically there was a very strong negative correlation between both fund expenses and returns and fund turnover and returns. The greater the expenses and the greater the turnover, the lower the returns. The authors hypothesized that because bonds, within each investment grade, are relatively homogenous investments (have relatively similar risk characteristics), there is little opportunity for fund managers to distinguish themselves. Since different bonds of the same investment grade are good substitutes for one another, costs only reduce returns. This is particularly true of short-term fixed income investments, where little or no value can be added by guessing right on the future direction of interest rates. This study certainly supports the theory that the bond market is highly efficient.[39]

Investors should also be aware that since fixed income returns are lower than equity returns, expenses have a greater relative impact on actively managed fixed income funds than they do on actively managed equity funds. The average actively managed bond fund has an expense ratio of 1.1%.[40] If bond yields are at 5%, then investors are paying out over 20% of the available returns. A fixed income fund that is passively managed should have an expense ratio of between 0.2% and 0.35%.

The lesson for investors: if you want to invest in a fixed income fund, choose the fund that has the lowest expense ratio from among those funds that meet your credit quality and maturity requirements. It is highly likely to be either an index or passively managed fund.

Investment Insights

- Current market prices reflect the total knowledge and expectations of all investors, and no investor can consistently know more than the market does collectively.
- New information is disseminated to the public rapidly and completely so that prices instantly adjust to new data.
- New information received by the market will be random,

not in the sense of being good or bad but in the sense of whether or not it surpasses or falls short of market expectations.

- While it is possible that anomalies may be discovered and profitably exploited, it is unlikely that any competitive advantage is sustainable.
- Economic growth rates of countries, in and of themselves, are uncorrelated with stock-market returns. What matters are the expectations embedded in security prices.
- There is no evidence that international markets are any less efficient than U.S. markets or that active management works any better internationally, or even in emerging markets, than it does domestically.
- Even if there are market inefficiencies, it is likely that the costs of exploiting them will exceed the rewards.
- If a fund has managed to outperform the market, it is highly likely that the success was a result of good luck. If it was a result of a competitive advantage, it is highly likely that the competitive advantage will rapidly erode.
- It is a long way from the theoretical results of an active strategy to actual deliverable results.
- If corporate insiders, trading in their own stocks, have difficulty outperforming the market, is it logical to believe that securities analysis can uncover mispriced securities?
- The cost of active management includes much more than just the expense ratio. Investors must also consider expenses for which they are not sent a bill. These include transactions costs, market impact costs, the "cost of cash," and for taxable accounts, the impact of distributions.
- Closet index funds (actively managed funds with high coefficients of correlation to their benchmark index) bear

the extra burden of very large fees for very little differentiation.

- Survivorship bias causes mutual fund performance to appear to improve with age as poor performers die off and their performance numbers magically disappear.
- Active management of fixed income portfolios is just as much a loser's game as active management of equity portfolios.

CHAPTER 3

◆

Increasingly Investors Are Shifting to Passive Management

I am a big believer in index funds.
        —Jane Bryant Quinn, in *The Vanguard*, Autumn 1998

Our stay-put behavior reflects our view that the stock market serves as a relocation center at which money is moved from the active to the passive.
                                                —Warren Buffett

By periodically investing in an index fund . . . the know-nothing investor can actually outperform most investment professionals.
                                                —Warren Buffet

Buy an index fund or stay out of the market. Period.
                        —UCLA professor Schlomo Benartzi,
                        InvestmentNews, December 14, 1998

Fees paid for active management are not a good deal for investors, and they are beginning to realize it.
—Michael Kostoff [Executive director of the Advisory Board, a
        Washington-based market research firm], *InvestmentNews*,
                                                February 8, 1999

Severe underperformance of active equity managers has raised the whole issue of performance for all asset managers, including bond managers.
                        —PIMCO managing director Brent Harris,
                        Institutional Investor, May 1998

The S&P 500 is a wonderful thing to put your money in. If somebody said, "I've got a fund here with a really low cost,

76

that's tax efficient, with a 15-to-20 year record of beating almost everybody," why wouldn't you won it?
—William Miller, Portfolio Manager, Legg Mason, *Wizards of Wall Street*, Kirk Kazanjian

The trend by investors away from active and toward passive management of portfolios began in the mid-1970s with the creation of the first index fund. The trend picked up momentum in the 1980s from an unexpected source: the arrival of high-speed computers. Their ability to analyze massive databases enabled financial economists, for the first time, to really analyze the performance of active managers. The data was both consistent and compelling: active managers delivered poor and inconsistent performance. After adjusting for investment style (growth vs. value or small-cap vs. large-cap) active managers, as a group, had consistently underperformed their true benchmarks. As Morningstar's John Rekenthaler put it: "Active management is a beauty contest in which the average contestant is kind of ugly."[1] Given the evidence of underperformance, institutional investors began to adopt passive investing.

The trend toward passive management gained further momentum in 1990 when the Nobel Prize in economics was awarded to Harry Markowitz, Merton Miller, and William Sharpe for their contributions to the body of work known as MPT. The major tenet of this theory is that markets are efficient at pricing securities, or at least efficient enough to make the practice of active management non- or even counterproductive because of the expenses incurred in the effort.

In 1992 the trend accelerated when the American Law Institute rewrote the Prudent Investor Rule, incorporating MPT into its definition of prudent investing for those with fiduciary responsibility. The vast majority of state legislatures have now passed legislation that adopts MPT as the standard by which fiduciaries invest funds.

Institutional investors have clearly taken notice. According to a survey in the September 6, 1999, issue of *Pensions and Investments*, tax-exempt institutional investors now have over $1.5 trillion of index-managed assets. Many major plans, including those of Philip Morris, Exxon, and Intel, have fired all active managers. An Intel spokesman explained the change in strategy: "Our goal had been to try to outperform the index fund and over the last five years we have failed to meet that goal." The outside advisors who picked stocks and timed the market for Intel's $1 billion of retirement plan assets were replaced by index funds.[2] Kimberly-Clark, by placing 90% of its $2 billion pension plan in index funds, estimates that it will save $100 million in investment expenses over the next decade.[3] The California Public Employees' Retirement System (CALPERS) indexes 85% of its over $40 billion plan.[4]

Perhaps most telling is the following: Douglas Dial is a portfolio manager of the CREF Stock Account Fund, the largest pool of equity money in the world. Dial was formerly a stock-picking manager who has seen the light. "Indexing is a marvelous technique. I wasn't a true believer. I was just an ignoramus. Now I am a convert. Indexing is an extraordinary sophisticated thing to do . . . If people want excitement, they should go to the racetrack or play the lottery."[5]

The poor and inconsistent performance of active managers, particularly on an after-tax basis, has not gone totally unnoticed by individuals. At the start of the 1990s index funds were barely on the radar screens of individual investors, attracting just 2% of assets.[6] By 1998 index funds were attracting 19% of the money committed to mutual funds.[7] In the first 8 months of 1999 this figure reached 38%.[8] The fastest growing fund is the Vanguard S&P 500 Index fund. While it took that fund 10 years to gather its first $1 billion and 10 more years to get to $10 billion, it took just 3 more years to get to $30 billion and about one more to get to $40 billion. By the end of the first quarter of 1999 it had crossed $80 billion. On April 5, 2000, it became the largest fund in the world.[9] By far the fastest growing sector of the retail mutual fund industry is index funds, growing at twice the rate of the industry.[10] Think of the dilemma facing the heads of marketing at T. Rowe Price or Merrill Lynch. On the one hand they now have to explain why investors should buy a T. Rowe Price or Merrill Lynch index fund. On the other hand, they must explain why investors should buy one of their actively managed funds (and probably pay 1% more in expenses and a lot more in taxes on distributions).

It is also worth noting the very surprising result that emerged from a survey of 1,100 Registered Investment Advisers (RIAs). Dalbar, a Boston research firm, asked the RIAs, who control over $40 billion in client assets, which fund companies they expect to perform the best in the coming years.[11] The survey includes the advisors' top 3 picks in 10 investment categories. The unexpected winner, particularly since it has no advertising budget and is virtually unknown to the public, was DFA. It was the top fund choice for large-cap and small-cap funds, the second choice for emerging market funds, and the third choice for taxable bond funds, index equity funds, and index bond funds. Dalbar reported that DFA was the top choice because it stressed quantitative research. The other major winner was Vanguard, another low-cost index, or asset class, fund provider. It seems like this is another case of "if you build it, they will come."

The Prudent Investor Rule

In May 1992, in response to the overwhelming body of academic evidence on the overall unsatisfactory performance of active managers and the benefits of passive asset class investing, the American Law Institute rewrote the Prudent Investor Rule. The institute stated:

- The restatement's objective is to liberate expert trustees to pursue challenging, rewarding, nontraditional strategies and to provide other trustees with clear guidance to safe harbors that are practical and expectedly rewarding.
- Investing in index funds is a passive but practical investment alternative.
- Risk may be reduced by mixing risky assets with essentially riskless assets rather than creating an entirely low-risk portfolio.
- *Active strategies entail investigation and expenses that increase transaction costs, including capital gains taxation.* Proceeding with such a program involves judgments by the trustee that gains from the course of action in question can reasonably be expected to *compensate for additional cost and risks*, and the course of action to be *undertaken is reasonable in terms of its economic rationale.*

By rewriting the Prudent Investor Rule, the American Law Institute recognized both the significance and efficacy of MPT. It also recognized the poor and inconsistent results delivered by active managers. The institute had the following to say about market efficiency:

- Economic evidence shows that the major capital markets of this country are *highly efficient*, in the sense that available information is rapidly digested and reflected in market prices.
- Fiduciaries and other investors are confronted with potent evidence that the application of expertise, investigation, and diligence in efforts to "beat the market" ordinarily promises little or no payoff, or even a negative payoff, after taking account of research and transaction costs.
- Empirical research supporting the theory of efficient markets reveals that in such markets skilled professionals have rarely been able to identify underpriced securities with any regularity.
- Evidence shows that there is little correlation between fund managers' earlier successes and their ability to produce above-market returns in subsequent periods.

The vast majority of states have already passed legislation with two major revisions to the Prudent Investor Rule:

- MPT is adopted as the standard by which fiduciaries invest funds.
- Fiduciaries can avoid liability if they exercise reasonable skill and care in making a delegation to an agent. The agent will be held to the same standards as the fiduciary.[12]

For those with fiduciary responsibility, adopting MPT makes sense because:

- It is expected to provide the maximum expected return for a given level of risk.

- It provides relief from liability for fiduciaries who are not in the investment business by appointing competent managers or advisors who invest according to its tenets.

Faced with this restatement, and the recent legislative changes, trustees began a major switch from active to passive portfolio strategies. As recently as 15 years ago, around $1 billion was invested in passive funds. Today the amount invested is over $2 trillion.[13] One reason for this rapid shift is that pension fund managers must now ask themselves: Do I want to invest in a way that has been recognized as prudent by the American Law Institute? Or would I rather try, with historical evidence against me, to beat the market through an active management strategy, knowing that if I fail I may be forced to justify why I took such a strategy in the face of an overwhelming body of academic evidence? Given the risk/reward tradeoff, I believe that the growing trend toward the use of passive asset class investing by institutional investors is not only inevitable but will accelerate.

Index Funds: Fair-Weather Friends?

Mutual Funds with a High Market Correlation Are All the Rage Right Now, but They'll Inspire a Different Kind of Rage When Stocks No Longer Soar.

This was the headline of an article by Craig L. Israelsen, Ph.D., an associate professor of economics at the University of Missouri in Columbia, that appeared in the April 1998 issue of *Financial Planning*. Unfortunately for investors, the article is filled with omissions and unjustified conclusions.

The article begins by pointing out the impressive performance of index funds over the past 3-, 5-, and 10-year periods. The author, while pointing out that index funds have the advantage of being low cost, suggests that their superior performance is a result of the superior performance of large-cap stocks over this time frame. The implication is that index funds would under-perform both in a bear market and when small-cap stocks out-perform large-cap stocks. He also points out that index funds have greater standard deviations than actively managed funds and are therefore more risky. Finally he points out that the high correlation of index funds to the market will make them a "foe to indexers and not a friend" during bear markets.

Let's examine the author's claims.

First, Israelsen actually understates the superior performance of index funds over the past 3-, 5-, and 10-year periods. He presents comparison performance data on funds with at least 5- and 10-year histories. For the 5- and 10-year periods the Van-guard Index 500 outperformed 90% and 82% of all funds, re-spectively. The reality is that this fund did even better, because Dr. Israelsen doesn't consider the issue of survivorship bias. Funds that have poor performance are made to disappear either by investors removing their funds or by fund sponsors merging a poorly performing fund into a better performing one. In the most comprehensive study ever done on mutual funds, covering the period 1962 through 1993, Mark Carhart found that by 1993 fully one-third of all funds in his sample had disappeared.[14] In 1996 alone, 242 (5%) of the 4,555 stock funds tracked by Lipper Analytical Services were merged or liquidated. The importance of survivorship bias is underscored in the following example. In 1986 the 586 stock funds returned 13.39% for the year. By 1996, the 1986 performance had improved to 14.65%. How did this happen? Twenty-four percent of the funds disappeared.[15] As another example, for the 10-year period ending in 1992, capital appreciation funds reported an average appreciation of 18.08% versus a return of only 17.52% for the S&P 500 Index. Once the survivorship bias is eliminated, the returns of all capital appreciation funds that existed during the same 10-year period drop to 16.32%. Actual returns to investors were not only almost 2% per annum worse then they initially appeared to be but they were also about 1% below the return available to investors in S&P 500 Index funds.[16] Two other studies confirm this view. The first, by Lipper Analytic Services, produced the following results: the return of all general equity funds for the ten-year period studied was 15.69%. This was 1.5% below that of the funds that existed at the end of the period (the survivors) and almost 2% below the return of the S&P 500 Index."[17] The second study found that over the 15-year period ending December 1992, the annual return of all equity mutual funds was 15.6% per annum. When you include all the funds that failed to survive the entire period, the annual return dropped to 14.8%. The cumulative difference in returns was 781% versus 689%.[18]

The survivorship bias problem has increased in recent years as mutual fund families try to bury poor performance. In 1998 alone 387 stock and bond funds were merged out of existence, an increase of 43% over the previous year. A further 250 funds were liquidated due to investor redemptions. In the first quarter of 1999 the number of vanishing stock funds jumped 74%.[19]

Second, Israelsen cites only pretax performance. I don't know any investor who gets to spend pretax dollars. Because of their passive strategy, index funds generate much lower distributions than do active managers. The higher turnover of active managers negatively impacts their returns, often in dramatic fashion. A study commissioned by Charles Schwab found that over a 30-year period the effect of taxes on fund distributions reduced the advertised returns of actively managed funds by almost 60%! That's right, almost 60%. While index funds are not 100% tax efficient, they are far more tax efficient than actively managed ones.[20]

Third, Israelsen states that the superior performance of index funds is due to the superior performance of large-cap stocks. The author is confused. He should be considering the relative performance of active versus passive funds on a style-adjusted basis. For example, he should compare large-cap active managers with S&P 500 Index funds and small-cap active managers with Russell 2000 or CRSP (Center for Research in Security Pricing) 9–10 funds. A study by Mark Carhart found that, after adjusting for style (value vs. growth and small vs. large), actively managed funds underperformed, on a pretax basis, by almost 2% per annum. Once taxes are considered, the performance differential would widen significantly. Carhart also found that stock selection and market timing efforts negatively impacted returns. Carhart's study clearly demonstrated that it is the asset allocation decision that determines the vast majority of returns.[21] In fact, a study by professors Eugene F. Fama and Kenneth R. French demonstrated that as much as 97% of all returns may be determined by asset allocations.

Fourth, Israelsen cites the fact that index funds have higher standard deviations than actively managed ones. That is hardly a startling observation. Actively managed funds tend to carry significant cash positions because of their market timing and stock selection efforts. Index funds, on the other hand, are always fully invested. Since cash has lower volatility than equities, actively managed funds, almost by definition, will have lower volatility than similar style index funds. If the author is seeking lower volatility, why not just invest in a money market fund? And, while I'm not suggesting you ignore volatility, you can't spend it. The fully invested position of index funds is one of the main reasons index funds outperform actively managed ones. (The other reasons are lower expenses, lower turnover, and greater tax efficiency.)

Fifth, Israelsen states that funds (like index funds) that have a high correlation to the market perform well during rising markets but suffer during periods when the market is falling. The author should check the facts. I am the first to admit both that during bear markets actively managed funds begin with an advantage over passively managed ones and that index funds will go down during bear markets. The active manager's advantage results from maintaining cash reserves averaging about 10% of assets. This cash reserve, because cash is a poorly performing asset class in bull markets, is one of the reasons active managers underperform in bull markets. In bear markets, however, cash becomes king. However, when you examine the performance of active managers, as Lipper Analytical Services did, you find surprising results. Lipper studied the 6 bear markets (defined as a drop of at least 10%) from August 31, 1978, through October 11, 1990, and found that while the average loss for the S&P 500 Index was 15.12%, the average loss for large-cap growth funds was 17.04%[22] While you would have to subtract about 0.2% from the index itself to account for an index fund's expenses, active managers would have still underperformed by almost 2% per annum in the very periods when they have the greatest advantage. The underperformance by active managers was repeated in the bear market of the third quarter of 1998, when the S&P 500 Index declined 10.1% and the average fund fell 11.7%.[23] As they say in the old Wendy's commercial, "Where's the beef?" Susan Dziubinski, editor of Morningstar's *Fund Investor* newsletter, stated it this way: "The average fund can't keep up with its index when it's sunny or when it's rainy."[24]

While passive index funds remain fully invested at all times, active managers have the "advantage" of being able to sell securities and hold cash during bear markets. Even with this advantage, it seems that the claims of active managers on their ability to add value appear to be another one of Wall Street's myths, created by its advertising machines. Unfortunately for Dr. Israelsen, he appears to have fallen under their spell. I should add that the fact that S&P 500 Index funds are highly correlated to the market is not a reason to avoid them (as he suggests) but it is a reason to create a broad globally diversified portfolio of passive asset class, or index, funds.

When the facts are brought to light, passive management clearly emerges as the winning investment strategy. Active management, while possibly providing excitement, is the losing strategy in both bull and bear markets. The winners in the active management game are few: the funds that get to charge investors 1.5% for a poorly performing actively managed fund instead of 0.2–0.5% for a superior performing passively managed one; the publications and rating services that advise you on the top funds to buy; and Uncle Sam, who collects more taxes.

The Triumph of Hope over Reason

Inactivity strikes us as intelligent behavior.
—Warren Buffett, 1996 Annual Report of Berkshire Hathaway

Actively managed funds do provide investors with the hope of outperforming their style benchmark (large-cap, small-cap, value, growth, international, emerging markets, etc.). The trade-off is that investors must also accept the risk, if not high probability, of underperformance. On the other hand, index funds, or the broader category of passive asset class funds, virtually guarantee that they will provide investors with the returns of the asset class they are replicating (less their expenses).

Investors should always prefer a guarantee of a return versus the possibility of a return with a similar mathematical value. For example, the vast majority of investors would prefer a guarantee of a 10% return to the equal possibility of a 0% or a 20% return. In order to prefer uncertainty, the mathematical value of the uncertain return would have to be greater than that of the guaranteed return. For example, a 60% chance of a 20% return and only a 40% chance of a 0% return might be preferred over a guaranteed 10% return, because the expected return of a series of events would be 12% [(60% $\times$ 20%) + (40% $\times$ 0%)]. Even then some investors would choose the certain return of 10% over the "uncertain value" of 12% because they want to avoid the possibility of a 0% return.

If actively managed funds had a history of on average matching the market's performance, and investors had some basis of predicting which actively managed funds would outperform in the future, choosing actively managed funds would make sense for investors willing to accept the possibility of underperformance in return for the possibility of outperformance. Investors who are risk avoiders would still prefer the guaranteed market return of an index fund. However, the evidence overwhelmingly demonstrates that actively managed funds underperform their benchmarks, by almost 2% per annum, and that is before taxes. In addition, since many studies have found that past performance has been shown to have no value as a predictor of future performance, there is no way for investors to pick which actively managed funds will be among the very few that will produce superior performance in the future.

Increasingly, investors are shifting to passive management.

They have begun to recognize that index funds should be the preferred choice, at least of those who are making rational decisions. The reasons are that they deliver market returns, at very low costs, and do so in a tax efficient manner. They also avoid style drift. This allows investors to construct a portfolio that keeps them in control of the main determinant of risk and returns.

Active Managers Lose Another Excuse

Index mutual funds have become the villains of an investment soap opera. Active managers have been blaming their underperformance on S&P 500 Index funds. The theory goes like this: money pours into the Index funds because of the dissatisfaction with the underperformance of active managers; the funds "blindly" buy the large-cap stocks and drive the market ever higher.

The problem is that this theory is based on a false premise. It is true that S&P 500 Index funds have grown rapidly, from $255 billion at the end of 1992 to $600 billion at the end of 1997. However, according to Melissa Brown, head of quantitative research at Prudential Securities, S&P 500 Index funds represented 6.7% of all U.S. stocks at the end of 1992 and only 6.1% by the end of 1997. Ms. Brown points out that since the total return (price appreciation plus dividends) of the S&P 500 Index was 152%, all of the gain in the amount of S&P 500 indexed assets was a result of price appreciation, not cash inflow. In fact, if the amount of funds in S&P 500 Index funds had grown as much as the 152% total return of the Index itself, the amount of money invested in these funds would have grown to almost $650 billion. This indicates there were actually net cash outflows from these funds. This clearly suggests that the underperformance of active managers is not due to inflows into index funds.[25]

The net cash outflow from S&P 500 Index funds should not be taken as an indication that investors are decreasing their commitment to passive investing. In fact, the contrary is true. Not all index funds are tied to the S&P 500. In recent years index funds have been created to replicate the performance of the Russell 2000, the S&P/Barra Value Index, the EAFE Index, and many others. When all passive funds are considered, their market share is growing at a rapid pace. By year-end 1999 their share of net new inflows into mutual funds was rapidly approaching 40%.

Clearly, active managers will have to find a different excuse for their poor and inconsistent performance.

Diamonds and Spiders and Webs, Oh My!

The dramatic increase in demand from investors for passive (i.e., index) investment strategies has not gone unnoticed by the investment community. Even such staunch advocates of active investing as Fidelity could not resist the demand from their investors to introduce index funds. Investors are now able to index not only the S&P 500 but also broader market indices such as the Wilshire 5000. Investors can also now invest passively in the full spectrum of asset classes, including real estate, small- and large-cap, value and growth, international, and even emerging markets. It should not be much of a surprise that the heightened demand for passively managed investment options has fueled the development and introduction of a new array of investment vehicles called Exchange Traded Funds (ETFs).

ETF Marketplace

The most popular and fastest growing segment of ETFs are traded predominantly on the American Stock Exchange (AMEX) and go by the following names:

- Spiders (SPDRs: tracking the various S&P and S&P/Barra indices)
- WEBS (World Equity Benchmark Securities: tracking various foreign country indices such as the U.K., German, and French equivalents of the S&P 500 Index
- Diamonds (tracking the Dow Jones Industrial Average)
- Qubes (or QQQ, tracking the NASDAQ 100).

Since it is possible to create an ETF for any index, and the demand for passive investment vehicles is growing at a rapid pace, it is likely that we will witness an explosive increase in the number and type of ETFs. As of February 2000, there were already 30 ETFs accounting for about $30 billion of assets.[26]

Structure

ETFs (or exchange-traded index securities) for all practical purposes act like open-ended, no-load mutual funds. Like mutual funds, they can be created to represent virtually any index or asset class. Thus, an ETF that represents the S&P 500 will look just like an S&P 500 Index fund, and an ETF that represents the S&P 500/Barra Value Index will look just like a similar index fund. However, ETFs are not actually mutual funds. Instead, these new vehicles represent a cross between an exchange-listed stock and an open-ended, no-load mutual fund.

Like traditional open-ended, index-based mutual funds, ETFs allow investors to purchase a portfolio of stocks through a single investment vehicle. Because of their unique operating structure, however, ETFs offer the potential for greater tax efficiency, lower annual operating expenses, and more flexible trading characteristics (although for individual investors this may prove to be more of a disadvantage as it might encourage increased trading, which is likely to prove counterproductive). In addition, the ability to purchase put-and-call options on ETFs allows investors to create risk/return profiles that are impossible to create with traditional mutual funds.

Unlike a traditional mutual fund, which sells shares of an individual fund to an investor in return for cash, the sponsor of an ETF exchanges large blocks of ETF shares, called "Creation Units," with large institutions for portfolios of securities that comprise the underlying index. Holders of these Creation Units can be institutional investors seeking to position them in their portfolio, broker-dealers seeking to break up the Creation Units and offer individual ETF shares to individual investors, or arbitrageurs seeking to profit from any disparity between the market price of the ETF and the price of the shares that constitute the underlying index. Redemptions of ETFs occur in a reverse manner. Sponsors exchange the underlying shares of the index plus a specified amount of cash in return for Creation Units of the ETF. It is this constant creation and redemption process that ensures that the ETF closely tracks, but may not exactly match, the underlying index. If the price of the underlying securities exceeds the price of the ETF, institutional investors/arbitrageurs will redeem their lower priced Creation Units to the sponsor in return for the more valuable individual securities. Conversely, when the price of the underlying securities is below the price of the ETF, investors/arbitrageurs will trade the lower priced securities for the more valuable Creation Units. The arbitrage process ensures that the price at which the ETF trades will not vary significantly from its NAV. This minimizes, if not virtually eliminates, one of the problems associated with closed-end mutual funds. Unlike open-ended funds that always trade at their NAV, closed-end funds can trade at substantial discounts and premiums.

Advantages

Taxes

Both ETFs and mutual funds must distribute virtually all (at least 98%) of realized capital gains and dividends to shareholders to avoid paying tax at the fund level. When applied to open-ended mutual funds, current (remaining) shareholders are responsible for all tax-related distributions, while redeeming shareholders, who may have benefited from gains, do not assume their proportionate share of the taxes. The Creation Unit structure and related redemption process of ETFs, however, have allowed them to substantially reduce taxable distributions for individual investors. During the redemption process, the sponsor takes in Creation Units and assigns out individual shares of the portfolio. With each individual security held by the sponsor having a unique cost basis, it is a relatively straightforward matter to assign out securities (to tax exempt entities such as pension plans) with the lowest cost basis. This process essentially "cleanses" the portfolio of its unrealized gains and the associated future tax liabilities. It is, therefore, the redeeming institutional investor (not the current shareholders) that is responsible for the taxes.

The redemption process can also be utilized to address the tax distribution implications of changes to the index the ETF tracks. In the case of an index fund being forced to sell the security being removed from the index, the sale of the outgoing security can often generate taxable distributions. Attentive assignment procedures during the redemption process can eliminate, or at least minimize, the need for a sale and capital gain realization. The structure of ETFs thus places the timing of taxable distributions more firmly in the hand of the individual investor. In effect, the tax issue is consistent with the holding of individual common stocks.

EXPENSES

Because of their passive nature, ETFs should generally have operating expense ratios that are very comparable to, or even lower than, the lowest cost open-ended mutual funds.

Other Advantages

- Continuous pricing throughout the trading day and even into extended trading hour sessions.
- Ability to sell short or to hedge an existing long position.
- Ability to place market and limit orders.
- Availability of put-and-call options to use as hedging vehicles.
- Because of tax and regulatory problems, most non–U.S. residents face restrictions on purchasing U.S. mutual funds. However, ETFs, because they trade as stocks, face no such problems.

I would add a caveat regarding these advantages: just as a little knowledge in the wrong hands can be a dangerous "advantage," so too can increased flexibility potentially lead to too-frequent trading in one's portfolio.

Disadvantages

Trading Costs

Investors in open-ended mutual funds incur no trading costs since the funds trade at their NAV. Because ETFs trade like stocks, bid/offer spreads will be incurred when buying and selling.

Brokerage Commissions

When an investor purchases a no-load mutual fund directly from the fund sponsor, no fees are incurred. Once again, since ETFs are like stocks, brokerage commissions are incurred. Investors may also incur brokerage expenses when they buy mutual funds indirectly through brokerage firms. For the buy-and-hold investor this should not present much of a problem since the expense will be incurred infrequently and the availability of discount brokerages should keep costs low. Where trading costs may make a difference is when investing on a frequent basis and/or in very small amounts. Examples might be dollar cost averaging programs and retirement and profit-sharing plans. For active traders, both the bid/offer spreads and the brokerage commissions must be weighed against the aforementioned benefits.

Summary

ETFs clearly represent a challenge to the mutual fund and brokerage industries alike. Whatever the outcome, the clear winners will be individual investors. First, competition is good. It usually leads to lower costs and product innovation (i.e., greater tax efficiency and more diversification choices). Given investor demand, and the sheer size of the market opportunity facing the investment community, the pace of change is likely to continue at a very rapid rate. Stay tuned.

Investment Insights

* It was the underperformance of active managers that raised the consciousness of the benefits of indexing in the pension community.
* The trend toward passive investing gained momentum in 1990 when the Nobel Prize in Economics was awarded to Markowitz, Miller, and Sharpe for their contributions to MPT.
* In 1992 the American Law Institute rewrote the Prudent Investor Rule incorporating MPT into its definition of prudent investing for those with fiduciary responsibility.
* Fiduciaries and other investors are confronted with potent evidence that the application of expertise, investigation, and diligence in efforts to "beat the market" ordinarily promises little or no payoff, or even a negative payoff, after taking into account research and transaction costs.
* Even if the markets are somehow inefficient, the costs of implementing an active strategy make active management a loser's game.
* Despite claims to the contrary, active managers underper-

form their benchmarks not only in bull markets, but in bear markets as well.

- Fed up with out-of-control outcomes, pension fund managers are adopting passive investment strategies as a means to reduce costs, control exposures to the marketplace, and get exact implementation of pension policies.
- The growth and influence of index funds is not a valid excuse for the failure of active managers to beat their benchmarks.
- Individuals choosing actively managed funds believe in the triumph of hope over reason.
- ETFs should be considered by investors as passive investment vehicles for building portfolios.

CHAPTER 4

◆

Neither Fund Managers nor Individuals Can Consistently Identify Mispriced Securities

Like everybody else in this industry, I have an ego large enough to believe I'm going to be one of the select few that will outperform.

—George Sauter,
Vanguard Group

The investment business is, by definition, a business of hope. Everyone hopes that he can beat the market, even if few people actually can.

—Avi Nachmany

I have a lot of friends who work in the securities business, and all of them just buy the stock market. I don't know any of them who are stock pickers.

—Benjamin Stein, TV host of
Win Ben Stein's Money, Smart Money,
March 1998

The ability to foresee that some things cannot be foreseen is a very necessary quality.

—Jean Jacques Rousseau

[Investors] think of the so-called professionals as having all the advantages. That is total crap. They'd be better off in an index fund.

—Peter Lynch, Barron's, April 2, 1990

The only way to beat the market is to exploit other investors' mistakes.

—Charles Ellis, *Winning the Loser's Game*

I'd compare stock pickers to astrologers, but I don't want to bad-mouth astrologers.

—Professor Eugene F. Fama,
University of Chicago, *Fortune*,
July 6, 1998

The fundamental belief of active managers is that markets misprice securities and that this mispricing allows them to identify and buy stocks that are somehow undervalued and sell short stocks that are somehow overvalued. These managers believe that markets don't work. Unfortunately for investors, as Nicholas Chamfort said, "There are well-dressed foolish ideas just as there are well-dressed fools." There is no evidence to support the view that markets systematically misprice securities. In fact, as this chapter will demonstrate, the evidence is compelling that the markets are very efficient at pricing securities. Louis Bachelier, a French economist, remarked long ago: "Clearly the price considered most likely by the market is the true current price: if the market judged otherwise it would quote not this price, but another price higher or lower."[1] With the vast majority of trading now being done by sophisticated institutional investors (who therefore determine market prices), it seems unlikely that all these smart investors could somehow systematically misprice securities. Even legendary investor Benjamin Graham, the man considered to be the father of fundamental security analysis, the basis of active management decisions, concluded that security analysis could no longer be counted on to produce superior results. Here is what he had to say in an interview in the *Financial Analysts Journal*:

I am no longer an advocate of elaborate techniques of security analysis in order to find superior value opportunities. This was a rewarding activity, say forty years ago, when Graham and Dodd was first published; but the situation has changed. . . . [Today] I doubt whether such extensive efforts will generate sufficiently superior selections to justify their cost. . . . I'm on the side of the "efficient" market school of thought.[2]

And he said this shortly before his death in 1976. Certainly with the advance in technology and the speed at which information now travels around the world, the markets have become even more efficient than when Graham came to his conclusion over 20 years ago. Here is another interesting perspective. Even Warren Buffett has stated that he is now happy if he can find just 1 or 2 stocks to buy every year. That means he must believe that all the other stocks are efficiently priced. Active manager Ted Aronson, of Aronson + Partners, in an interview with *Money* magazine, was asked: "Why don't more funds beat the market?" His response was simply: "Because they can't." When asked why not, he again responded simply: "Costs."[3]

An excellent example of why investors shouldn't believe that active managers can somehow find the stocks that other investors have somehow mispriced is the results of *Business Week*'s 1998 annual stock picker's contest. Each year they ask 4 "gurus" to pick their 10 best stocks. For the period of the contest (through December 14, 1998) the S&P 500 Index was up 17.6%. The best performance of the 4 "gurus" was only +3.8%. The others were −9.3%, −23.5%, and −45.2%.[4]

John Rekenthaler, Morningstar's research director, stated:

"With the odds of being right at 50% in every transaction, picking stocks that beat the benchmark is no different from correctly calling a coin toss. Accordingly, over time, active managers tend to earn a market return—minus management fees and transaction costs."[5] This statement takes on great significance considering it comes from the head of research of a firm that rates actively managed funds. John Bogle provides the proper perspective: "A winning coin flipper commands no press interest; a winning fund manager is acclaimed a genius."[6] Bogle's conclusion: "The chances that individual investors will find the holy grail that will identify in advance the future's superior performers seem dismal."[7]

Even advocates of efficient markets and MPT admit that it is possible to beat the market. Since luck does not provide us with any guidance as to how to accomplish this objective, W. Scott Simon, in his book *Index Mutual Funds*, points out that the only requirements for success are:

1. You must be consistently accurate in predicting the future to overcome the costs of active management.
2. You must take the same information that is available to the general public and interpret it differently. In other words, all other investors, collectively, are wrong, and you are right. Remember that if everyone interprets information in the same way, then all securities are correctly priced, and there is no reason to prefer one security to another.
3. All other investors must be making "mistakes" in pricing securities that can be exploited while incurring costs that are less than the gains that can be achieved.

If you do not believe you can accomplish these simple objectives, you can always attempt to hire the *next* Warren Buffett.

The only problem with that approach is that we do not have any reliable way to identify the next successful money manager. We only know today that Warren Buffett was successful. Out of all the money managers who existed 20 years ago, how would you have known to pick him or, say, Peter Lynch? Twenty years from now there will probably be another Buffett and another Lynch. Unfortunately, we have no way to know, today, who they will be.

This chapter documents the results of investment strategies that are based on the belief that investors and/or fund managers have the ability to consistently identify securities that the market has mispriced. I believe that once you have finished reading this chapter you will come to the same conclusion that I did: active managers have the *disadvantage* of being able to buy and sell whatever they want. Perhaps you will also agree with this variation on an old saying: those whom the gods would destroy they first make active fund managers.

Stock-Selection Skills of Brokerage Firms

One of the most persistent beliefs held by investors is that brokerage firms and their research teams have the ability to select stocks that will outperform the market. If investors don't believe that, why do they pay those large brokerage fees? Unfortunately for investors, as Anatole France said: "If fifty million people believe a foolish thing, it is still a foolish thing." As the October 29, 1998, edition of the *Wall Street Journal* demonstrated, there is no evidence to support the Wall Street wisdom on stock selection skills.

On a quarterly basis, the *Journal* reports on the stock selections of 15 large brokerage firms, including all of the major ones, like Merrill Lynch, Salomon Smith Barney, Prudential, and Paine Webber. Let's look at the facts:

- For the quarter ending September 1998, investors who bought the stock selections of the 15 firms would have lost between 10.5% and 31.7%. This compares to a loss of 9.9% for the S&P 500. Obviously, the only one doing well was the broker, who made money whether he added value or not.
- For the 12-month period the S&P 500 was up 9.0%. The selections of only a single firm managed to outperform that benchmark, with a return of 12.3%. The next closest figure was 3.6%. Only 3 even showed positive returns, and 3 lost more than 16%.
- Over the 5-year period the S&P 500 was up 147.9%. The selections of only 2 of the 15 managed to outperform that benchmark. The selections of 4 firms managed to produce returns of less than 96%.

Doubly damaging for the brokerage firms was that during 1998's third-quarter bear market, not a single firm's selections outperformed the S & P 500. Supposedly, it is in bear markets that active managers add value. And this was not the first time this type of underperformance occurred. During the last bear market—third quarter of 1990—when the S&P 500 fell about 14%, the stock selections of the 10 brokerage firms then included in the study lost between 14.3% and 28.7%. Importantly, the *Journal*'s study includes estimates for hypothetical trading costs and taxes.

Further evidence against Wall Street's ability to protect investors by moving to cash ahead of a bear market comes from a *Wall Street Journal* study on asset allocation skills. The headline of the *Journal*'s October 28, 1998, study was: "Strategists Post Worst Results in 8 Years." Here are a few of the facts:

- Of the 13 firms, 6 raised their equity allocations for the quarter, just as the bear was about to visit.
- Only 5 of the 13 managed to outperform a robot portfolio (55% stocks, 35% bonds, 10% cash), and none did so by more than 2%.
- The average portfolio performance was −4.11% versus −3.25% for the robot portfolio.
- For the 12-month period only 2 of the 13 outperformed the robot portfolio, and none did so by even 1%.
- For the 5-year period not a single strategist managed to outperform a robot portfolio by as much as 1% per annum.

Investors should ask themselves: If the brokerage firms with all their great research can't find securities that are so undervalued that they can overcome the costs of trading, how are individual investors supposed to? The best advice for investors: while trying to find the next Microsoft may be exciting, you should get your excitement from something other than your investment portfolio.

All the Wrong Moves

Terrance Odean, of the University of California at Davis, studied the performance of individual investors by examining over 100,000 trades covering the period 1987 through 1993. Odean's conclusion: individual investors aren't as bad at stock-picking as many people think. They're worse! The study found that stocks individual investors buy trail the overall market and stocks they sell beat the market after the sale. The more the time span the study covered increased, the more their performance trailed the market. Investors shot themselves in the foot with their trades even before taking into account the transaction fees and taxes they paid for the privilege of "playing the market." These costs would further depress trading performance. The author's conclusion: individuals shouldn't be trying to pick stocks. He further stated that investors probably don't realize just how badly they are doing. Since they were trading in a rising market, their portfolios generally showed gains. Unfortunately, the time and money they spent trying to pick stocks cut into their profits instead of enhancing them.[8]

Odean, along with Brad Barber, also at the University of California at Davis, followed up that study with another that looked at how the frequency of trading affected individual investor returns. MPT states that stock trading and market timing is a loser's game. Thanks to Odean and Barber, we now know just how much of a loser's game it actually is. The researchers looked at a large unnamed discount brokerage firm's trading records for 78,000 households from February 1991 through December 1996. They broke the households into 2 groups, those that averaged 4 trades per month and those that averaged less. The 20% of households that were in the most active trader group produced returns of 10% per annum. This was over 5% per annum less than the 15.3% per annum return of those that traded less frequently.[9] Even these investors would have been better off by not even trying in the first place, as the S&P 500 Index produced a rate of return of about 17% per annum. Individual investors, on average, were heavily weighted to riskier small value stocks that outperformed the overall market during the study's time frame. Once risk was accounted for, the underperformance increased to over 10% per annum.[10] While this study did include all trading costs, it did not include the negative impact of taxes created by the trading activity of these active investors. Obviously, if taxes were considered, the pain of trading activity would have increased.

Odean and Barber also studied the relative investment performance of men and women. In a study covering 35,000 investors, they found that women earn higher investment returns. Before you attribute this feat to a superior genetic makeup, women were not better stock pickers. In fact, the stocks that both men and women sold tended to outperform the ones they bought. The reason men did worse was simple: they traded more often. The increased costs of turnover (both bid/offer spreads and commissions) accounted for the entire difference in investment results. If taxes were considered, the disparity in returns would only get larger. On a risk-adjusted basis (using a statistical formula that takes into account that higher risk asset classes should produce higher returns) women outperformed men by 1.4% per annum. Single men did even worse. They underperformed women by 2.3% per annum (or 0.6% worse than married men). Behavioral economist Meir Statman, a professor of finance at Santa Clara University, attributed both the greater trading activity and the purchasing of riskier stocks by men to overconfidence. "More so than women, men simply think that they are better at investing than they actually are. Men also get a thrill from trading, and thrill seeking is likely to be biologically based."[11]

Odean and Barber decided to pursue their gender study after their research showed that men tend to feel more competent in financial matters, as well as in tasks that involve math and science. This feeling of confidence leads to a false sense of competency in stock-picking abilities. Their *mis*guided confidence in skills they did not have led to excessive trading. Women, on the other hand, often feel intimidated by the market and, therefore, tend to stay put.[12]

With the advent of do-it-yourself on-line trading, Odean and Barber decided to investigate the performance of individual investors who were clients of a discount brokerage firm that used the telephone to implement their own stock picks and then switched to e-trading. They studied the performance of over 3,000 accounts, half of which switched to e-trading. The assumption is that those that switched were motivated by their excellent investment results—trading more would only improve their results. Unfortunately, it appears that these investors confused skill with luck. Those who switched to e-trading did substantially increase their trading activity—annualized turnover leaped about 70% within the first month and 2 years later was still 80% greater than the turnover of investors who continued to use the telephone. The result of all that trading activity: before expenses e-traders managed to match the returns of the market. Unfortunately, after costs were considered (though not taxes) they trailed the market by 3.5% per annum.[13]

Odean and Barber concluded that it was the cost of trading and the frequency of trading, not portfolio selection, that explains the poor investment performance of individual investors.[14] Legendary investor Peter Lynch offered this sage advice: "To the rash and impetuous stockpicker who chases hot tips and rushes in and out of equities, an 'investment' in stocks is no more reliable than throwing away paychecks on the horses with the prettiest names, or the jockey with the purple silks . . . [But] when you lose [at the racetrack, at least] you'll be able to say you had a great time doing it."[15]

Investors would benefit by following this advice from Jonathan Clements, columnist for the *Wall Street Journal*: "Ignore market timers, Wall Street strategists, technical analysts, and bozo journalists who make market predictions. . . . Admit to your therapist that you can't beat the market."[16] Investors would also benefit by remembering this simple phrase: trading is hazardous to your wealth.

Do Hedge Fund Managers Deliver Superior Performance?

Hedge funds, a small and specialized niche within the investment fund arena, attract lots of attention. Hedge funds differ from mutual funds in several ways.

- They are generally available only to high net worth individuals.
- Unlike the typical broadly diversified mutual fund, they generally have highly concentrated large positions in just a few securities.
- They have broad latitude to make large bets, either long or short, on almost any type of asset, be it a commodity, real estate, currency, country debt, stocks, and so on.
- Management generally has a significant stake in the fund.
- Management has strong financial incentives (fees heavily related to performance).
- Management has very limited regulatory oversight.

Hedge fund managers seek to outperform market indices such as the S & P 500 by exploiting what they perceive to be market mispricings. Therefore, studying their performance would seem to be one way of testing the EMT and the ability of active managers to outperform their respective benchmarks.

Roger Ibbotson, Stephen Brown, and Will Goetzmann investigated hedge fund performance in their study "Offshore Hedge Funds: Survival and Performance 1989–1995." Their conclusions were as follows:

- When looking at past returns, there is little evidence of consistently outstanding performance.
- There was no evidence of persistent ability of managers in a particular style classification to earn returns in excess of their style benchmark.
- Of the 108 offshore funds that were listed in a 1989 U.S. Off-Shore Funds Directory, only 25 survived the study period. The probability of a fund lasting 7 years was very low.
- Most of the funds underperformed the S&P 500 Index.[17]

A *Forbes* article by columnist David Dreman presented a performance index of 2,600 hedge funds (1,500 domestic and 1,100 international) for the period January 1993 through October 1998. After deducting for fees, the average annualized returns of the hedge funds was 13.4%, trailing the 19.9% return of the S&P 500 Index.[18]

Very similar results were found in a study by Carl Ackermann, Richard McEnally, and David Ravenscraft.[19] Their study covered 906 hedge funds for the period 1988 through 1995. They concluded:

- Hedge funds provided greater returns than mutual funds but provided no advantage over indexing on a risk-adjusted basis.
- Hedge funds are more volatile than both mutual funds and market indices.

- Hedge funds may have a place in diversified portfolios because of their low correlation with other asset classes.
- Survivorship bias was so great that if it had not been taken into account, hedge fund returns would have magically improved by 3% per annum.

They also found that while hedge funds did not provide greater net returns to investors, they did provide greater gross returns. This finding conforms to an important part of the EMT: any excess returns over the market rate of return should equal the cost of that effort (otherwise why undertake the effort?). One might conclude that the only ones who benefited from their efforts were the hedge fund managers themselves.

Hedge fund investing appeals to many investors because of the exclusive nature of the club and because it has the potential of great rewards. The media conveys instant celebrity status on the latest superstar performer. The few successful ones make for great cocktail party stories. Unfortunately, the evidence is that these fund managers demonstrate no greater ability to deliver above-market returns than do active mutual fund managers. A recent example of a candle that once burned brightly is Julian Robertson's Tiger fund. Its great track record led to huge inflows of funds. The fund hit a peak of $22 billion in 1998. While the S&P 500 Index was up over 21% in 1999, Tiger Management fell 19%. This led to a huge outflow of cash, and fund assets fell to $7 billion.[20] In early 2000, continued underperformance and fund outflows led to the closing of the fund. Yes, a few hedge managers succeed. However, the real tests are: Do more succeed than is randomly expected? Is there persistence in performance? As the historical record suggests that the answers to these questions are no, maybe the markets don't misprice asset values after all?

"Enhanced" Indexing

Capitalism is a wonderful thing. Suppliers of product respond to demand. As more and more consumers become aware of the superior performance of index funds, mutual fund companies are rolling out new products, including enhanced index funds. Most enhanced index funds, while basically trying to replicate an index such as the S&P 500, attempt to enhance returns (beat their index) by overweighting certain stocks the fund manager believes will perform better than the other stocks within the index. The managers of these enhanced index funds may also use complex options and futures contracts to make further "bets" on the direction of the market. In other words, inside sheep's clothing (a passive manager), there really is a wolf (an active equity manager) charging higher fees for the so-called enhanced returns. Before reviewing the performance of these enhanced funds, I should point out that the entire logic behind their creation eludes me. Here's my problem: If active management really worked, why not own only those stocks that you are going to overweight? In other words, why own any amount of the ones you expect to underperform? To me it seems like the investing equivalent of putting both a humidifier and a dehumidifier in the same room and letting them fight it out.

If you ever hear that the performance of index funds is disappointing, the creation of enhanced funds is probably the main culprit. In trying to make it outperform its benchmark, the manager of the enhanced fund is engaging in the loser's game of stock selection and market timing. Using the Morningstar database, I found that there were 16 "enhanced" S&P 500 Index funds that had survived the entire 5-year period ending December 1999. I then compared the returns of those 16 funds on both a pre- and after-tax basis to the returns of the Vanguard S&P 500 Index fund. As sports announcers are fond of saying: "Let's go to the videotape." The actively managed funds provided per annum pretax returns ranging from 11.82% to 30.01%. The average pretax return was 24.74%. This compares to a pretax return of the Vanguard fund of 28.49%. The Vanguard fund outperformed all but 3 (or 19%) of the so-called enhanced funds. The average outperformance was a very significant 3.75% per annum. The cumulative 5-year difference was over 20%! It seems the hope of outperformance was greatly exceeded by the likelihood of underperformance.

On an after-tax basis the numbers are even more compelling. The 16 actively managed funds provided returns ranging from 28.49% to as low as 11.04%. The average after-tax performance of the actively managed funds was 21.55%. This compares to the after-tax return of the Vanguard fund of 27.5%. Once again the average per annum underperformance was a very significant 5.95% per annum. The cumulative impact on 5-year returns was over 33%!

For investors in taxable accounts it is important to note the drag on returns due to taxes. The average actively managed fund provided its investors with just 87% of its pretax return. Contrast this to the 96.5% tax efficiency of the Vanguard 500 Index fund. Keep in mind that these figures do not include any impact from state and local taxes. Once these were considered, the Vanguard fund would look even more attractive, particularly to investors in such high tax states as New York and California.

One reason for the underperformance is the greater expenses

of the enhanced funds. Another reason is that the much greater turnover of the actively managed enhanced funds increased trading costs (bid/offer spreads, market impact, and commissions) and, therefore, negatively impacted returns. The final reason is that the markets are very efficient, making it difficult to gain a competitive advantage.

Charles Ellis points out another problem with enhanced index funds. He asks the questions: How much do the actual portfolios differ from the index? What fees are investors paying *relative* to the assets composing this differentiated portfolio? The answers are daunting. If the typical enhanced index fund is even 20% differentiated from its index, then even a 0.5% apparent incremental fee is really a 2.5% (0.5% × 5) marginal fee for the incremental differentiated portfolio.[21] If active managers have been unable to overcome their average expense base of 1.5%, how will they overcome a 2.5% handicap?

It should be pointed out that there are other types of enhanced S&P 500 Index funds that have actually been able to enhance returns. However, these funds do so by purchasing S&P 500 Index futures (making no stock or market timing bets whatsoever) and investing their cash in fixed income strategies. The combination of the use of futures and a fixed income strategy has allowed them to exceed the returns of owning the actual stocks in the Index. In other words, all of the "enhancement" efforts are on the fixed income side, not the equity side, of the equation. DFA, PIMCO, and Smith Breeden all run successful funds in this manner. (To learn more about enhanced indexing using fixed income strategies and to gain insights into how futures markets and arbitrage work, see appendix B.)

It seems that the only thing that the enhanced index funds that focus on enhancing equity returns manage to enhance is the income of the fund managers. Like plastic silverware and jumbo shrimp, the term "equity enhanced" index fund should be added to the list of oxymorons.

The Class of '95, '96 . . .

Each year *Business Week* selects "The 100 Best Small Companies." An investor believing in *Business Week*'s skill in stock selection would be tempted to build a portfolio of these 100 great companies. For the period ending April 30, 1997, the Russell 2000, a benchmark for small companies, rose 33%. *Business Week* reported that a Class of '95 portfolio would have returned −4.5%. An investor believing that *Business Week* somehow possessed more knowledge than the market as a whole underperformed, by 37.5%, the return every investor could have achieved simply by buying a Russell 2000 Index fund.[22]

In case you think this poor performance was an anomaly, *Business Week* repeated their performance with the Class of '96. While the Russell 2000 Index was rising 38% (and the S&P 500 Index was up 71%) over the 2-year period ending April 30, 1998, the class of '96 showed a cumulative return of just 2.6%. Despite occurring during the greatest bull market in history, stocks with negative returns outnumbered stocks that rose in value by a 3 to 2 margin. In fact, at least 10 of the 100 "hot growth companies" lost at least 72% of their value. Quite a feat! Investors believing that *Business Week* could evaluate companies better than the market would have underperformed a simple small company index strategy by 35.4%[23]

Business Week did manage to do somewhat better with its Class of '97. It produced a return of 30.3%, just slightly better than the Russell 2000 Index's return of 29.5%. However, 10 of the top 100 lost at least 75% of their value during the period.[24]

After being exposed to the facts, hopefully you will be convinced to read stories such as "The 100 Best Companies" from a skeptical viewpoint. Does it make sense to believe that *Business Week* can somehow identify great companies that the rest of the market has somehow mispriced?

Another Legend Bites the Dust

A group of lovable grandmothers became instant legends and heroes to millions of investors when their book *The Beardstown Ladies' Investment Guide* was published. The book was such a bestseller that the ladies followed it with 5 more. Their claim of 23.4% per annum investment returns for the period 1984 through 1993 was "proof" that investors could beat the market. Investors wanted so badly to believe that these ladies held some secret investment formula that their *seventh* book was about to be published when, sadly, everyone's dreams were squashed. It seems that the Beardstown Ladies made a computer error when calculating their returns. As it turned out, the 23.4% figure was only for the period 1991 through 1992. Their actual returns for 1984 through 1993 were 9.1% per annum, or 5.8% per annum below that of the S&P 500 Index. The Beardstown Ladies' returns through year-end 1997 were 15.3% per annum, again underperforming the S&P 500 Index by 1.8% per annum.[25]

While this is a tale with a sad ending, what is even sadder is that it seems most investors place more emphasis on hope than on reason. There are well over 10,000 investment clubs registered in the United States. Just as it is likely that randomly 10 in every 10,000 people will flip 10 heads in a row, we should expect that just as randomly 10 in every 10,000 investment clubs should beat the market 10 years in a row. If just 10 investment clubs accomplished that feat, no one would claim that it was "proof" that investors could beat the market. However, when just one investment club produces superior returns, publishers rush to capitalize on investors' greed and hope. Just as popular trade publications know that all they have to do to sell lots of magazines is put on the cover "The Ten Best Funds" or some similar title, publishers know that investors are willing to believe in almost any claim of a superior investment strategy.

Investors should have asked the question: How likely is it that a group of grandmothers, or any other investment club, would discover some investment strategy that the brightest minds in academia and Wall Street, let alone the other 10,000 investment clubs, had not discovered? Alternatively, wasn't it more likely that these women were following the same formulas and strategies that most investment clubs were using and were just lucky in their choice of individual stocks? It certainly seems more logical to believe that over time the Beardstown Ladies results would have regressed to the mean, or average return, of all investment clubs. With thousands of clubs trying, a few are likely to produce superior performance, particularly when the time frames are short. However, that doesn't necessarily mean that the "winners" used a superior strategy or superior skill to produce that result. Believing that would have no more basis in reality than believing that someone who just rolled 10 sevens in a row at the craps table had skills that would allow him or her to roll 10 more in a row.

Supporting this theory is the research of Terrance Odean and Brad Barber, finance professors at the Graduate School of Management at the University of California at Davis. They studied the performance of 166 investment clubs that traded with discount brokers (at least they were keeping commission expenses low) for the period February 1991 through January 1997. The average investment club earned a respectable 14.1% per annum. The only problem was that the investment clubs underperformed the broad market index that the professors used as a benchmark by 3.7% per annum. And that was before taxes were considered! The study concluded that the stocks the clubs sell tend to subsequently outperform the ones they buy. They found if the investment clubs had simply held for the entire year their beginning portfolios, their returns would have improved by more than 4%.[26] It is worth noting that this poor performance is at odds with the data reported by the NAIC (National Association of Investment Clubs). There are two logical explanations. First, we have the likelihood that clubs that do poorly are less likely to report their results. Second, it is also likely that we have the same survivorship bias in the data that we have observed with mutual funds. A third possibility also exists—there are more Beardstown Ladies out there. The bottom line is simply that while investment clubs may serve some social function, they aren't good investment vehicles.

When you hear about the next investment legend or buy the next investment book based on some legend, ask whether their strategy is based on academic evidence. If it isn't, then it's likely that their investment returns were the results of random luck— if not a computer error—and will probably regress to the mean over time.

Not Worth the Paper on Which
They Are Printed

The headlines on the cover pages of the growing plethora of personal financial magazines scream out the latest hot stocks and mutual funds. Headlines such as "Six Stocks Pegged to Earn 47% within the Next Year" (*Money*, June 1997) attempt to grab the reader's interest. Unfortunately for readers, there is no evidence that these publications provide any overall value, other than the profits they generate for the publishers. For example, I have never seen any accountability of performance that would demonstrate that the advice of trade publications has any value whatsoever.

The *Los Angeles Daily News* performed a valuable service for investors by tracking the performance of 141 randomly selected stock picks from 21 articles in issues of 4 popular personal finance magazines—*Money, Smart Money, Kiplinger's,* and *Worth*. The period covered was April 1997 through January 1998. Keep in mind that if investors, instead of buying the magazines' picks, had purchased an S&P 500 Index fund on the first day of that month's issue, they would have earned about 46%. Here is what they found:

- Despite a strong bull market, 73 (52%) of the 141 picks lost money.
- Comparing the stock recommendations with the appropriate benchmark (such as the Russell 2000 for small-cap stocks), 82 (58%) out of the 141 stocks underperformed.
- When you took the average return of each article's stock picks, the result was that none of the 4 magazines added value; 50% of *Worth*'s, 56% of *Money*'s, and 75% of *Smart*

Money's picks failed to outperform the market. Amazingly, none of *Kiplinger*'s picks outpaced the market.

Investors really shouldn't be surprised. All these headlines that scream about short-term opportunities come from the same magazines that preach long-term investing. A conflict arises, since if you invest long term, you don't need the monthly advice touted in their publications. As Samir Husni, head of the magazine program at the University of Mississippi at Oxford, puts it: "Readers take 2.5 seconds to decide whether to pick up a magazine. Publishers must, therefore, grab the reader's attention. The audience wants immediate recommendations. What should I buy now?"

It is obvious that plenty of investors are buying the advice because the 4 magazines together have a readership of over 4 million. How many of the 4 million know that these magazines add no real value, at least in terms of stock selection?

The following is advice from Rene Stulz, editor of the prestigious *Journal of Finance*: "Buy index funds, watch out for costs, diversify and watch out for tax consequences." She chuckles at the idea of journalists predicting the market. "Mass media is entertaining, but it strikes me as very unlikely that you will find information you could make money on.[27]

Investors Need Filter to Screen Investment *Mis*information

"Beyond the S&P, index funds aren't a sure thing." This was the headline of an AP story in the May 26, 1998, *St. Louis Post-Dispatch*. The article began by singing the praises of the S&P 500 Index funds that have outperformed the vast majority of active managers over almost every period studied. The article then questioned the use of index funds in the "less efficient" small-cap markets. It pointed out that over the 20-year stretch ending March 1998, a small-cap index fund ranked next to last among all small stock funds that operated throughout the period.

This article contains information that could be misleading. Since *mis*information generally leads to poor investment decisions, investors need to be careful in accepting poorly researched stories at their face value. Unfortunately, with the popular press, stories like this one are the rule—rather than the exception. Let's examine the article's claims using corrective lenses.

First, investors need to beware of studies that claim that active managers beat their benchmarks. The reason for caution is that such studies have almost invariably been "polluted" by what is called survivorship bias. Unsuccessful funds usually are made to disappear before their performance becomes embarrassing. This "magic act" makes the performance of active managers appear far better than the reality. For example, the AP story covered just 12 small-cap funds. Do you really believe that in 1978, at the beginning of the 20-year stretch examined, there were just 12 small-cap funds in existence? Isn't it more likely that there were many other small-cap funds that did so poorly that they were made to disappear by either their sponsors or by dissatisfied investors?

The second problem with the article is that it really is comparing apples with oranges. Articles like this one typically use the very misleading style definitions of Morningstar or Lipper. They are misleading because many self-defined actively managed small-cap funds aren't really small-cap funds. For example, stocks with a market capitalization of more than about $900 million are in the upper half of all stocks ranked by size. Of the small-cap funds that existed for the entire 20-year period, 3 had average market caps of greater than $2 billion (top 40%) and another 4 had average market caps of between $1 and $2 billion (certainly placing them in the top half). This left just a handful of funds with a market cap that would even place them in the bottom half. Even these had an average market cap of $650 million, placing some of them just barely in the top 60%.

The AP article claimed that actively managed small-cap funds were dramatically outperforming their passive rivals. With the right pair of lenses, we can look at the facts. First, since large-cap stocks have outperformed small-cap stocks over the past few years, we would expect funds with a larger average market cap to outperform funds with smaller market caps. This has nothing to do with active versus passive management and everything to do with asset allocation. Using the Morningstar database, the small-cap funds with a market cap of less than $1 billion had an average annualized 10-year return of 15.87%. For the same 10-year period, the truly small-cap DFA U.S. 9–10 Small Company fund (it buys the smallest 20% of stocks as ranked by market cap—average of about $160 million) provided a return of 15.68%. Since the pretax difference is very small, I think it is safe to say that on an after-tax basis the passively managed DFA fund, with its lower turnover, would have provided higher after-tax returns. Over the previous 5 years, the actively managed funds provided pretax returns of 19.68% versus 21.48% for the DFA 9–10. It doesn't seem to me that these actively managed funds managed to add value even during a period when their larger market cap should have provided them with an advantage.

The final claim of the article is that indexing doesn't work in the "less efficient" international markets. The AP story cited the fact that an international index fund had underperformed the vast majority of active managers. This is also misleading for the following reason. Index funds are typically market cap weighted by country. Japan, because of the size of its market, carries a very high weighting in such an index. For example, during the glory days of the Nikkei, Japan carried a weighting in the EAFE (Europe, Australasia, and Far East) Index of almost 70%. Given the Nikkei's poor performance in the 1990s, that figure is now closer to 25%. Active managers have been very reluctant to allocate that much exposure to any one country. The result is that international index funds carry a much higher exposure to Japan than does the average actively managed fund. From a returns perspective, when Japan provides high returns, active managers look bad. When Japan does poorly, they look good. It has nothing to do with stock selection or market timing skills. If an investor doesn't want exposure to Japan (although I don't think anyone can predict when Japan will outperform and when it will underperform), he or she can buy a European index fund or an emerging markets index fund. Selectively purchasing a passively managed fund, instead of seeking an active manager, is the solution to this problem. To prove this claim, David G. Booth of DFA studied the performance of closed-end country funds and compared their performance to their benchmark country index. His study covered 9 countries and 26 funds in developed markets and 18 countries and 30 funds in emerging markets. If active managers were able to add value, we would see them consistently outperforming market indices. All results are for the period ending December 1996. Booth found that while the average developed market country fund outperformed its benchmark by 0.7% over a one-year period, it managed to underperform by 7.9% and 1.4% over 3- and 5-year periods, respectively. The average emerging market country fund also underperformed its benchmark country index by 11.8%, 5.8%, and 1.6% over 1-, 3-, and 5-year periods, respectively. The average underperformance for all 56 funds covering 27 countries was 7.9%, 6.6%, and 1.5% for 1-, 3-, and 5-year periods, respectively. The value added by active managers is clearly negative. In addition, the negative value added is greatest in the "inefficient" emerging markets.

Again we see that, despite the claims of active managers, there is no evidence that active management works in either efficient or "inefficient markets." Booth concluded: "Even these dismal results overstate the value of active management, since the [benchmark] index returns are price-only, rather than total-return indices [which would include dividends]."[28] Booth's insight on total returns is not the whole story. For taxable accounts, the value added by active managers is likely to be even more negative because of the greater turnover, and probably greater distributed income, of an active versus a passive management strategy.

The next time you read stories claiming that index or passively managed funds underperform active managers, remember the source, and be sure to wear those "corrective lenses."

Ten Ways to Beat an Index

This was the title of a brochure for the value fund of the well-known and highly regarded *active* manager Tweedy Browne. On the surface it explains why the firm's active management style should provide superior returns to "the index." The document is very interesting in that an advocate of *passive* management could have written almost all of it.

The introduction, a letter from the 3 managing directors of the firm, begins with a summary of the academic studies that have found that the vast majority of active managers underperform the simple S&P 500 Index. For example, they cite their own study, which found that over the 16-year period ending December 31, 1997, less than 10% of the *surviving* equity funds beat the S&P 500 Index. It is important to note that even this low percentage is misleading, since many poorly performing funds didn't survive the entire period and the returns are pretax. Despite this evidence, the firm then presents their arguments for active investing, the Tweedy Browne way.

Many of their arguments are those of passive investing advocates. They state that their strategy includes attempts to keep transactions costs low because costs reduce returns. They also attempt to keep turnover low, as turnover increases costs and reduces returns. Perhaps the most interesting point they make is that they stay as fully invested as possible. They state that "empirical research has shown that 80–90% of investment returns have occurred in spurts that amount to 2%–7% of the total length of time of the holding period. The rest of the time stock returns have been small." The most telling point is the note that follows: "It is a little painful for us to write this section because, in our past, we have often sat on our thumbs with too much cash in client's portfolios before empirical research and our own analysis convinced us of the error of our ways."

These three strategies—low expense, low turnover, and being fully invested at all times—are passive management strategies. Tweedy Browne then adds that they do no index mimicking. They focus only on stocks likely to generate excess returns. And they use statistical methods to identify these "value added" companies. First, they state that research has demonstrated that stocks classified as value stocks, those with a higher-than-average book-to-market value (the stocks of distressed companies), produce higher returns. They state that the stocks they purchase are generally in the extreme 10 to 20% of the value rankings. They further state that they can be expected to out-perform "the index" by broadening their investment universe to include the smaller-cap stocks that are excluded from the S&P 500 Index. Once again they state that academic research has shown that small-cap stocks outperform large-cap stocks.

Tweedy Browne's statements are all correct. Over long periods of time investors can beat "the index" What they are missing is the following: you can expect to beat the index if you define your benchmark as the S&P 500 Index and you buy and hold stocks of the higher *expected* returning asset classes of small-cap and value. For the 16-year period 1982 through 1997, the S&P 500 Index rose 17.8% per annum. Tweedy Browne found that less than 10% of all active managers beat the S&P 500 Index. However, during this period when so few active managers were beating "the index," an index of small value stocks rose 20.3% per annum and an index of large value stocks rose 18.6% per annum. Tweedy Browne got it right. You could beat "the index." This is what MPT is all about. Markets reward for risk, and small-cap and value stocks are riskier and therefore provide higher *expected* returns. Unfortunately for Tweedy Browne, beating "the index" probably had little to do with stock selection skills (active management) and everything to do with asset al-location. Tweedy Browne is also right about low costs, low turn-over, tax efficiency, and avoiding market timing. The only problem with their analysis is that they arrived at the wrong conclusion. Their conclusion is that they can somehow discover the few large value and small value stocks that the rest of the intelligent fund managers have somehow mispriced. What they neglect to tell investors is that the very same academic research they cite also concludes that there is absolutely no evidence that anyone can consistently identify undervalued securities that will in the future outperform securities with similar risk characteristics of size and value. If there were such evidence, we would see active managers consistently outperforming their appropriate benchmark. And there is no such evidence.

The problem with Tweedy Browne's analysis is that they are defining the rules of the game incorrectly. They are comparing apples to oranges. Since the risky value stocks Tweedy Browne buys have outperformed the less risky S&P 500 Index over time, Tweedy Browne's fund *should* beat "the index." Their benchmark, however, *shouldn't* be the S&P 500 Index; it should be a value index. Using a value benchmark, the winning strategy is to own a value-oriented index fund or a passive asset class value fund. By doing so you are following all of the tenets of Tweedy Browne's strategy without paying Tweedy Browne's fees. Tweedy Browne's research (trying to find those few undervalued stocks within the value asset class) and other expenses result in an expense ratio of about 1.4%. You can buy value-oriented index funds with expense ratios of about 0.4%, or a full 1% less than Tweedy Browne charges. You will get to implement the same investment strategy, at lower cost.

Let's examine Tweedy Browne's statement about getting exposure to the 10 to 20% most distressed value stocks. According to the Morningstar database, as of April 30, 1998, the Tweedy Browne American Value Fund had far less exposure to the value risk factor than did a similar DFA Large-cap Value Fund. As measured by book-to-market value, the stocks in the DFA fund were almost 60% more distressed than those in Tweedy Browne's portfolio. As measured by P/E ratio, the DFA stocks were over 20% more distressed. It is worth noting that the DFA fund uses an academic definition of asset classes. This determines which stocks they own. The Tweedy Browne fund uses subjective judgment. Tweedy Browne's average market capitalization is smaller than the DFA Large-Cap Value Fund (by about $5 billion as compared to $12 billion). However, those investors wanting exposure to both of the risk factors of size and value can find that exposure in the DFA Small-cap Value Fund. This fund has an average market cap of under $500 million. This fund would achieve a far greater exposure than the Tweedy Browne American Value Fund does to the combined risk factors of value and size that are expected to produce the highest returns. An even better choice for investors would be to diversify their risk by allocating a portion of their assets to both of the two DFA value funds.

Surprisingly, Tweedy Browne provides investors with another important piece of academic evidence: past performance is not a predictor of the future performance of active managers. "Unfortunately, there is no way to distinguish between a poor 3-year stretch for a manager who will do well over 15 years, from a poor 3-year stretch for a manager who will continue to do poorly." They could have added that the same thing is true about a good 3-year track record. There is simply no way to know whether that performance will continue or deteriorate. The question for Tweedy Browne is, since they are an active manager, how can investors know ahead of time whether Tweedy Browne will be one of the very few who, they themselves admit, will beat their benchmark?

Tweedy Browne gave investors *almost* all the facts. In fact, they gave investors just enough facts to draw the wrong conclusion. Perhaps they did so because they want to charge you 1.4% per annum for an actively managed fund instead of being able to charge about 0.4% or less for a passively managed one. It is also interesting to note that as of year-end 1997 Tweedy Browne's value fund was still holding 11% of its assets in cash. Maybe this was before they discovered the error of their ways and decided to be "fully invested" at all times. Or maybe they think 11% cash is fully invested. Of further interest is the fact that Tweedy Browne's value fund, American Value, had almost 13% of its assets in foreign stocks. I wonder how many of their investors knew about, and/or wanted, this foreign stock asset allocation from their "American" fund.

This brochure is an example of why investors need to be fully informed about how markets work in order to be able to separate truth from half-truth. Investors should also beware of whose interests the authors have at heart when reading investment advice. Without the full knowledge of how markets work it is easy to fall prey to what appears to be sound advice.

Tweedy Browne deserves praise for concluding their brochure with the following: "You are more likely to reap the rewards of a value strategy if you stick with it through good and not-so-good periods over a long period of time. . . . It is all too human, in the field of investing, to extrapolate recent results, which have no statistical significance, rather than emphasizing long-run odds and empirical data. Your own psychology and ability to handle the emotional ups and downs of investing are likely to be important determinants of your long-run investment success." Sound advice, certainly in keeping with all the tenets of passive investing.

Investment Insights

- There is an overwhelming body of evidence to support the view that active management is a loser's game in both equity and fixed income markets.
- Efforts to outperform the market are not only nonproductive, they are counterproductive because of the expenses and taxes incurred.

- There is absolutely no evidence to support the view that markets systematically misprice securities.
- The price considered most likely by the market is the correct price: if the market judged otherwise it would not quote this price but another price, higher or lower.
- Individual investors (and their investment clubs) aren't as bad at stock-picking as many people think. They're worse!
- Trading is hazardous to your financial health.
- Despite the claims of active managers, there is no evidence that active management works in either efficient or inefficient markets (small-cap, international, or emerging markets).
- Glamorous hedge funds do not provide superior performance.
- Enhanced indexing (using active equity management strategies) is an oxymoron.
- Investment industry trade publications make more money selling their advice than investors do by following it.
- Scrutinize advertising claims to make sure funds are making apples to apples comparisons against the appropriate benchmark.
- Beware of survivorship bias in studies purporting to show superior performance of active managers.

CHAPTER 5

◆

Timing the Market Is a Loser's Game

Investors are overpaying for virtually all stocks.
>   —Warren Buffett, Berkshire Hathaway
>   1996 Annual Report

It must be apparent to intelligent investors that if anyone possessed the ability to do so [forecast the immediate trend of stock prices] consistently and accurately he would become a billionaire so quickly he would not find it necessary to sell his stock market guesses to the general public.
>   —*Weekly Staff Letter*, August 27, 1951,
>   David Babson and Company, quoted in Charles Ellis,
>   *The Investor's Anthology*

Market timing is impossible to perfect.
>   —Mark Rieppe, vice president, Charles Schwab Center for
>   Investment Research, November 27, 1998

Index funds decline in bear markets. So do managed funds . . . only more so.
>   —John C. Bogle, senior chairman, Vanguard Group,
>   keynote speech at Intelligent Investor Conference,
>   Philadelphia, October 3, 1998

We've found people tend to buy what has done well recently. But, in fact, studies have shown that they cost themselves money with poorly timed purchases and sales.
>   —Scott Cooley, analyst at Morningstar,
>   *St. Louis Post-Dispatch*,
>   February 11, 1999

Advice from Jonathan Clements on what to do when the market goes down: Read the opinions of the investment gu-

*rus who are quoted in the WSJ . . . And, as you read, laugh.
We all know that the pundits can't predict short-term market movements. Yet there they are, desperately trying to
sound intelligent when they really haven't got a clue.*
                        —*Wall Street Journal,* January 13, 1998

*I think that it is at least possible that we will be sitting
here around 6,000 for some years. The market fundamen-
tals just aren't very good.*
                    —John Bogle, chairman, Vanguard Mutual Funds,
            Smart Money, October 1997 (Less than 10 months later
                    the Dow Jones Industrial Index had risen above
                            8,300—almost 40% higher.)

*The big declines to come are in the big-cap tech stocks,
specifically Microsoft.*
                            —Barton Biggs, Morgan Stanley,
                        Wall Street Journal, March 19, 1997

*In the 46 markets around the world, we don't see a single
positive signal.*
            —Alan Shaw, director of technical research, Salomon Smith
                        Barney, *Barron's,* August 31, 1998

One of the most popularly held beliefs of individual investors is that market timing strategies can add to returns.
Market timers believe that they can determine when to increase
their equity investments prior to the market rising and reduce
their exposure to the market prior to the onset of a bear market. Unfortunately, *what Wall Street doesn't want investors to
know* is that an idea is not responsible for the people who believe
in it.

The evidence is very clear that professional mutual fund managers cannot predict the stock market. A Goldman Sachs study
examined mutual fund cash holdings from 1970 through 1989.
In their efforts to time the market, fund managers raise their cash

holdings when they believe the market will decline, and lower their cash holdings when they become bullish. The study found that mutual fund managers miscalled all 9 major turning points.[1]

One powerful example of the huge odds against the success of a market timing strategy comes from a Smith Barney study covering the 3,541 trading days of 1980 through 1993. An investor who built and held a portfolio consisting of the S&P 500 would have realized annualized returns of 15.5% per annum. (This figure is based solely on the price appreciation of the Index and does not include dividends.) If, in an attempt to time the market, an investor missed out on just the best 10 days, the annualized return dropped to 11.9%. Being absent from less than 0.3% of the trading days would have cost an investor over 23% of the returns available for the entire period. If an investor had the misfortune of missing out on the best 40 days (or about 1% of the total trading days), annualized returns would have dropped to 5.5%, a loss of almost two-thirds of the returns earned by a passive investor who had stayed the course. The returns of the investor who missed out on just the best 40 days could have been matched by owning risk-free certificates of deposit.

Peter Lynch offers another example. He points out that an investor who followed a passive investment strategy and stayed fully invested in the S&P 500 over the 40-year period beginning in 1954 would have achieved an 11.4% rate of return. If that investor missed just the best 10 months (2%), the return dropped (27%) to 8.3%. If the investor missed the best 20 months (4%), the return dropped (54%) to 6.1%. Finally, if the investor missed the best 40 months (8%), the return dropped (76%) all the way to 2.7%.[2] Do you really believe that there is anyone who can pick the best 40 months in a 40-year period? Lynch put it this way: "Far more money has been lost by investors in preparing for corrections, or anticipating corrections, than has been lost in the corrections themselves.''[3] One great example of this is that with the Dow Jones Industrial Average (DJIA) at the 2000 level, the September 26, 1988 issue of *Time* had the cover story ''Buy Stocks? No Way.'' Almost immediately thereafter the greatest bull market in history began.

A final example is perhaps the most compelling. An analysis of monthly investment returns of the S&P 500 from 1926 through 1993 by Sanford Bernstein showed that, out of the 816 months in this period, the returns of the 60 best months (just 7% of the time) averaged an amazing 11%. In the remaining 756 months (93% of the time) the returns averaged only 1/100 of 1% per month.[4] Trying to time investment decisions is likely to prove to be a futile endeavor because most of the action occurs over such brief, and unexpected, periods of time.

As this chapter will demonstrate, there is an overwhelming body of both academic and anecdotal evidence to support the view that believing in the ability of market timers is the equivalent of believing astrologers can predict the future. The following is from *Fortune's* May 12, 1997, issue: "Let's say it clearly: No one knows where the market is going—experts or novices, soothsayers or astrologers. That's the simple truth." What is truly amazing is that these words of wisdom come from the same magazine that advises you on whether or not the market is overvalued and on which active managers to choose when building your portfolio. *Fortune* speaks with forked tongue.

Speaking out against what he called the "Persistent Delusion" of successful stock market forecasting, Henry Dunn of the investment firm of Scudder, Stevens and Clark believed that every reasonable effort should be made to disabuse the public of the unwarranted and erroneous yet widespread belief that competent investment management is largely a matter of anticipating stock-market movements. His long experience had taught him that "various systems may at times have appeared to work fairly well for periods just long enough to mislead the unwary."[5]

John Bogle, Vanguard's legendary founder, stated: "After nearly fifty years in this business, I do not know of anybody who has done it [market timing] successfully, and consistently. I don't even know anybody who *knows* anybody who has done it successfully and consistently.[6] Legendary investor Bernard Baruch said it best: "Only liars manage to always be out during bad times and in during good times."

In my opinion, all market forecasts should be required to carry a warning from the surgeon general: ''This forecast may be dangerous to your financial well-being.'' Investment advisor John Merrill suggests that an even stronger disclaimer be required whenever the financial media interviews one of the so-called experts:

The views expressed are the views of our guest and not of this network. They may be unfounded, biased, self-serving and completely at odds with your long-term investment success. No due diligence on all past recommendations has been attempted.

Or

Warning! The following market analysis will likely be hazardous to your long-term investment strategy if acted upon. It is designed to motivate you to be a short-term trader (most of whom eventually fail) instead of a long-term investor (most of whom succeed).[7]

The bottom line is that stock market forecasts have about as much value as George Carlin's Hippy Dippy Weatherman's forecast: ''tonight's weather is dark, followed by widely scattered light in the morning.'' Investors are well served to heed this warning from behavioral economist Richard Thaler in his book *The Winner's Curse*: If you are prepared to do something stupid repeatedly, there are many professionals happy to take your money.

It Doesn't Take a Genius

With the major financial problems faced by the Asian economies in 1998, market gurus were telling investors that it didn't take a genius to see that the U.S. stock markets were where you wanted to invest in 1999. It was also clear that the markets of Japan and the other Pacific Rim countries should be avoided. Their rationale went something like this: the U.S. economy is strong, and employment, wages, and productivity are all rising. Our technology is the envy of the world. Not only is inflation falling, but the government budget deficit has all but disappeared. Both commercial and residential real estate prices are rising across the country, and the stock market has risen over 20% each of the last 4 years. Our free enterprise model has clearly proven to be superior to the managed capitalism of the Asian economies and the socialist and communist models of Europe and Asia. On the other hand, across Asia asset values are falling rapidly, unemployment is rising, and government budget deficits are exploding. Since every investor knows how large the disparity is in economic performance, it must be painfully obvious to everyone that they should invest in the U.S. and avoid the Asian markets. It sounds like good advice. But was it? Let's take a short trip down memory lane.

It's 1989, and Japan is the envy of the world. Asset prices are rising rapidly. The Nikkei is at 40,000 and no top is in sight. Land values have risen so high that the land under the Imperial

Palace is worth more than all the real estate in California. The Japanese "managed capitalism" model, with a few government officials deciding how assets will be allocated, is viewed as superior to our free enterprise model. Japan's technology and product quality is clearly viewed as superior to ours. They are running huge budget and trade surpluses. On the other hand, the United States is running huge budget deficits, our economy is growing very slowly, the market is about to fall again in 1990, and Sony's president states: "It's obvious the U.S. is in for a gradual economic decline."

Ten years later, despite the painfully obvious superiority of the Japanese economy in 1989, the Nikkei fell over 60%, while the U.S. market had tripled. While these facts should not be the basis for any predictions, this analogy should be a strong warning to investors about accepting the advice of so-called market experts. Remember, the markets were fully aware of the pain the Asian economies were experiencing. The EMT tells us that market prices already reflected all the information that was then currently known. Specifically, the stock markets of the Pacific Rim already reflected the current bad news and the market's current expectations. And, as the example helps to illustrate, very few, if any, investors have shown the ability to forecast which markets will perform the best in the future.

My advice is to build a globally diverse portfolio that reflects your investment horizon, financial goals, and appetite for risk and then stick with your allocations through both good and bad times. And, very important, avoid acting on the forecasts of so-called gurus. Just enjoy their commentary for whatever entertainment value you might find and heed the following advice from the January 5, 1998, edition of the *Wall Street Journal*: "Judging by the results of the past few years, New Year's stock market forecasts have a useful life span similar to those of other holiday paraphernalia like greeting cards, noisemakers and funny hats." And remember that the obvious is not always obvious when it comes to investing.

"Market Timing: A Perilous Ploy"

This was the headline of an article in the March 9, 1998, issue of *Business Week*. The appeal of market timing is obvious. As *Business Week* pointed out: "Who, after all, wouldn't want to ride the bull and dodge the bear?" The problem for those playing the market timing game is that they are depending on the triumph of hope over reason. First, most of the market's dramatic upward moves come over very short periods of time. Therefore, unless you are always fully invested you are highly likely to miss out on much of the market's gains. Second, over long periods of time, the market goes up much more than it goes down. However, market timers, in fear of bear markets, spend much of the time with substantial investments in cash and miss out on much of the market's gains. Let's look at the empirical evidence.

The *Business Week* article described a study conducted by Mark Hulbert. Hulbert studied the performance of 32 of the portfolios of market timing newsletters for the 10 years ending in 1997. During this period the S&P 500 Index was up over 18% per annum. Here is what he found:

- The timers' annual average returns ranged from 5.84% to 16.9%.
- The average return was 11.06%
- *None of the market timers beat the market.*

The *Business Week* article presented a study by another research firm, MoniResearch, which tracks 85 managers with a total of $10 billion under management. Here are its findings:

- The timers' annual average return ranged from 4.4% to 16.9%.
- The average return was 11.04%.
- *None of the market timers beat the market.*

For believers in market timing, the actual performance was probably worse than that presented by these figures. One reason is survivorship bias. Market timing newsletters, money managers, and mutual funds that performed poorly may have disappeared (and so did their poor results) because they were "fired" by investors. A second reason is that the returns of the newsletters ignore all transaction costs. A third reason is that the trading activity generated by the market timers would have further reduced returns. Unless market timing activities are confined to a tax deferred account, Uncle Sam will confiscate a large share of the gains (and most states want their share too) in the form of capital gains taxes. On the other hand, passive investors remaining fully invested continue to benefit from the deferral of taxes on unrealized gains.

What I found most interesting is that an article warning of the dangers of market timing was found in the very same magazine that provides advice from so-called market gurus on when to be in or out of the market.

A fitting conclusion to this tale is that the very next issue of *Business Week*, March 16, 1998, carried the headline "Beware the Trades of March: Signs point to a 'short and nasty pullback' for the stock market.... Wall Street soothsayers warn that there's trouble in the alignment of record-high stock prices, a backup in interest rates, and a slowdown in corporate profits growth." *Business Week* should have warned readers of this article to read the previous week's issue. They would then know that the use of the term "soothsayer" was appropriate.

We're So Sorry, Mutual Fund Managers, It Still Pays to Be an Index Investor

This was the headline of an article in the *Wall Street Journal*, October 5, 1998. After many years of underperforming their benchmarks, actively managed mutual funds have been left with hanging their hats on their ability to offer some protection from severe bear markets. After all, unlike index funds, they have the ability to move to cash and avoid the stocks that will suffer the most. Well, the third quarter of 1998 witnessed a very sharp decline in equity prices, and, as the *Journal* stated, "one of the biggest prejudices against index investing was shattered."

In almost all asset classes index funds outperformed their active counterparts. For example, mutual funds tied to the S&P 500 (which account for 70% of all index funds) declined 10.11%. This compared to an average fall of 11.69% for actively managed funds in the large-cap asset class. What is even more discouraging for supporters of active managers is the superior performance of index funds in asset classes in which active managers are the most confident of their ability to outperform their benchmarks. Active managers of large-cap international funds underperformed their benchmark EAFE Index by 14.93% versus 16.51%. Active managers in the "inefficient" asset class of U.S. small-cap stocks underperformed their benchmarks as well.

The article quoted one financial advisor as stating: "I hate index funds, because there's not a manager to protect you." Given the evidence, maybe active managers are the ones needing protection—from themselves!

The underperformance by active managers in 1998's bear markets was not unique. During the worst bear market of the postwar era (January 1973 through December 1974) only 5 of the top 25 funds outperformed the S&P 500 Index, and 3 of them were balanced (holding both equities and fixed income assets) funds. None of these 3 outperformed a balanced 60% (S&P 500)/40% (Lehman Bond Index) strategy.[8] This leaves just 2 (8%) that outperformed the S&P 500 Index.

"Every Time"

These are highly influential words to most investors; as a result they may also be the most dangerous to their financial health. A good example of the "every time" phenomenon is this statement: *"Every time* the dividend yield has fallen below x% it has been a signal that the market is overvalued and that a correction will follow." You can readily see how such a statement can scare an investor into action. However, there are two fundamental problems with the "every time" statement.

The first problem is a result of what is known as "data mining." If you look hard enough for a correlation, you will probably find one. In other words, if you torture the data enough, eventually it will confess. However, unless there is a logical reason for a correlation to exist, it will not have any predictive value. For example, many investors are aware that there has been a very high correlation between which conference of the NFL won the Super Bowl and the performance of the stock market in that year. Despite that high correlation, I am sure, or at least I hope, no serious investor would make investment decisions on the basis of which team won a sporting event. Serious investors know that it is a coincidence that the NFC has won most of the recent games and the market has been mostly up in recent years. Thus there is no predictive value in this information. David Leinweber, of First Quadrant, illustrates this point with what he calls "stupid data-miner tricks." Leinweber sifted through a United Nations CD-ROM and discovered that historically, the single best predictor of the S&P 500 Index was butter production in Bangladesh.[9] His example is a perfect illustration of the fact that the mere existence of a correlation does not necessarily give it predictive value.

The second problem with the "every time" statement is that even if a correlation existed for a logical reason, things change. For example, since bonds are competing investments for stocks, there is some logic behind believing that when the dividend yield of stocks reaches historically low levels investors would sell stocks and buy bonds. In 1996 many experts urged investors to sell when the dividend yield broke below 3%. That used to be a good indicator. Unfortunately, investors who followed this advice (as dividend yields fell to historically very low levels) missed out on the greatest bull market in history. The problem for investors using that indicator was that they failed to recognize that the world had changed. There are very valid reasons why dividend yields have dropped. First, companies are paying out less of their earnings as dividends because there is greater recognition and concern over the double taxation of dividends, first as corporate earnings and then as dividend income to the individual. Instead of raising dividends or paying them in the first place, companies are instead using their earnings to buy back their own stock. Investors also may be becoming more aware that equities are only relatively high-risk investments when the investment horizon is short. With this recognition, investors may be willing to accept a lower current yield.

Investors must be careful to remember that even a relationship that has worked for a very long time and has a rational basis can stop working. The question that investors must ask is: What, if any, relevant economic fact may have changed to alter historical relationships? The following is an example of where I believe it is simple to determine that the relationship is likely to continue. Equities have historically provided a premium return over Treasury bills. The premium has averaged about 7% per annum. The fundamental reasoning behind this phenomenon is that investors demand this premium as compensation for the extra risk inherent in equities. For you to believe that this risk premium will no longer exist, you must believe that investors will stop demanding a risk premium. That doesn't sound logical. Therefore, you have a high degree of confidence that equities will continue to provide a risk premium. The only question remaining then is whether or not that 7% premium will increase, decrease, or remain relatively constant over the long term. And no one knows the answer to that one.

Investment Newsletters and Other Fairy Tales

Individual investors flock to investment newsletters the way racetrack attendees flock to tout sheets. The financial press satisfies investors' apparently insatiable appetite with a proliferation of newsletters promoting the next hot stock or hot fund. Unfortunately, subscribers to these newsletters meet with the same degree of success as the purchasers of tout sheets.

Two researchers, from Duke University and the University of Utah, collaborated on a study examining the performance of the stock selections of 237 market timing newsletters over the 12.5 year period June 1980 through December 1992.[10] They used a database supplied by Mark Hulbert, publisher of *Hulbert's Financial Digest*. If an investor held an equally weighted portfolio of all the newsletters, he or she would have earned an 11.3% rate of return. This compared to the rate of return of 15.8% earned by an S&P 500 Index fund. As we have seen, when considering the costs associated with the trading recommendations of these financial tout sheets, the results get even worse.

- Transaction costs would have to be subtracted.
- The negative impact of the taxes generated by all of the trading activity must be considered.
- Adding insult to injury, the cost of the newsletters themselves would have to be subtracted from returns.

Perhaps most telling is that only 5.5% (13 of 237) of the newsletters survived the entire 12.5-year period. How would an investor, at the start of the period, have known which 13 would survive?[11]

Another study, by Andrew Metrick, found similar results. Metrick studied the equity portfolio recommendations of 153 newsletters covering the 17-year period ending December 1996. His conclusions:

- There was no evidence of stock-picking ability.
- There was no evidence of abnormal short-run performance persistence ("hot hands" didn't stay hot).

Metrick noted that there were over 2 million subscribers to over 500 newsletters. He also noted that while the publishers were making millions for themselves, they weren't adding any real value for their readers.[12]

A third study, by Mark Hulbert, examined the performance of 27 mutual fund portfolios for which he had 10 years of data. During that time, only 1 of the 27 (3.7%) was able to beat the market as measured by the Wilshire 5000 Index, through June 1996. When he studied 106 newsletter portfolios with at least 5 years of data, he found that just 12 (11.3%) had managed to outperform the Wilshire 5000 Index. Not surprisingly, the longer the time frame covered by Hulbert's study, the lower the percentage of newsletters that were able to beat a market benchmark.[13]

You can avoid falling prey to the "investment pandering" of investment newsletters by simply adopting this perspective: if racetrack tout sheets really could add value, the publishers would make far more money following their advice then selling it. The same is true of investment newsletters. As proof I offer this advice from Steve Forbes, quoting his grandfather, who founded the magazine that bears their name: "You make more money selling the advice than following it."[14] Economist and Nobel laureate Merton Miller agrees with the Forbes family: "I make my money writing about the stock market, not playing it."[15]

Individual Investors and Market Timing

As hard as it may be to believe, the average investor in mutual funds consistently underperforms the very same mutual funds in which he invests. The reason is simply that market timing efforts produce negative results. The following may be my favorite story on market timing. A Morningstar study evaluated 199 no-load growth mutual funds for which they had performance data for the period 1989 through 1994. The average total return for the 199 funds over this 6-year period was 12.01%. Keeping in mind that the average no-load mutual fund investor holds his funds for only 21 months, the individual owners of those same funds received a return of just 2.02% for their various periods of ownership. Either market timing or chasing the hot manager turned their 12% returns into 2%.[16] A similar study by Dalbar found that from 1984 to 1996 investors in equity mutual funds earned on average 10% less than the funds themselves.[17]

Looking at an even longer time frame, 1982 through 1997, Charles Ellis found that while the average mutual fund returned about 15%, mutual fund *investors* averaged only 10%. Trying to time the market and jumping from one fund to another resulted in investors missing out on fully one-third of the returns earned by the funds.[18] A similar Dalbar study covering the period 1984 through 1997 found that while the S&P 500 Index had an annualized return of 17.1%, the average equity fund investor achieved an annualized return of just 6.7%.[19]

Perhaps the most compelling evidence of investors chasing yesterday's winners was provided by a Morningstar study, covering the period 1987 through 1994. In comparing returns each year with the returns for the next 1, 2, and 3 years, Morningstar found that funds from the 3 *least* popular equity categories (based on net cash inflows) outperformed funds from the 3 *most* popular categories 22 out of 24 times.[20]

Institutional investors have fared no better. A study of 100 large pension funds and their experience with market timing found that while they all had engaged in at least some market timing, *not a single one* had improved its rate of return as a result. Their losses averaged an incredible 4.5% over the 5-year period. Maybe the results of these activities is one of the reasons we have seen institutional investors shifting assets in a dramatic fashion from active to passive managers.[21]

Both individuals and professionals miss out on available profits because they are overconfident of their market timing skills. Ellis offered the following excellent advice: "Investors would do well to learn from deer hunters and fishermen who know the importance of 'being there' and using patient persistence—so they are there when opportunity knocks."[22]

The Sky Is Falling

The fear of the spread of the "Asian contagion" combined with the collapse of commodity prices led many gurus and financial commentators to warn investors of a coming deflation. The "logical" conclusion from this forecast is that while deflation will be good for bonds, it will be very bad for stocks. Advice to "SELL STOCKS NOW!" filled the airwaves and the covers of financial publications. For investors, this is understandably unsettling, if not downright scary.

As John Merrill, author of *Outperforming the Market*, points out, investors need to be aware of the bias of the financial press. Investors must remember that the job of the media is to maintain and increase readership. They must get listeners and readers "hooked" on the daily drug of financial information. In order to be successful the media must have investors believe that all the daily information has value and isn't really just noise. However, contrast the headlines with their own advice that the road to success lies in a *buy-and-hold* strategy!

Thanks to Merrill we can actually examine the claim that deflation is good for bonds but bad for stocks. Merrill examined the returns of stocks (as represented by the S&P 500) and

5-year Treasury bonds for the full period 1926 through 1997. He then divided the full period into 2 subperiods, 1926 through 1959, when inflation averaged just 1.5% per annum (he called this the deflation era) and 1960 through 1997, when inflation averaged 4.6% per annum (the inflation era). The following are his findings:

- For the full period, bonds provided per annum returns of 5.3%, versus 2.8% for the deflation era and 7.5% for the inflation era.
- For the full period, per annum returns for stocks were 11%, versus 10.3% for the deflation era and 11.6% for the inflation era.

These return figures are, however, *nominal* returns. They do not reflect real purchasing power, or *real* returns. To arrive at the real returns investors earned, Merrill subtracted the inflation rate from the nominal returns. The results provide a very different picture.

- For the full period, bonds provided per annum real returns of 2.2%, versus 1.3% for the deflation era and 2.9% for the inflation era.
- Stocks provided per annum real returns of 7.9%, versus 8.8% and 7%, respectively.

While stocks have provided consistent long-term returns, the real returns are exactly the opposite of the "conventional" wisdom. The real returns for stocks were 1.8% higher in the deflation era than in the inflation era. Whenever investors hear or read such forecasts they should check to see if they are backed by real data, not just hype.

A fitting conclusion is the following factual tale. The worst period for stocks was clearly the Great Depression. For the purpose of this discussion, let us examine the period 1930 through 1938. The nominal return for the S&P 500 was 0%. For investors who had the patience to wait just 8 years, they would have realized no loss of principal. However, the story for real returns (the only kind that matter) is actually much better. The reason is that this was a period of deflation. Because of falling prices, the real returns to investors were +2.9% per annum. In fact, in real terms, investors only had to wait until 1935 to realize positive real returns. While this doesn't guarantee that stocks will provide positive real returns in a future deflationary environment, it does provide some perspective on the value of forecasts of doom and gloom.

Investment Insights

- There is an overwhelming body of evidence to support the view that believing in the ability of market timers is the equivalent of believing astrologers can predict the future.
- We have two classes of forecasters: those who don't know—and those who don't know they don't know.
- Trying to time investment decisions doesn't work because most of the action occurs over brief, and unexpected, periods of time. Unless investors are always fully invested, they are highly likely to miss out on much of the market's gains.
- Far more money has been lost anticipating corrections than has been lost in the corrections themselves.
- Active managers do not protect investors from bear markets.

- Ignore "every time" statements.
- If the advice of market timers had any value, they would make far more money following their own advice than selling it.
- Treat "expert" opinions as entertainment.
- Perhaps the most amusing thing about the stock market is that for every buyer there is a seller and both think they are doing the right thing.

CHAPTER 6

◆

Exposure to Risk Factors Determines Investment Returns

Knowledge is power.
> —Thomas Hobbes, *Leviathan*

The more original a discovery, the more obvious it seems afterward.
> —Arthur Koestler

Fortune favors the bold.
> —Virgil, *Aeneid*

Value criteria act like a chaperone at a party making sure you don't fall for some sexy stock with a great story.
> —James O'Shaughnessy, *What Works on Wall Street*

There are 2 main theories about what determines the returns of a portfolio over the long term. The Wall Street establishment wants investors to believe that it is the ability to pick individual securities and time the market that determines the vast majority of returns. If the Wall Street establishment were correct, stock selection and market timing efforts would add value beyond their costs and active managers would consistently deliver superior results *once style was accounted for*. In addition, Wall Street could justify its large management fees and the brokerage commissions it collects. The other theory on the determinants of portfolio returns comes from the academic community. Financial economists believe that the vast majority of returns are not a result of stock selection or market timing skills. Instead, they believe that the vast majority of a portfolio's returns results from the specific allocations to the 3 asset classes of equities in general, and then, within the equity asset class, the asset classes of small-cap companies (vs. large-cap) and value (vs. growth) companies. Small-cap companies are riskier than large-cap companies, and value (distressed) companies are riskier than growth companies.

The theory is that the low (distressed) prices of small-caps and value stocks are a reflection of the concern over the potential for financial distress. It seems very logical that investors are concerned that in the event of a credit or liquidity crunch, a severe economic recession, or a general flight to quality, these asset classes will do very poorly. The problem for investors is that this distress factor will evidence itself just when investors are most concerned about losing money. Think of the owner of a small or value company. The company is already exposed to the types of distress risks just mentioned. If the owner now has exposure in her portfolio to these same risk factors of distress, she compounds the problem. It would seem very logical for that investor to want to avoid, or at least severely limit, her exposure to those asset classes. The same logic could be used for an employee working for a small or value company. This logic provides a natural explanation for the value and size premiums. Many investors will want to avoid the distress risk factor. They will prefer stocks (or asset classes) that will do relatively well in recessions. They thus bid up the prices of those stocks (or asset classes) and are willing to accept the resulting lower future returns. This risk preference is what creates the risk premiums. William Sharpe, the father of the Capital Asset Pricing Model, put it this way: Consider a security that is expected to do badly in bad times. It should have high expected returns since more of its payoff comes in states of high aggregate consumption (a strong economy). Thus there will be a relationship between expected return and the extent to which a security "does badly in bad times."[1] Think of it this way: the market acts as a big insurance company. It transfers risk from those that want to avoid it to those that are willing to accept it, assuming they receive an insurance, or risk, premium.[2]

Not only are small companies riskier, but the market for their stocks is less liquid, and trading in them is more costly (much wider bid/offer spreads). A 1996 study by Donald B. Kiem and Ananth Mandhavan found that the market impact cost of block sales (large amounts of stock) was 1.86% for NYSE stocks but 3.28% for NASDAQ stocks (which on average have much smaller market caps).[3] Given the greater cost of trading and the lower level of liquidity (making it harder to sell large amounts of stock quickly), it is logical for investors to demand a liquidity (risk) premium.

Investors accepting greater risk are rewarded with greater returns in the form of risk premiums. For the period 1964 through 1999 the risk premium for equities, above the risk-free rate of return, was 7.25%. The additional risk premium for investing in small-cap stocks (smallest 50% as ranked by market cap) and value stocks (highest 30% as ranked by book-to-market) was 3.05% and 4.17%, respectively.[4]

Mark Carhart's 1994 University of Chicago dissertation concluded that it is the asset allocation decision (exposure to the risk factors of size and value) that determines the vast majority of returns. In addition, he found that stock selection and market timing efforts are not only *nonproductive*, they are *counterproductive* because of the expenses incurred in the effort. The conclusions of his paper, "On Persistence in Mutual Fund Performance," can be summarized as follows:

- Once common risk factors (investment style) such as size and value are accounted for, the average fund underperformed by 1.8% per annum.
- Any persistence in fund performance was easily explained by common factors such as expenses, transaction costs, and exposure to the aforementioned risk factors.
- There was little evidence of stock selection skills.
- Expenses have a one-for-one negative impact on performance. The more dollars expended on research and trading, the lower the returns.
- Turnover costs approximate 1% of the value of the assets traded.

The results of Carhart's study provide powerful evidence on the efficiency of the markets. They also strike a major blow to the claims that active managers are likely to add value over the long term.

This chapter examines the evidence on the risk factors of first size and then value—to help you understand how markets really work, as opposed to how Wall Street would like you to think they work.

Is the Small-Cap Effect a Myth?

Given the relative performance of U.S. large-cap stocks (as represented by the S&P 500 Index) compared to small-cap stocks from 1995 through 1998, some investors have questioned whether the size effect (small-cap stocks provide higher returns than large-cap stocks) on equity returns really exists. Professor Jeremy Siegel, in his book *Stocks for the Long Run*, even made an argument that if we ignore the 9-year period of 1975 through 1983, the greater returns provided by small-cap stocks relative to large-cap stocks disappears. First, a word of caution. Excluding the boom period (1975 through 1983) and saying that the small-cap effect doesn't exist would be like saying that if you exclude the month of September when he hit 17 home runs, Babe Ruth would not have hit 60 home runs. No one would accept that proposition. The following statistics also throw cold water on Siegel's claim. For 5-, 10-, and 20-year periods spanning 1926–1998, the CRSP 9–10 (smallest 20% of stocks) has outperformed the S&P 500 51%, 61%, and 82% of the time.

The following chart provides additional evidence that if investors have a sufficiently long investment horizon, they are highly likely to be compensated for the risk they take by investing in small-cap stocks, both domestically and internationally.

Best-Performing Asset Class
5-Year Periods

Annualized Returns 1970–1999				
Int'l Small Companies	US Small Companies	US Large Companies	Int'l Large Companies	US Treasury Bills
Best performer in 12 periods	Best performer in 8 periods	Best performer in 5 periods	Best performer in one period	Best performer in no periods
1987–1991 (19.9) 1986–1990 (28.3) 1985–1989 (46.2)				

1984–1988 (41.6)			
1983–1987 (43.0)	1992–1996 (19.5)		
1981–1985 (17.5)	1991–1995 (24.5)		
1977–1981 (29.9)	1990–1994 (11.8)		
1974–1978 (28.0)	1980–1984 (18.2)	1995–1999 (28.6)	
1973–1977 (12.4)	1979–1983 (28.7)	1994–1998 (24.1)	
1972–1976 (11.1)	1978–1982 (26.1)	1993–1997 (20.2)	
1971–1975 (20.6)	1976–1980 (37.4)	1989–1993 (14.5)	
1970–1974 (11.4)	1975–1979 (41.7)	1988–1992 (15.9)	1982–1986 (28.8)

International Small Companies asset class is represented by the DFA International Small Index fund; U.S. Small Companies is represented by DFA 9–10 Small Company fund; U.S. Large Companies is represented by the S&P 500 Index; International Large Companies is represented by the EAFE Index; U.S. Treasury Bills are one-month. For periods prior to fund inceptions, simulated CRSP data is used, including estimated hold ranges and trading costs.

The lesson for investors: Patience and discipline are keys to financial success. As studies demonstrate, the longer the investment horizon the greater the likelihood that the expected will occur.

Evidence of the Size Effect in International Markets

There have been many studies that have demonstrated that in the U.S. markets small-cap stocks have provided higher returns than large-cap stocks. The following 5 studies provide evidence that the size effect is a risk factor in international markets as well. Adding to their credibility is that, despite covering various time frames and various regions, all the studies come to the same conclusion: small-cap stocks provide higher returns (as compensation for their increased risk) than large-cap stocks. As these studies provide "out of sample" (non-U.S.) data, they further support the theory that small-cap stocks provide higher returns.

John Chisholm examined the relationship between size and returns in the United Kingdom, France, Germany, and Japan.[5] The study covered the period December 31, 1974–December 31, 1989. Companies in each country were sorted into quintiles according to market capitalization at the end of each year. Equal investments were made in each stock, and the portfolios were reconstructed at the end of each year. All results are in U.S. dollars. As you can see, in each country, the smaller-cap stocks provided superior returns.

Annual Compound Returns 1975–1989

	U.K.	France	Germany	Japan
Smallest stocks	33.7%	29.5%	21.6%	32.1%
Largest stocks	24.3%	21.4%	20.2%	23.6%

Mario Levis, professor at the School of Management of the University of Bath, England, and John Moxon examined the relationship between size and returns in the United Kingdom for the period 1956 through 1987.[6] Each year they sorted all stocks on the London Exchange into deciles as determined by market capitalization. There was an almost perfect negative relationship between size and returns: the smaller the stocks, the higher the returns. The smallest cap stocks outperformed the largest cap stocks by 10.18% per annum (21.58% to 10.4%). A study of small-cap stocks in Canada, covering the 2 periods 1951 through 1972 and 1973 through 1980, found similar results. Stocks on both the Toronto and Montreal stock exchanges (391 in total) were sorted into quintiles as determined by market capitalization. In this case there was perfect negative correlation between size and returns: the smaller the market cap, the higher the returns. For the period 1951 through 1972 the smallest cap stocks outperformed the largest cap stocks by 24.24% to 10.80% per annum. For the period 1973 through 1980, the smallest cap stocks outperformed the largest cap stocks by 20.04% to 14.76% per annum.[7]

A study covering all Australian industrial, mining, and oil stocks for the period 1958 through 1981 found similar results. Once again, there was almost a perfect symmetry between risk and return. The stocks in the first 3 deciles (the smallest) provided average annual returns of 81.05%, 26.77%, and 20.92%. This compares to returns of 12.88%, 14.17%, and 14.65% for the stocks in the largest three deciles.[8]

Finally, a study that examined the size factor for Japanese stocks for the period 1966 through 1983 found the same results. The study sorted stocks into quintiles as ranked by market capitalization. In this case there was a perfect negative correlation between size and returns: the smaller the stocks, the greater the returns. The smallest quintile stocks outperformed the stocks of the largest quintile stocks by 10.7% per annum (24.4% to 13.7%).[9]

Taken as a body of evidence, these studies provide powerful persuasion that size is a risk factor, and therefore a determinant of returns, in international markets. Investors seeking higher returns should seek greater exposure to this risk factor.

Turtle Eggs

Many academic studies have demonstrated the existence of a negative relationship between market capitalization and returns. Large-cap companies provide lower returns than do small-cap companies. When you rank stocks by market cap into deciles you find amazingly consistent results: the smaller the market cap, the higher the return. Financial economists explain this phenomenon as the market's way of pricing assets in an efficient manner. Investors perceive smaller cap stocks as riskier than larger cap stocks and, therefore, demand greater returns as compensation for accepting higher risk.

A study by Peter J. Knez and Mark J. Ready, published in the September 1997 issue of the *Journal of Finance*, examined the size effect in a different light. They used a mathematical technique called least trimmed squares. Put simply, this technique "trims," or removes, a fraction of the data and then examines the behavior of the remaining data. Their findings were not only very interesting but also provided investors with valuable insights into developing the winning investment strategy.

Knez and Ready found that the negative relationship between size and returns is driven by a very few extreme positive returns in each month. Most of the excess returns from small-caps came from a very small number of stocks. In fact, when only 1% of each month's observations are trimmed, there is a significant positive relationship between firm size and returns (large-caps now outperform small-caps). They called this the "turtle eggs" effect: investors who own small-cap stocks anticipate a few major successes and many minor disappointments. That is, they lay many "turtle eggs," hoping a few will hatch and make it to the ocean. This analogy helps explain why small-cap stocks should, and do, provide a risk premium over large-cap stocks. This finding also provided a valuable insight for investors in terms of choosing between active and passive management as the winning investment strategy. There are thousands of small-cap firms. No researcher or active manager can possibly follow all of them. Investors must ask themselves: If the excess returns from small-cap stocks come from just 1% of the companies, is it likely that an active manager will be able to identify the few "turtle eggs" that will make it to the sea? It seems clear to me that the winning strategy is to own all the "turtle eggs."

Knez and Ready provided another valuable insight for investors in developing the winning investment strategy. They found that the negative relationship between firm size and returns could be entirely explained by the 16 months (out of over 30 years of data) with the most extreme returns. I believe that this finding has powerful implications for investors. For active managers to believe that they can add value through market timing strategies (knowing when to buy small-caps and when to buy large-caps), they would have to believe that they could somehow identify the 16 months out of over 30 years that provided all the excess returns.

For investors, Knez and Ready's study provides strong support for adopting a passive strategy as the one most likely to provide the highest return. Since almost all the excess returns from owning small-cap stocks come from just a few "turtle eggs," the winning strategy is to not waste money on trying to identify the few that will make it to the sea. Instead, just own them all. Furthermore, because the vast majority of the small-cap premium occurs over such short periods, the most likely way to earn it is to be there all the time.

The Value Effect: Strong, Persistent, and Global

In their paper *The Cross-section of Expected Stock Returns*, professors Eugene F. Fama and Kenneth R. French examined the effect of book-to-market value ratios (value stocks vs. growth stocks) on returns in the U.S. markets. Their study covered the period July 1963 through December 1990. Fama and French broke the market down into deciles, ranking stocks by book-to-market value (btm) ratios. The results were amazingly consistent. Progressing through the deciles, from growth stocks to value stocks, average annual rates of return increased. The study found that value stocks, defined as the top 30% of stocks as ranked by book-to-market value, provided a risk premium of about 5% above the return on equities overall.[10]

The study created quite a stir in both the academic and financial communities. One reason was that the results flew in the face of the conventional Wall Street wisdom that growth stocks provide better returns than value stocks. Fama and French postulated that the value effect was a "risk premium"—the extra returns were compensation to investors for accepting the extra risk of owning stock in relatively distressed companies. The study, however, did receive some criticism. The critics' view was that Fama and French were guilty of data mining—the results were period specific and would not stand the test of time.

The issue of whether the value premium was period specific was addressed in a followup study by James Davis, Eugene F. Fama, and Kenneth R. French entitled *Characteristics, Covariances and Average Returns: 1929–1997*. The study broke the 68-year period into 2 separate periods, July 1929 through June 1963 and July 1963 through June 1997. The monthly value premium was 0.5% for the first period and a very similar 0.43%

for the second period. The conclusion: the value premium is robust.[11]

Fama and French performed an "out-of-sample" study that confirmed the existence of a value premium. They examined the impact of the value risk factor on stock returns for the period 1975 through 1995 in the developed country markets of the United States and 12 major EAFE countries. Using a variety of value measures, they concluded that the value premium was just as strong in other developed country markets as it was in the United States. For example, using btm as the measure of value, value stocks outperformed growth stocks by 7.68% per annum.[12] At an October 1997 conference at the University of Chicago, Fama and French presented a paper that extended their studies on the value effect to the emerging markets. For the period 1985 through 1996, emerging markets value stocks returned 34.6%, while the emerging markets overall returned 28.69% and the emerging markets growth stocks returned just 22.36%. Fama and French concluded that a U.S. value premium in excess of 5% is neither unusual nor unjustifiably large. Instead, the value premium is a global phenomenon.

In 1993 Carlo Capaul and Ian Rowley, both of Union Bank of Switzerland, and William Sharpe, a Nobel Prize–winning economist at Stanford University, analyzed stock returns from France, Germany, Switzerland, the United Kingdom, Japan, and the United States from January 1981 through June 1992. They found that global value stocks outperformed global growth stocks by 3.3% per annum. In fact, the value effect was greater in the Japanese and European markets than it was in the U.S. market.[13] Other studies on international markets confirm the Fama-French findings.

A study by Independence International Associates examined 20 equity markets in Europe and the Pacific Rim. For the 20-

year period ending December 31, 1994, they found that the value index they created outperformed a growth index by 4.7% per annum. In addition, growth stocks also underperformed their overall market index by 2.3% per annum.[14]

A study by John Chisholm, covering the period December 31, 1974 through December 31, 1989, examined the price-to-book value and investment results for companies in the United Kingdom, France, Germany, and Japan. At the end of each year, companies in each country were sorted into 5 quintiles according to their ratio of price-to-book value. Equal investments were made in each company, and a new portfolio was constructed each year. Chisholm then compared the returns of the growth stocks (those in the first quintile—highest price-to-book value ratio) to the returns of the value stocks (those in the fifth quintile—lowest price-to-book value ratio). His results provide further support for the theory that value stocks provide higher returns than growth stocks.

Annual Returns 1975–1989

Price-to-Book Category	United Kingdom	France	Germany	Japan
Lowest price-to-book	32.7%	28.2%	22.5%	30.9%
Highest price-to-book	24.4%	17.0%	20.1%	19.4%

In each country the value stocks provided superior returns, with the outperformance ranging from 2.4% per annum to 11.5% per annum.[15]

In his study on emerging market returns, K. Geert Rouwenhorst of Yale University provided further evidence of the value risk premium. He studied the performance of 1,705 firms in 20 emerging market countries covering the period January 1982 through April 1997. He found that value stocks provided a risk premium of almost 1% per month (0.93%). This study provided further "out-of-sample" support for the value risk premium.[16]

Another study, published in the spring 1998 issue of the *Journal of Investing*, "The Dimensions of International Equity Style," confirmed the existence of both the size and value effects in international markets. The study divided the market into 4 categories: value (top 50% as ranked by book-to-market value); growth (bottom 50% as ranked by book-to-market value); small (bottom 30% as ranked by market cap); and large (top 30% as ranked by market cap). The study covered the period 1975 through 1996 and 20 countries. The study also examined 3 different subperiods (1975 through 1981, 1982 through 1989, and 1990 through 1996) and 6 geographic regions. Here are its findings:

- For all 6 geographic regions and all 4 periods (the whole period and the 3 subperiods), value stocks outperformed growth stocks.
- For all periods, except the last subperiod, small-cap stocks outperformed large-cap stocks.
- Large value stocks generally outperformed large growth stocks.
- Small value stocks generally outperformed small growth stocks.

The following chart presents annualized returns of each asset class.

Asset Class	World	World Ex-U.S.
Value	16.99%	16.87%
Growth	12.35%	12.07%
Small	16.39%	15.43%
Large	13.92%	14.00%

Not only was the value premium robust, it was also very persistent. In fact, U.S. large value stocks have outperformed the S&P 500 with greater persistency than the S&P 500 Index has outperformed riskless 1-month Treasury bills. While the periods are different, the data is of great interest, as it surely will surprise most investors. For the period July 1963 through December 1998, large value stocks outperformed the S&P 500 Index in 5-, 10-, and 15-year periods 82%, 93%, and 98% of the time, respectively. For the 73-year period ending December 1998, the S&P 500 Index outperformed 1-month Treasury bills over the same 5-, 10-, and 15-year periods just 80%, 84%, and 94% of the time, respectively. Note that as the investment horizon increased, so did the likelihood of stocks outperforming T-bills and value stocks outperforming growth stocks. That is the nature of risk: the longer the horizon, the more likely it is that the expected (riskier assets will outperform less risky assets) will occur.

Another study, *Contrarian Investment, Extrapolation and Risk*, also examined the consistency of the value effect. The study covered the period 1968 through 1990 and examined the returns of the low price-to-book (value) stocks as compared to the returns of high price-to-book (growth) stocks. Defining value as the lowest 2 deciles and growth as the highest 2 deciles, the study examined the relative performance of these 2 groups of stocks over 1-, 3-, and 5-year time periods. The results were striking:

- Growth stocks outperformed distressed value stocks in just 6 of the 22 1-year periods (27% of the time), 2 of the 20 3-year periods (10% of the time), and not once over any 5-year period.
- During the market's worst 25 months value stocks fell about 10%, outperforming growth stocks, which fell by about

11%. For the remaining 88 months (in total) when the market declined, value stocks also outperformed growth stocks by −2% to −2.9%.

- For the market's best 25 months, value stocks outperformed growth stocks by about 14% to about 11%. In the remaining 122 months when the market rose, both value and growth stocks provided similar returns of close to 4%.

The study's conclusion: "Overall, the value strategy appears to do somewhat better than the glamour strategy in all states and significantly better in some states."[17]

Taken as a body of work, these studies provide further support to the EMT. Markets do compensate investors with returns in proportion to the amount of risk taken. Value stocks are riskier investments and therefore can be expected to provide greater returns. It works both domestically, internationally, and in emerging markets.

Are Value Stocks More Risky?

There is no doubt that value stocks have outperformed growth stocks over long periods. For example, for the period 1964 through 1999 small value stocks outperformed small growths stocks by 17.6% per annum to 12.9% per annum. For the same period, large value stocks outperformed large growth stocks by 14.8% per annum to 11.9% per annum.

While there can be no disagreement as to performance, there is, however, a great debate over whether or not the higher returns are compensation for a distress risk factor. If the greater returns are compensation for greater risk, then it could be said that the markets are efficient. Some academics, however, claim that value stocks do not entail greater risk since they have produced lower standard deviations. Standard deviation, a measure of volatility, is the most commonly used definition of risk. Therefore, some academics claim that, because value stocks have produced higher returns with a lower standard deviation, the market is inefficient (at least in pricing for risk). The logic is that if markets are efficient, greater returns must be accompanied by greater risk (i.e., higher standard deviation). Professor Robert A. Haugen even wrote a book on this seeming anomaly—*The New Finance: The Case against Efficient Markets.*

Those arguing that the market is efficient make the case that standard deviation, while a convenient measure, is not the only, or even necessarily the correct, measure of risk. Some focus on cost of capital as a better measure. Value companies have to pay more to attract capital. For example, their lower credit ratings result in a higher cost of debt. Their lower P/E ratios result in having to give away more of their future earnings when they sell equity. Keep in mind that the flip side of a higher cost of capital is a higher expected return to the providers (investors) of that capital.

The October 1998 issue of the *Journal of Business* contains a study, "Risk and Return of Value Stocks," by Naifu Cheng and Feng Zhang, that makes the case that value stocks do contain a distress factor. The study examined 3 factors of distress present in value companies:

1. DIV—firms cutting dividends by at least 25%.
2. LEV—a high ratio of debt to equity.
3. SEP—a high standard deviation of earnings.

The authors found that the 3 factors all captured the returns information (produced high correlations) contained in portfolios as ranked by book-to-market value. In other words, when these 3 factors were present, returns were greater. Since all 3 factors have simple intuitive risk interpretations (are associated with firms in distress), they state that it isn't surprising that the risk factors they studied were highly correlated and were also highly correlated with book-to-market rankings. Their conclusion was that value stocks are cheap because they tend to be firms in distress, with high leverage, and face substantial earnings risk. Therefore, they provide higher returns as compensation for their greater risks.

Baruch Lev and Theodore Sougiannis offered another possible explanation. They theorized that a research and development (R & D) risk factor might explain the enigma of the book-to-market (value) effect—at least for companies where R & D was a significant expenditure. There are fundamentally two types of scientific research—basic (innovative) and developmental (applied). Innovative scientific research is riskier than developmental research. Because of the greater risk inherent in innovative research, companies that engage in a high degree of such research have higher costs of capital than those that spend a greater amount on developmental research. The higher cost of capital translates into higher expected returns.

To test their theory, Lev and Sougiannis studied 1,200 firms, covering the period 1968 through 1989, that spent a minimum of 2% of sales on R & D. They found that the ratio of research capital to market value is closely associated with the book-to-market effect. In fact, it subsumes the role of btm in the Fama-French 3-Factor Model. Their conclusion was that, at least for the fastest growing sectors of the economy, the enigma of the book-to-market effect could be explained by the higher returns to risky basic research.[18] The market is perfectly rational: risk and reward were related. It just doesn't show up in standard deviation.

"Come Rain or Come Shine"

This was the headline of the winter 1997 issue of the Heartland Advisors' research report on value investing. Heartland examined the performance of low P/E (value) stocks and high P/E (growth) stocks in the 12 major market declines from 1937 to 1995 and the 12 recovery periods. Major market declines were defined as a loss of 20% or more. A recovery was defined as one in which at least 65% of the loss was recovered over at least a 3-month period. Value stocks were defined as those ranked by P/E ratio in the bottom 20% and growth stocks as those ranked in the top 20%. The study concluded that:

- Value stocks beat the market in 8 of the 12 declines.
- Value stocks beat growth stocks by an average annualized rate of almost 8%.
- Value stocks actually delivered positive returns in 8 of the 12 declines and in all 6 of the most recent declines.
- Value stocks outperformed growth stocks in 7 of the last 12 recoveries and did so by an annualized adjusted rate of almost 9%.

In another study, using P/E ratios to distinguish value versus growth stocks, Heartland compared the average annual returns of low P/E (value) stocks and high P/E (growth) stocks over 3-year holding periods following 13 market tops between 1950 and 1995. As in the aforementioned study, Heartland defined low P/E and high P/E, respectively, as the lowest 20% and the highest 20% of P/Es in the S&P 500 Index. Heartland found that low P/E stocks returned, on average, 7.12% for the 3-year holding periods following each of the 13 market tops studied—a figure more than 8 times the return of 0.88% produced by the high P/E stocks during the same periods.

It is clear that value stocks have outperformed growth stocks over the long term. They have also provided, on average, a significant advantage, in terms of performance and risk reduction, during bear markets.[19]

Heartland's results provide compelling rationale for including value stocks as a core portion of a portfolio.

Value *versus* Growth Stocks

It gives you a comfortable feeling when your theories are confirmed by all studies in which they are tested. "No matter how you define 'value,' out-of-favor value stocks have outperformed glamour growth stocks. It does not matter whether glamour is defined as a high ratio of stock price-to-book value; a high ratio of price-to-cash flow; a high ratio of sales growth; or a high ratio of price-to-earnings. For the 22-year period ending in April 1989, the average rate of return of glamour stocks was between 9% and 13%, while the rate of return of unglamorous value stocks was between 16% and 20%"[20]

Further evidence was provided by a study that covered all bear markets between 1978 and 1997. The best performer was small-cap value stocks. Large-cap value stocks also far outperformed the S&P 500 Index and both the large- and small-cap growth stocks.

* Small-cap value stocks fell an average of 4.8%.
* Large-cap value stocks fell an average of 11.8%.
* The S&P 500 Index fell an average of 18.1%.

- Large-cap growth stocks fell an average of 21.2%.
- Small-cap growth stocks fell an average of 23.9%[21]

Adding to the evidence on value stocks are 2 studies done by the mutual fund manager Heartland Advisors, using data from Prudential Securities. The first study looked at the performance of value stocks across various market capitalization levels. Heartland found that for the period 1976 through 1996, no matter what the market capitalization class, value provided superior returns to a growth strategy.

- Small-cap value stocks outperformed small-cap growth stocks by 20.4% to 18%.
- Mid-cap value stocks outperformed mid-cap growth stocks by 18% to 16.7%.
- Large-cap value stocks outperformed large-cap growth stocks by 15.9% to 12.1%[22]

The second study examined the returns of value stocks across various holding periods in order to determine how likely it is that a value strategy will outperform either an index or growth strategy. This is important because one of the risks of investing in risky asset classes is that if your investment time horizon is short, the expected outcome, in terms of returns, may not occur. The corollary to that risk is that the longer the investment horizon, the more likely it is that the expected outcome will occur. Heartland found that, even when the holding period is as short as one year, value strategies are likely to outperform either index or growth strategies. In addition, the longer the holding period, the more likely it was that value would prevail. If the holding period was at least 8 years, a value strategy outperformed an index strategy over 97% of the time and outperformed a growth strategy almost 91% of the time.[23]

There are 2 important lessons here for investors. First: value stocks should play an important role in an investment portfolio. Second: patience, and the discipline to stick with your investment strategy, are very important elements of a successful investment strategy.

Low Price-to-Book Determines Value

If you were to ask individual investors whether the stocks of the great growth companies (those with low book-to-market values and high P/E ratios) or the stocks of distressed companies (those with high book-to-market values and low P/E ratios) have provided investors with higher returns, the vast majority would vote for the great growth companies. Unfortunately, this is just another legend unsupported by fact.

Roger Ibbotson, in a 1986 Yale School of Management working paper titled "Decile Portfolios of the New York Stock Exchange, 1967–1984," studied the relationships between stock price as a percentage of book value and investment returns and P/E ratios and investment returns. On December 31 of each year, Ibbotson sorted all NYSE stocks into deciles as ranked by their market capitalization-to-book value and by P/E ratios. The table above shows the compound annual returns for each decile.

Over the 18-year period the market cap weighted return for all NYSE stocks was 8.6%. The almost perfect correlation between price-to-book value ratios and returns and P/E ratios and returns is impressive. The table is also evidence that the com-

Investment Results of NYSE Companies 1967–1984

	Compound Annual Return	
Decile	Price-to-Book	P/E
1 (Lowest price-to-book and P/E)	14.4%	14.1%
2	14.4%	13.8%
3	14.4%	11.0%
4	12.4%	10.3%
5	8.8%	9.2%
6	8.4%	6.4%
7	7.7%	7.0%
8	5.6%	5.6%
9	5.3%	5.5%
10 (Highest price-to-book and P/E)	6.1%	5.6%

monly held belief that the great growth stocks provide the best returns is false.

Professors Eugene F. Fama and Kenneth R. French provided further evidence on the value effect. In their famous paper "The Cross-section of Expected Stock Returns," they examined the effect of market capitalization (large-cap vs. small-cap) and stock price-to-book value ratios (growth vs. value) on returns. Their study covered the period July 1963 through December 1990. Fama and French broke the market down into deciles, ranking stocks by both market capitalization and stock price-to-book value ratios. The results were amazingly consistent. As you went up deciles, from large-cap stocks to small-cap stocks and from growth stocks to value stocks, average annual rates of return increased. Within every size decile the highest returns came from the highest btm (value) stocks. In 7 of the 10 deciles the lowest return came from the stocks with the lowest btm (growth stocks) ratios. In the other 3 cases the lowest returns were in the second and fourth deciles. With great consistency, the smaller the market capitalization, the higher the returns. The highest returns, 23% per annum, came from the stocks with the smallest market cap and the lowest price-to-book ratios. These stocks outperformed the largest cap growth stocks by almost 12% per annum.[24]

Investors should be aware that mutual funds use different definitions of risk. For example, most retail-oriented funds, like those of Vanguard and Schwab, base their definition of value on the S&P/Barra indices. These indices split the market equally (50/50) into growth and value stocks. The institutional style funds run by DFA, however, define value as the top 30% of stocks as ranked by btm and growth stocks as the bottom 30%. One definition isn't necessarily better than the other or one fund better than the other. However, investors seeking the highest expected long-term returns should purchase funds that achieve the greatest exposure to the value risk factor.

The "Black" Box

"I've known Scott Black for 23 years. . . . To me he's simply one of the brightest stock pickers in the business. For the past 19 years, Scott's firm, Delphi Management, has been managing money for large institutional clients. . . . I've always wanted to tap into Scott's expertise, and finally I've convinced him to make his skills available to individual investors." So begins a marketing brochure for the Kobren Delphi Value Fund. The brochure continues with an interview with Scott Black, the fund's investment manager, focusing on his investment style. Scott describes his value approach as buying companies with the following characteristics: 15% after-tax return on equity; low debt/ equity ratios; revenues and earnings growing faster than inflation over a 3- to 5-year time horizon; conservative accounting methods; strong management; and especially low P/E ratios. He also stays relatively fully invested with an 85 to 100% equity exposure. Sounds like a good strategy—one that accounts for Scott Black's excellent reputation. But is Mr. Black's excellent reputation for adding value truly deserved? To answer that question we need to examine his performance and then have an appropriate benchmark against which to judge it.

The marketing brochure provides us with the historical performance of Mr. Black's investments using the assumption that his returns would have been reduced by the Kobren Fund's expected expenses (since the funds that Mr. Black has previously managed may have had different internal expense ratios). We are provided with the returns earned by Mr. Black for the 5- and 10-year periods ending June 30, 1998, and since inception, which was January 1, 1980. We can now compare his performance to appropriate benchmarks.

Since we are not provided with knowledge of whether Mr. Black is a large-cap value investor or small-cap value investor, we need to look at benchmarks for both of those asset classes. Appropriate benchmarks are the passively managed asset class funds of DFA. They are similar to index funds in that they basically buy and hold all of the stocks in the asset class of small value and large value. The small value fund basically buys and holds all stocks within deciles 6 to 10 (the smallest half), as ranked by market capitalization, and the top 30% of stocks, as ranked by book-to-market value. The large value fund basically buys and holds all stocks within deciles 1 to 5 (the largest half), as ranked by market capitalization, and the top 30% of stocks, as ranked by book-to-market value. Mr. Black's performance can also be compared to that of the S&P 500, although that is a less appropriate benchmark, since it is basically a large-cap growth index. Here are the facts:

	Delphi Management	DFA Small Value*	DFA Large Value**	S&P 500 Index
5 years ending 6/30/98	20.35%	20.43%	19.78%	23.06%
10 years ending 6/30/98	15.62%	17.21%	17.86%	18.54%
Since inception 1/1/80–6/30/98	17.58%	19.53%	18.56%	17.76%

*Returns are actual since 3/20/92 and simulated prior to that.
**Returns are actual since 2/18/93 and simulated prior to that.

As can be readily seen, despite his great acclaim, Mr. Black has not shown any real ability to add value through superior stock selection or market timing skills. In fact, his returns only look great when compared not to appropriate benchmarks but instead to other active managers—the vast majority of whom underperformed the S&P 500. Once you subtract operating expenses, Mr. Black actually underperformed (added negative value compared to) an appropriate benchmark. The table also is another piece of evidence that the vast majority of a portfolio's returns are a function of exposure to an asset class and not stock selection or market timing skills. The conclusion for investors: once you have decided on the asset class to which you want exposure, choose a low-cost passively managed fund to implement your strategy.

Another legendary value investor is David Dreman. Bill Bernstein's winter 2000 issue of the *Efficient Frontier* put Dreman's returns to the same factor analysis tests. For the period April 1988 through October 1999, Dreman's fund returned 16.58%, almost 2% per annum less than that of the S&P 500 Index's return for the same period. When a 3-factor analysis (exposure to the risk factors of size and value) was applied to Dreman's returns, his alpha (value added) was precisely zero. Keep in mind that when looking at Dreman and Black, we are looking at 2 legends that survived the period. Imagine what the returns of the rest of the active managers must look like.

The main purpose of this tale is not to ridicule either Mr. Black or Mr. Dreman in any way. In fact, compared to most active managers they have exemplary records. However, their benchmarks shouldn't be other active managers any more than it should be the S&P 500. Investors need to make sure that they are comparing apples to apples when looking at the performance of active managers.

Technology and Other Sector Funds

One of the most frequent theories we hear about investing goes like this:

- It is *obvious* that technology companies will experience much faster growth rates than the economy in general.
- The *obvious* result is that technology companies will experience much greater growth in earnings than will firms in other sectors.
- Thus, technology stocks should be overweighted in a portfolio.
- Investors can accomplish this overweighting by purchasing a technology sector fund.

176

The argument for overweighting a fast-growing sector such as technology (or biotechnology, or whatever sector is the "flavor of the moment") is really just another version of the argument that growth stocks will outperform value stocks because of their superior sales and earnings performance. Unfortunately for those "betting" on technology, or growth stocks in general, there is no logical or factual support for this view.

The most important tenet of MPT is that the market is highly efficient in processing information. The result is that current market prices reflect the total knowledge and expectations of all investors in a free market, and no one investor can know more than the market does collectively. Given the highly efficient flow of information that exists in the U.S. capital markets, it seems illogical to believe in the proposition that if technology companies are indeed expected to produce much higher earnings growth, their stocks don't already reflect those great prospects. For technology stocks to be "undervalued" (giving an investor a reason to buy them), the market must be unaware of their great prospects relative to companies in other sectors of the economy. That doesn't seem like a logical proposition. Yet for investors to overweight technology that is exactly what they must believe.

Even if we know with certainty that technology companies will produce superior earnings, it does not guarantee that the stocks of those companies will provide superior investment returns. In fact, the evidence suggests just the opposite. For example, from 1964 to 1998, while large growth stocks produced annual returns of 11.4% per annum, the S&P 500 stocks returned 12.3% per annum, and large value stocks returned 15.1% per annum. For small stocks the evidence is even more compelling. Small growth stocks returned just 12.1% per annum to 17.7% per annum for small value stocks. These historical return figures demonstrate that earnings growth rates are not the major determinant of investment returns of either individual stocks or economic sectors. Instead, it is the exposure to the risk factor of value (and/or size—small companies are perceived as riskier than large companies) that is the major determinant of returns.

Let's look at the specific evidence on technology funds. Using the Morningstar database, there are just 7 technology funds that survived the 15-year period ending June 1999. The average *pretax* return for the 7 funds was just 0.5% greater than the 19.2% return of the S&P 500 Index. Not a very statistically significant difference, and probably far less than the average investor would have guessed. If we go back just a bit further and examine the 19-year period ending December 1998, of the 3 technology sector funds that survived the period, not one outperformed the 16.94% return of the S&P 500 Index. The average underperformance was over 2% per annum. In addition, despite investor perception of the superior recent performance of tech stocks, the fact is that for the 3-year period ending December 1998 the S&P 500 was up over 28% per annum while the 37 tech sector funds in the Micropal universe returned just over 23% per annum. Once again, these figures are pretax returns. Since the average actively managed fund is far less tax efficient than a passively managed index fund (because of greater turnover and the resulting distributions of realized gains), it is highly likely that the relative after-tax performance of the technology funds would have looked even worse. In addition, the Morningstar and Micropal databases suffer from survivorship bias. Various studies have shown that over long periods of time, survivorship bias causes actively managed mutual fund returns to be inflated by between 1% and 2%. Since it is unlikely that a fund that outperformed would have disappeared, it is highly likely that the actual returns of all tech sector funds would have been even lower.

There is another often-overlooked bit of logic on why tech stocks do not outperform the overall market: technology doesn't just benefit the inventors any more than the invention of the telephone or electricity benefited just their inventors. The benefits of technology flow throughout the economy. For example, one reason that Walmart has achieved its superior results is the way it benefited from its implementation of computerized inventory systems. Over the past 20 years, for example, Walmart's stock has far outperformed the stock of Intel, the maker of the chip inside many computers. And Intel has been one of the best performing stocks over the past 20 years. Many other examples can be cited.

Jane Bryant Quinn, in her syndicated column of April 14, 2000, provided more evidence against the "Technology Is King" myth. She found that of the 34 leading tech stocks back in 1980 only one—Intel—emerged a winner. Of the rest, 22 were no longer trading; the other 11 trailed the S&P 500 Index; and 3 lost over half their value (even without consideration of the impact of inflation over 20 years).[25]

There is another reason investors should think twice before overweighting any economic sector, be it technology or health care. ("Isn't it obvious that with an aging population health care companies will have to outperform?") When an investor overweights a sector, he or she is *betting* (not investing) that sector will outperform. In return for the hope of outperformance, investors must also acknowledge that they are accepting the risk that the sector they have chosen to *over*weight will *under*perform. Logical investors only accept risk if they can be expected to be compensated with greater returns. There is no logical reason to expect those greater returns. There is also significant historical evidence supporting the illogic of such a conclusion. The logical conclusion: ignore those ads for tech funds, or any other sector fund.

Dunn's Law

The Schwab Center for Investment Research published a research paper, *Core and Explore—An Effective Strategy for Building Your Portfolio.* The paper begins by stating that it is Schwab's belief that asset allocation is the key to building an effective portfolio. The study concludes that the best way to implement an asset allocation plan was to use broad-based index funds for the "Core" of the portfolio. Investors would then add a layer of actively managed or "Explore" funds, providing the potential to outperform the market.

There were 3 main research findings:

* The Core and Explore (C & E) approach reduced the risk of underperforming versus an all-explore approach.
* C & E provided more potential to beat the market versus an all-Core approach.
* Emphasizing actively managed funds in the small-cap and international asset classes tended to increase a portfolio's potential to beat the market.

Schwab concluded that the right mix was:

Large-cap	80% Core/20% Explore
Small-cap	40% Core/60% Explore
International	30% Core/70% Explore

This study received wide press coverage. However, there are many problems with the study. First, it covers a very brief period, just 3 3-year periods beginning in 1993. No financial economist worth his salt would draw any real conclusions from such a short period. In addition, Schwab should be criticized for what was really nothing more than data mining. The period the study covered was one in which large-caps outperformed small-caps and domestic equities outperformed international equities. Thus the study ignores what is rapidly coming to be called Dunn's law (named after a Southern California attorney who provided the insights).

Dunn's law states that when an asset class does well, index funds will outperform active managers in that asset class. However, when an asset class does poorly, active managers have a greater chance to outperform their benchmark index. The logic is simple. Index funds generally achieve the greatest exposure to the relevant risk factor responsible for the vast majority of the returns. In other words, when large-cap stocks are the leading asset class index funds will dramatically outperform large-cap active managers. This was true from 1995 to 1998. The reason is that active managers tend to style drift (i.e., large-cap funds often own mid- and small-cap stocks, and small-cap funds often own mid-and large-caps). Thus active managers lose some of their exposure to both the "winning" and "losing" asset classes. Thus we see results like those from 1995–1998 when the S&P 500 Index outperformed about 80% or more of active managers each year (and about 94% for the entire period, even before taxes). The reverse is also true. For example, from 1977–1982, when small-caps outperformed large-caps by about 16% per annum, in only one single year did less than 60% of active managers outperform the S&P 500 Index. The reason is simple. Active managers, even active managers of large-cap mutual funds, tend to own some stocks that are smaller cap stocks than those in the S&P 500 Index—thus they held some of the "outperformers." Conversely, from 1995–1998 they held some of the "underperformers."

In periods when the S&P outperforms, you hear claims like "it wasn't a stock picker's year." Stock-picking has virtually nothing to do with it. It's all about asset allocation. The academic evidence is very clear that, as a group, active managers fail miserably at *intentionally* style drifting to the asset class that will outperform.

Let's examine two examples. The first is the recent "superior performance" of the Janus 20, a very concentrated fund, holding just 20 of the largest stocks (not all of the S&P 500 stocks). Its outperformance relative to the S&P 500 can be traced to its owning a larger percentage of the very largest of stocks than the index does itself. When large-caps do well, the very largest generally perform the best and the very smallest the worst. The reverse is also true. When small-caps outperform large-caps, the very smallest generally do the best and the very largest the worst. Thus, unless it style drifts, when small-caps outperform large-caps again, the Janus 20 fund is likely to underperform the S&P 500. A second example is the dramatic underperformance in the 1970s and 1980s of international actively managed funds versus their benchmark EAFE index. This underperformance could largely be traced to their style drifting— in this case, holding throughout the period a much lower percentage of Japanese stocks than did the EAFE index. In the period of the Schwab study, Japan underperformed the EAFE Index overall. The result is that active managers, because of their underallocation (style drifting), looked good. Again, it's all about asset allocation.

Returning to the results of the Schwab study, since the period covered was one in which large beat small and domestic beat international, Dunn's law tells us that it is not surprising that the Schwab study concluded that you should own more actively managed funds in the asset classes of small and international. Unfortunately for Schwab, if they had studied a period like 1977 through 1982, they would have come to the exact opposite conclusion. The study is really nothing more than an exercise in data mining. It may also be another example of having to be careful whose interests the study has at heart. The Schwab One-Source supermarket is mostly made up of active managers. It probably would not have been good for Schwab if their study showed that investors should only use index funds.

The 2 other conclusions of the Schwab study are so ludicrous that they almost don't even warrant comment, but I can't resist. The first is that by adding Core (index) funds to an all-Explore portfolio, you reduce the risk that an all-Explore approach will underperform. That is an obvious conclusion, because the Core funds are the benchmark itself. Therefore, they can't underperform. If you don't want the risk of underperformance, why own any active managers? The second is the claim that adding Explore funds increases the chance of outperformance. If you own only Core funds, you hold only funds that are their own bench marks. Obviously, you can't get outperformance. Therefore, by adding Explore funds you obviously increase the chance of outperformance. The more relevant conclusion is that you increase your chance of underperformance by a far greater amount!

Dunn's law also provides us with the winning strategy. If you can forecast which asset classes will outperform the others, the best chance of capturing those returns is by purchasing an index fund. You would avoid the asset classes that perform poorly—where active managers have a better chance of outperformance. If you can't forecast which asset classes will do best, then you should choose index funds anyway, because that is the only way you can control your asset allocation, the major determinant of returns and risk.

Defining a Fund's Investment Style Is Hard?

Clint Willis, a freelance writer who covers mutual funds for Reuters, asked the question: "What should you consider when choosing a mutual fund?"

Most investors look at past performance and expense ratios. However, the academic evidence is clear that the vast majority of a fund's performance is determined by its asset allocation, or fund style. Fund style is determined by whether a fund invests in large-cap or small-cap companies, value or growth stocks, and domestically or internationally. If asset allocation is the determinant of the vast majority of a fund's performance, every investor should know the style of his or her fund.

Willis states that the simple task of choosing a fund according to its "style" isn't easy because most funds don't have a consistent asset allocation. "Many funds don't have a consistent style. Instead, their managers simply invest on a case-by-case basis." Willis adds: "Other funds are downright misleading about their styles. For example, many so-called small-cap funds invest mostly in mid-sized or even large companies. And some so-called value funds are quick to shift to growth stocks when growth is in vogue."[24]

Unfortunately for investors, since the vast majority of a portfolio's return is determined by asset allocation, if fund managers switch styles, investors lose control over the most important determinant of the risk and expected return of their portfolios. A good example of investors losing control over their portfolio's asset allocation occurred in February 1996 when Fidelity Magellan's asset allocation was only 70% equity, 20% bonds, and 10% short-term marketable securities. As a result of Magellan's style shift, investors had a lower equity exposure and a higher fixed income exposure than they desired.

What Willis failed to point out is that there is a very simple solution to the style drift problem: avoid actively managed funds, because by owning them you lose control of the asset allocation decision. Instead, buy only passive asset class and/or index funds. By definition these funds own only the stocks that meet the definition of the asset class in which you are seeking to invest or are part of an index. Investors in these funds never have to worry about being subject to style drift.

Investment Insights

- The vast majority of returns are determined by an investor's exposure to the risk factors (or asset classes) of equities, size, and value.
- Markets reward investors with returns commensurate with the degree of risk they are willing to accept.
- The same risk factors—size and value—that determine returns in the domestic equity markets are also present in the international and emerging markets.
- When looking at the performance claims of active managers, make sure to compare their performance to the appropriate benchmark.
- Any persistence in fund performance (the repeating of a fund as a top performer) is easily explained by common factors such as expenses, transaction costs, and exposure to the aforementioned risk factors.

- Investors seeking above-market returns should allocate more of their assets to the high-risk asset classes of small-cap and value stocks.
- It does not matter whether a glamour (growth) company is defined as a high ratio of stock price to book value, a high ratio of stock price to cash flow, a high ratio of stock price to sales or a high ratio of stock price to earnings. Out-of-favor value stocks have outperformed glamour growth stocks.
- The longer the holding period, the greater the likelihood that the value and size effects will prevail.
- The fact that large-cap and growth stocks provide lower returns than small-cap and value stocks does not make them "bad investments." Their lower returns are just a reflection of their lower perceived risk.
- Value stocks have generally outperformed growth stocks in most bear markets. Small-cap value stocks generally have been the best relative performer in bear markets.
- Investors should avoid sector funds.
- Most of the risk premium from small-cap stocks comes from a very small percentage of the small-cap universe. Since security analysis is unlikely to find the very few winning "turtle eggs," owning the whole asset class is the winning strategy.
- The only way to ensure that your portfolio maintains the asset allocation you chose is to avoid actively managed funds.

CHAPTER 7

◆

Investors Should Focus on the Long, Not the Short Term

My favorite time frame is forever.
 —Warren Buffett

Don't just do something, stand there!
 —Charles Ellis, *Winning the Loser's Game*

In the main, therefore, slumps are experiences to be lived through . . . with as much equanimity and patience as possible.
 —John Maynard Keynes

Do you know what investing for the long run but listening to market news every day is like? It's like a man walking up a big hill with a yo-yo and keeping his eye fixed on the yo-yo instead of the hill.
 —Alan Abelson

One of the major tenets of MPT is that over the long term, markets reward for risk. Historically, equities have outperformed risk-free short-term Treasury bills by about 7% per annum. On the other hand, while Treasury bills never go down in value, over the last 70 years stocks have generally experienced a bear market—a loss in value of at least 10%—one out of every 3 or 4 years. From 1926 to 1998 the S&P 500 has outperformed one-month Treasury bills for 1-, 5-, 10-, and

15-year periods 69%, 80%, 84%, and 94% of the time. Over the same time frame, stocks have outperformed the risk-free one-month T-bills over every 20-year period. The explanation is simple: stocks provided that extra 7% per annum return as compensation for the risk that there will be periods, even long ones, when they not only underperform but, as they did in 1973 through 1974, lose as much as 40% of their value. If stocks outperformed fixed income investments every year by that same 7%, then investors would not be taking any risk. What investors must accept is that the risk premium is there for a reason. Investors can use this knowledge to develop the winning investment strategy by understanding one simple point: the longer the investment horizon, the greater the likelihood that the expected outcome will occur. With this information investors can construct a portfolio that fits their unique tolerance for risk and the investment time horizon. All other things being equal, the longer the investment horizon, the greater should be the willingness to accept risk.

While Wall Street would like investors to focus on the short term, this chapter describes why a very important part of the winning investment strategy is to have a long-term perspective.

The Longer the Investment Horizon, the More Likely It Is That the Expected Will Occur

Most investors understand the relationship between risk and reward: riskier assets must provide greater *expected* returns as compensation for their extra risk. What many investors fail to understand is that those extra returns are not guaranteed. In fact, if they were guaranteed, there wouldn't be any risk, nor would there be any risk premium. The key to maximizing the opportunity to achieve those higher *expected* returns is to understand the relationship between risk and holding periods.

Undoubtedly, stocks are much riskier than bonds. They provide excess returns as compensation for that risk—but only if the holding period is long enough. In fact, there have been 20 down years for the S&P 500 between 1926 and 1998. In 1973 the S&P 500 dropped 15% and then fell another 27% the following year. On the other hand, even during the depression the S&P 500 never had a period of longer than 7 consecutive years when cumulative returns were negative. In the post–World War II era that figure dropped to just 3 years. Consider this evidence, based on research conducted by Baylor University professors William Reichenstein and Dovalee Dorsett. For a one-year holding period, there is a 5% chance that the stock market will fall at least 25% and a 5% chance that it will rise more than 40%. On the other hand, over 30 years, there is only a 5% chance that a 100% stock portfolio will grow by less than 20% and a 5% chance that it will increase in value by over 50 times.[1]

What we learn from these statistics is that when the investment horizon is short, the *unexpected actually occurs fairly frequently*. The longer the investment horizon, the less likely it is that the unexpected will occur. These are important concepts to incorporate into an investment strategy. If an investor's horizon is fairly short, then a relatively low allocation to equities is appropriate. For most investors there are two reasons why the allocation to equities should increase as the investment horizon increases. First, as the investment horizon increases, so does the likelihood that equities will outperform the "safer" fixed income alternative. Second, as the investment horizon increases, so does the risk that inflation will outrun the returns that fixed income assets provide. For 20-year holding periods, stocks have always produced positive *real* (after inflation) returns. The same cannot be said for bonds or T-bills, which have lost as much as 3% per annum in *real* terms over a 20-year period.[2] In other words, the nature of risk changes as we increase the investment horizon, and the disparity between returns on "risky" equity investments and "conservative" fixed income instruments widens dramatically. Reichenstein and Dorsett also concluded that, over 20 years, there is only a 5% chance that a fixed income portfolio will more than quadruple, while there is a 50% chance that an all-equity portfolio will grow at least eightfold.[3] With a long-term horizon, bonds or any other fixed income investment become the risky investment because equities provide protection against the erosion of purchasing power by inflation. The bottom line for investors is that equities are risky when the investment horizon is short, but fixed income assets become the riskier asset class when the investment horizon lengthens.

While most investors know that riskier stocks outperform safer Treasury bills, they may not know that riskier value stocks outperform safer growth stocks. In fact, value stocks have outperformed growth stocks with even greater persistency than equities have outperformed T-bills. Comparing the returns of large value stocks to that of the S&P 500 over 5- and 10-year periods, we find that since 1963 large value stocks have outperformed the S&P 500 82% and 93% of the time, respectively. This compares to the S&P 500 beating 1-month Treasury bills just 80% and 84% of the time, respectively.[4]

Further evidence that "the longer the investment horizon the greater the likelihood that the expected will occur" is the performance of riskier small-cap stocks compared to safer large-cap stocks. Morningstar examined the 72-year period beginning in 1926 and found that small-caps outperformed large-caps in 40 of the 72 calendar years, or 56% of the time. When the investment horizon was extended to 5- and 10-year periods, the figures increased to 59% and 65% of the time, respectively. When the investment horizon was extended to 20-year periods, small-caps outperformed a "whopping" 94% of the time.[5]

Oliver Wendell Holmes said: "A page of history is worth a volume of logic." Unfortunately, investors are often blinded by the light of recent returns and forget the lessons of history. This often causes them to lose discipline and chase yesterday's winning asset classes or to sell during bear markets.

Investors should draw 2 conclusions from the preceding data:

1. The longer the investment horizon, the more likely it is that riskier assets will provide greater returns. Discipline to stay the course is required to achieve the greater returns. And sometimes you have to wait a very long time to be rewarded for your discipline.
2. When investment horizons are very long, fixed income assets become the riskier asset class in terms of maintaining purchasing power.

Far Horizons

In order to have the greatest likelihood of achieving financial objectives, investors must have very long investment horizons. The premium returns investors receive for allocating assets to higher risk asset classes are premiums for accepting the risk that even over fairly long time frames those asset classes will underperform. Think of it this way: if the equity, small-cap, and value asset classes always provided premium returns, then they wouldn't be risk factors. For example, in 1966 the DJIA crossed the 1,000 mark for the first time. Not until 1983 did it finally reach that level again. For 17 years investors received higher returns by investing in far less risky bank certificates of deposit. Having experienced that poor performance, an investor choosing to avoid the high-risk and "obviously" low returning equity asset class would have missed out on an 800% return over the next 15 years. Other noteworthy examples:

- The difference in performance between U.S. large-cap and international large-cap stocks was almost 30% in 1997 and over 10% per annum for the 10-year period ending in 1997. However, over 15, 20, and 25 years, the difference in returns drops to 1.5%, 1.3%, and 0.5% per annum, respectively.
- While Japanese stocks dramatically outperformed U.S. stocks in the periods 1971 through 1978 and 1983 through 1988, they dramatically underperformed in 1979 through 1982 and 1989 through 1998.

As John Merrill points out, investors should keep three important facts in mind:

1. *Bull markets*, no matter how apparently sound the underpinnings, no matter how good the economic conditions, are followed by bear markets.
2. *Bear markets*, no matter how pernicious the economic conditions, no matter how deep the damage, are followed by bull markets.
3. *There are no guarantees.* Even a full market cycle does not guarantee that stocks will always be the best portfolio investment. It takes 20 years for history to prove stocks are always the better investment over bonds and cash.[6]

When You Get What You Wish For, Remember Why You Made the Wish

The years 1995 through 1999 were record-breaking ones for the U.S. stock market. For the first time ever the S&P 500 Index rose over 20% for 5 consecutive years. During the same period, returns from investments in international markets lagged well behind. In fact, in many markets, including Japan, returns were negative. This has caused some investors, and even some "market gurus," to question the wisdom of investing in "risky" overseas markets. Roger Lowenstein, a columnist for the *Wall Street Journal*, even cited the recent performance of global markets as "proof" that international diversification was unnecessary and even unwise.[7] Given recent events, I think it is important for investors who wisely included an allocation of international equities when they constructed their portfolios to consider why they originally did so. Investors can then decide if the rationale for their original decision is still valid.

To assist in this process let us consider an investor with a portfolio consisting of a single asset, stock in Ford. I think that everyone would agree that this "portfolio" is too risky. No matter how safe you considered an investment in Ford to be, putting all your eggs in one basket is simply too risky. So we advise our investor that in order to reduce risk, he needs to diversify.

Suppose, in an attempt to diversify, we added Chrysler to the portfolio. While reducing the risk of the portfolio somewhat, this type of diversification would not be very effective because Chrysler and Ford are subject to the same economic risks (gasoline prices, interest rates, U.S. consumer spending, etc.). Economists would say this attempt at diversification is ineffective because the "coefficient of correlation" between the stock prices of Chrysler and Ford is so high that risk is hardly reduced at all.

Therefore, in order to reduce risk an investor must add assets to the portfolio that have a low degree of correlation. Successful diversification results from finding assets that do not move up and down at the same time or, at the very least, do not move up and down to the same degree at the same time. For example, we might want to add an oil company to the Ford portfolio. Oil companies tend to do well when gasoline prices are rising, while the reverse is true of auto companies. We might then consider adding companies from other industries such as banking, retailing, pharmaceuticals, and so on. Finally, we should add international equities to the portfolio because they tend to have low degrees of correlation with U.S. equities.

By adding assets that have low degrees of correlation we expect the returns of the portfolio to be less volatile. Not only will the portfolio be less risky, but because volatility reduces returns, the compound growth rate of the portfolio will probably increase. The cliché that there is no such thing as a free lunch is incorrect because effective diversification provides higher returns and lower risk—a free lunch. If you don't believe it, try this test. Portfolio A grows 10% every year. Portfolio B grows 20% one year and then 0% the next. Both average 10% per annum returns. Despite the same average return, at the end of any even number of years Portfolio A will have provided a higher compound growth of every dollar invested.

Once an investor diversifies away from a single asset such as Ford, or an asset class such as the S&P 500 Index, then he must acknowledge that there will be periods when the single asset, or asset class, he began with will outperform the overall portfolio. This subjects the investor to what is called tracking error regret.

For example, if an investor has had an allocation of small-cap or value stocks (both of which over the last 70 years have out-performed large-cap stocks) over the past several years, his portfolio would have significantly underperformed the S&P 500 Index. The investor might regret that the portfolio's performance didn't match or exceed that well-known benchmark. Does this mean that it was a bad decision to diversify away from holding only large-cap stocks? Of course not. Thus, it is very important for investors to not only be aware of the benefits of diversification, but also what risks you accept to get those benefits. Investors must understand that, particularly in the short term, diversification guarantees neither a successful outcome nor even the elimination of losses.

These asset classes were included in a portfolio because they provided diversification that was expected to reduce the volatility of the portfolio and improve its performance *over the long term*. Obviously, if it were possible to predict the future with certainty, investors would never diversify—they would only own the asset class, or single stock, that would perform the best. It is the lack of certainty that makes diversification the winning strategy (ex-ante). Since few, if any, investors have shown the ability to move in and out of asset classes in anticipation of which will be the best performers, investors should construct a portfolio that meets their tolerance for risk and is appropriate for their investment horizons.

Turning back to the question of including international equities in a portfolio, there is no reason to expect that U.S. equities will provide either a higher or lower return over time than will international equities. In fact, the returns over long periods of time have been amazingly similar. For the 27 years ending 1996, while the S&P 500 Index was returning an average of 12.3%, the EAFE Index returned an average of 12.0%, an insignificant difference. It is important to understand that with the relative freedom of capital to move around the globe in search of returns, if investors thought that U.S. markets were likely to provide higher returns, today's prices would have already been bid up to reflect those greater expectations.

Despite the amazingly similar returns of the EAFE and S&P 500 Indices over long periods, the variance in returns over short time periods has been dramatic. One-year return differences have approached 30%. We shouldn't be surprised, therefore, when for even relatively long periods we experience wide divergences in returns. The periods of relative under- and outperformance are not only expected but are, in fact, the reasons why we diversify. In order to reduce the risk of our portfolio, we want to add low correlating assets. We should not be surprised or disappointed, therefore, when what occurs is exactly what we expected to occur. While it might be unpleasant during periods of divergent returns, there are only 2 alternatives. First, investors could create a portfolio with only 1 asset class. While this would avoid any tracking error regret, the portfolio would certainly be more risky. Alternatively, investors could try to time the market by guessing which asset classes will be the next winners. Not only will this strategy prove to be highly tax inefficient due to the turnover created, but, remember, over the past 20 years only a very small percentage of all the actively managed U.S. equity funds have outperformed S&P 500 Index funds. And that's even before taxes are considered.

Here is an analogy that might help. We buy homeowner's, life, and auto insurance every year because we seek to reduce risk. Most years we never receive any return on our investment. Yet we never complain. When a loss occurs, we are of course pleased that we were smart enough to have bought insurance (diversified our risk). From 1995 to 1998 investors who have included small-cap stocks, value stocks, and international stocks in their portfolios have been faithfully paying their insurance premiums. At some point, the S&P 500 will end its reign as the best performing asset class. Investors who remembered why they diversified in the first place will then be rewarded for their discipline.

The "Fifteen-Year Trend" of Large Growth Outperformance

As we entered the new millennium, many trade publications, pundits, gurus, and individual investors were touting the obvious 15-year trend of superior performance of the S&P 500 Index. For example, for the 15-year period 1985 through 1999 the S&P 500 Index (consisting predominately of large-cap growth stocks) outperformed small value stocks by 18.9% per annum versus 16.6% per annum. The conclusion some drew from this data was that it was obvious that we were in a "new economy" where large growth stocks will deliver superior performance. Whenever I hear claims like this, my first inclination is to "go to the videotape." Let's examine whether there has in fact been a 15-year trend and how investors could have exploited such a trend. We will then look at what, if any, implications "the trend" has for investment policy decisions going forward. For our analysis we will compare the performance of the S&P 500 with the performance of the small value asset class.

Let's begin by examining the data prior to 1985. This will give us insight into what conclusion investors were drawing as we entered the "new economy." Let's examine the 5-, 10-, and 15-year periods prior to 1985.

Period	S&P 500	Small Value
1981–1985	14.7%	25.4%
1976–1985	14.3%	28.8%
1971–1985	10.5%	19.5%

As we can clearly see, small value stocks dramatically outperformed the S&P 500 Index for each of the periods. And if we had looked all the way back to 1928 through 1984, small value outperformed by 14.0% to 9.0% per annum. Using the same logic as today's pundits, it would seem obvious that entering 1985 investors should have loaded up with small value stocks and avoided the S&P 500 Index.

Let's now turn to the post-1984 period, the latest 15 years. As we began the period, small value stocks continued their outperformance. In 1985 small value outperformed by 34.7% to 32.2%. No new trend yet. In 1986 the S&P 500 Index did outperform by 18.5% to 16.9%. Surely 1 year of outperformance would not convince us to ignore the previous 16 years, let alone the previous 58 years. So investors wait to see what 1987 brings. Again, the S&P 500 Index outperformed by 5.2% to −6.3%. However, 1988 provided a reversal with small value again outperforming by 28.8% to 16.8%. Investors thinking 2 years was enough of a trend to convince them to ignore longer term data were badly burned.

For the full 5-year period 1986 through 1990, the S&P 500 Index did outperform small value by 13.1% to 6.0%. It is important to note that in 1990, a year during which the markets experienced credit and liquidity problems in the banking sector (periods when the risk of value, and in particular small value, stocks becomes apparent), while the S&P 500 Index fell 3.2%, small value stocks fell 20.8%.

With a full 5-year period behind them, investors might have concluded that we had entered the "new economy" where large growth stocks would outperform. Having experienced 5 years of poor relative performance of small value stocks, investors might abandon them in favor of the S&P 500 Index.

Let's now look at the next 4-year period. In 1991 through 1994 small value stocks outperformed the S&P 500 Index by 23.9% per annum to 11.9% per annum, or 12% per annum. What do investors conclude now? Maybe they should switch back to small value. Maybe 1986 through 1990 was not a new era. Instead, maybe it was either an anomaly or simply just a normal (but unpredictable) cyclical rotation.

Continuing our journey through time, the cycle reversed again. From 1995 to 1997 the S&P 500 Index did manage to outperform small value, but not by much. Certainly not enough to convince anyone that a new era existed. For the period the S&P 500 Index returned 31.1%, compared to 29.6% for small value stocks.

Let's pause at this point and look at the returns for the full 13-year period 1985 through 1997 and see if we see any evidence of outperformance by the S&P 500 Index. First, I think you will agree that there clearly was no trend at all. Second, for the full period, small value stocks returned 18.6%, and the S&P 500 Index 18.1%. So for the first 13 years of this so-called new era, small value actually outperformed the S&P 500 Index. So what would investors have concluded at this time? I don't see how anyone could have drawn any conclusion about a new era. In fact, the only conclusion one might draw is that all of the outperformance of the S&P 500 Index for the full 15-year period 1985 through 1999 is accounted for by the performance of just the last 2 years of the entire period. For the period 1998 through

1999 the S&P 500 Index outperformed small value by 24.7% to just 3.9%.[8]

	S&P 500	*Small Value*
1985	32.2%	34.7%
1986–1990	13.1%	6.0%
1991–1994	11.9%	23.9%
1995–1997	31.1%	29.6%
1998–1999	24.7%	3.9%
1985–1997	18.1%	18.6%
1985–1999	18.9%	16.6%

I certainly am not suggesting that the last 2 years should be ignored, or even that we should ignore the results of the entire 15-year period. However, I think it is obvious that there is no trend in favor of large growth stocks. There have been many short periods when one asset class outperforms by significant margins. However, it is impossible to tell whether those periods will abruptly reverse or continue. What we do know is that, in general, periods of outperformance tend to be followed by periods of underperformance. Let's look at the historical evidence.

The average historical P/E ratio for the market has been around 15. For the period 1926 through the second quarter of 1999, an investor buying stocks when the market traded at P/E ratios of between 14 and 16 earned a median return of 11.8% over the next 10 years.[9] This is remarkably close to the long-term return of the market. The S&P 500 returned 11.3% per annum for the 74-year period 1926–1999.

Let's now look at the returns investors received when they bought stocks when the perception of risk was low, and when it was high. Investors purchasing stocks when the P/E ratio was greater than 22 earned a median return of just 5% per annum over the next 10 years.[10] The high P/E ratios generally reflect a strong economy and a bull market. During such times investors perceive relatively low levels of risk. Low levels of risk translate into high prices and a low risk premium. The low risk premium, however, translated into low future expected returns.

Let's now look at the returns that investors received when they purchased stock when the perception of risk was high. Investors who purchased stocks when P/E ratios were below 10 earned a median return of 16.9% per annum over the next 10 years.[11] The low P/E ratios generally reflect a weak economy and a bear market. During such times investors perceive relatively high levels of risk. High levels of risk translate into low prices and a high risk premium. The high risk premium, however, translates into high future expected returns. Investors buying stocks when the P/E ratios were below 10 (when perceived risk was high, and seemingly no one wants to own stocks) outperformed investors who bought stocks when P/E ratios were above 22 (when perceived risk was low, and everyone is jumping on the equity bandwagon) by almost 12% per annum.

In that light it is worth noting that over the past 6 years we have seen a collapse in the risk premium for the large-cap stocks that dominate the S&P 500 and NASDAQ indices. At year-end 1994, the P/E ratio for the S&P 500 was just under 16, not much higher than its historical average. However, by the end of the first quarter of 2000, it had risen to just under 30, well above the 22 P/E ratio that historically has produced returns of just 5% per annum over the succeeding 10 years. The NASDAQ was trading at a P/E ratio of well over 100. It is worth noting that the P/E ratios for the other asset classes have remained virtually unchanged. For large value stocks (as represented by the DFA LV fund) the P/E ratio rose from 10.3 to just 11.3. For small-cap stocks (as represented by the DFA 9–10 fund) the P/E ratio actually fell from 14.1 to 13.7. And for small value stocks (as represented by the DFA 6–10 value fund) the P/E remained virtually unchanged, falling from 11.7 to 11.6.

The decreased perception of risk for large-cap growth stocks can also be seen by examining btm values. For the S&P 500, the btm fell by almost 50%, from 0.4 to 0.21. However, the btm of large value stocks actually rose from 0.85 to 1.02, the btm of small-caps remained unchanged at 0.61, and the btm of small value stocks rose from 0.93 to 0.98. Low btms reflect low perception of risk (and a high risk premium), and vice versa.

Investing is all about risk and reward. There are no certainties. If there were certainties, there would be no risk and no risk premiums. If equities always outperformed bonds, there would be no equity risk premium. The same is true for value and small-cap stocks when compared to growth and large-cap stocks. Even long periods, such as 15 years, are not long enough to know a trend is in place. Again the nature of risk is that returns are uncertain, even for very long time frames. Even if you thought that after the evidence just presented that the full 15-year period 1985–1999 was enough to convince you that we were in a new era, the following example should convince you otherwise.

Investors know that stocks are far more risky than one-month bank certificates of deposits (which carry no risk as they are insured). Therefore, stocks should provide higher returns, especially over the long term. Yet, for the 19-year period 1966–1984, one-month CDs outperformed the S&P 500 Index by 8.5% to 7.6%. Even more compelling is that one-month CDs outperformed the asset class of large growth stocks (top 50% by market cap and bottom 30% by book-to-market value) over the even longer 23-year period 1966–1988 by 8.3% to 7.6%. What would you have concluded after these very long periods? With the DJIA at just 875.26, the August 13, 1979 issue of *Business Week* concluded: ''For better or worse, then, the U.S. economy probably has to regard the death of equities as a near-permanent condition.'' It was obvious, wasn't it? How many more years of evidence would you need to convince you? If you were convinced, you had concluded that risk and reward are no longer likely to be correlated. You also would have missed out on the greatest bull market ever.

If investors should not conclude that we are in a new era, what should they conclude? First, markets are both volatile and unpredictable (risky) even over fairly long periods. This makes diversification across asset classes a very important part of any strategy. Second, "trends" come and go in unpredictable fashion. Thus, the winning strategy is to adhere to a well-articulated investment plan (asset allocation) and have the discipline to regularly rebalance to your targeted allocations. This will ensure that you avoid chasing yesterday's returns. Rebalancing also ensures that you do what all investors attempt to do, sell high and buy low.

Is the Market Too High? And What, if Anything, Should I Do About It?

This question, or some version of it, is probably the question most asked by investors. One version goes like this: since we have just experienced the greatest bull market in history and with P/E ratios at all-time highs, isn't the market overvalued, and how can it possibly go higher? The first response is to point out that this is exactly what many, if not most, market gurus have been saying since 1994. Those listening to such advice missed out on the returns available to passive investors—those who remained fully invested throughout the period. With that in mind, it is worth reviewing the market's performance to see what caused the rally, as well as examining the likelihood of either a repeat performance or a reversal.

To begin, we need to examine what drives the market. There are basically three factors: earnings, the risk-free rate of return, and the equity risk premium. Let's begin with earnings. Clearly, we have been through a period where earnings growth has been very strong. This has been a positive influence on the market. In addition, the market may be expecting the recent higher earnings growth rates to continue.

The 2 other factors impacting stock prices, the risk-free rate and the equity risk premium, together determine how the market values expected future earnings. Since the *expected* earnings stream is in the future and subject to risk, a discount rate is applied to arrive at a present value. Since every investor can earn at least the rate of return on short-term Treasury bills without being subject to any principal or interest rate risk, we begin with this "risk-free" rate. We then have to add to the risk-free rate a risk premium for the risk of investing in equities. The greater the risk perceived, the greater the risk premium. The greater the risk premium, the greater the discount that will be applied to the expected earnings stream, and the lower the current valuation of that earnings stream. It is important to note that from 1964 to 1996 the risk-free rate (the rate on short-term Treasury bills) averaged about 6.5%, and the equity risk premium (investor's subjective judgment of the risks of equity investing) averaged about 5.5%.[12]

The relationship between value and earnings, expressed as a mathematical formula, looks like this:

$$\text{Current Value} = \text{Total Future Earnings}/(\text{risk-free rate} + \text{equity risk premium})$$

In English, this formula states that the current value of a company (its stock price multiplied by the number of shares) is equal to the total value of all future earnings divided (or discounted) by the sum of the risk-free rate and the equity risk premium. The greater the numerator (total future earnings), the greater the current value (and vice versa). The greater the denominator (the greater the rate at which we discount future earnings) the lower the current valuation, and vice versa. Let's look at a couple of examples to clarify the issue.

- When interest rates rise, the denominator increases and the current value of a future earnings stream falls (and equity prices fall). This is because investors demand that equities now provide a higher return in order to compensate them for foregoing the now higher fixed income alternative.
- When the perception of the risks of equity investing increases, the denominator increases, again causing the current value of future earnings (and equity prices) to fall because investors demand higher returns as compensation for the greater risk now perceived.

Let's now examine the market's performance in light of the 3 factors of earnings, risk-free rate, and the equity risk premium. First, earnings growth was very strong from 1995 to 1999. This was one of the main forces driving up stock prices. Second, the risk-free rate had fallen as short-term Treasuries fell to about 5% (before rising again in 1999 through 2000). By lowering the rate at which the future earnings stream was discounted, the current value of that stream of earnings increased (causing P/E ratios to rise). Third, the strong economy (low inflation, high productivity, reduced budget deficits, etc.) that we experienced led to a lowering of investor perceptions of both economic risk and the risk of equity investing. This, too, has caused a reduction in the rate at which future earnings are discounted (again causing P/E ratios and stock prices to rise). The following example will show how even small changes in either of these factors (risk-free rate or equity risk premium) can lead to dramatic changes in equity valuations.

Let's begin with a company with current earnings of $1. If we assume a growth rate of future earnings of 10% per annum, a risk-free rate of 7%, and an equity risk premium of 6%, we arrive at a current value of about $22, or a P/E ratio of 22. If we reduce the risk-free rate and the equity risk premium each by just 1%, the current value would be about $31, creating a P/E of 31. Despite the fact that forecasted earnings did not change, the current value of the company (stock price) increased by about 40%. The company isn't overvalued any more at a 31 P/E than it was at a 22 P/E. If both the risk-free rate and the equity risk premium each were to fall another 1%, the "fair value" of the stock would rise to $45, a further increase in value of about 45%. As you can see, small changes in either current short-term rates or the equity risk premium demanded by investors can have a dramatic impact on stock prices.

Since the crash of 1987, we have seen P/E ratios and stock prices soar because earnings have risen dramatically, interest rates have fallen, and investor perceptions about economic risk have fallen. In addition, investors may have also become more knowledgeable about the risks of equity investing. They may have become more accepting of the view that since equities have always outperformed bonds when the investment horizon has been at least 20 years, equities aren't really that risky. Investors, therefore, may no longer require such a large risk premium. This kind of change may have been one of the driving forces of the post–World War II bull market. Investors once demanded that stocks pay larger dividends than bonds because they were clearly perceived as being more risky. Today we take for granted the fact that the dividend yield on stocks will be less than that on bonds. With this change P/E ratios and stock prices soared. It is worth noting that when the dividend yield on stocks fell below the bond yield, many gurus of the time forecasted a market crash, citing this apparent anomaly in equity and bond yields and the record high P/E ratios. Investors listening to these gurus missed out on one of the greatest bull markets in history. The lesson for investors: while those who forget the past may be doomed to repeat it, things change. These changes in investor perceptions created a one-time benefit to equity prices.

Let's look at an interesting hypothetical example. One can certainly imagine the following scenario. With inflation at 1% we could see the rate on short-term Treasury bills fall from 5% to 4% (lowering the risk-free rate by 1%). As a result of lowering the denominator, the rate at which future earnings are discounted, P/E ratios and stock prices could rise about 20%. If we combined lower short-term rates with a further lowering of expectations about the risks of equity investing (lowering the equity risk premium by 1%), this could result in P/E ratios of 40 to 50. And the market would be fairly valued. (In case you thought this scenario is unlikely, it is worth noting that in previous periods of price stability the equity risk premium was very slim, being just 1.9% per annum from 1816 to 1870 and just 2.8% from 1871 to 1925.)[13] Conversely, interest rates could rise, the perception of economic risks could rise, and the equity risk premium could rise. The result would be that future earnings would be discounted at a much higher rate. The result would be a dramatic collapse in equity prices.

In summary, we only know after the fact whether the market is under- or overvalued. Just because something hasn't occurred before doesn't mean the market is either under- or overvalued. Current market prices reflect current expectations of earnings and economic risks. When someone states that the current market is too high because P/E ratios are too high, he or she is really saying that the rest of the market is wrong. I don't accept the proposition that anyone can consistently know more than the market.

It is impossible to know whether future earnings will be greater or less than the market currently expects; whether interest rates (the risk-free rate) will rise or fall; or whether investors in the future will demand a higher or lower equity premium than they are currently demanding. The result is that the costs of active management of portfolios have resulted in negative impacts on returns. The winning strategy is passive investing.

Equity Prices Cannot Grow Faster Than the Economy Forever! (Investor Expectations Are Too High)

Beginning after the crash of October 1987, investors in the U.S. equities markets experienced the greatest bull run in history with 12 straight years without a major correction. In fact, there was only a single down year, 1990, when the S&P 500 dropped just over 3%. Furthermore, 1995 through 1999 has been the first 5-year period in history when the S&P 500 rose over 20% each year. The returns since the crash of 1987 have been far in excess of the rate of growth of the economy. The question, then, is: Can the equity markets continue to grow faster than the overall economy? The obvious answer is NO. Stock prices reflect 3 factors. These factors are future earnings expectations, the risk-free rate of return, and the equity risk premium. Let's examine how the 3 factors impact returns and the implications for future returns.

Let's begin with the risk-free rate of return. The benchmark for the risk-free rate of return is the 3-month Treasury bill rate. As interest rates rise, the value of future earnings falls. As interest rates fall, the value of future earnings rises. However, interest rates cannot fall to 0. Thus, there is a limit to the impact falling interest rates can have on stock prices.

Investing in equities entails risk. This results in equities carrying a risk premium as compensation for that risk. Over the 70-year period 1930 through 1999, equities provided a risk premium of about 7%. The risk premium, of course, has not been stable. It has been much higher during times of economic distress (recessions) as investors perceive greater risk in equity investments. The higher equity risk premium drives the value of future expected earnings, and therefore equity prices, lower. However, the higher risk premium results in higher future expected returns. The reverse is true in good times, when investors perceive less risk. The equity risk premium falls, driving the value of future expected earnings and equity prices higher. It should be obvious that while the equity risk premium could rise to infinity, it cannot fall to 0 (since equities are riskier than risk-free instruments).

Understanding the impact of rising and falling risk premiums (and rising and falling interest rates) helps us understand why periods of high returns are generally followed by periods of low returns, and vice versa. This process is called reversion to the mean (long-term average).

Now let's address the third factor, earnings growth. Historically, corporate earnings have grown in line with both the GNP and overall income. While there are short-term fluctuations around averages, the tendency for corporate earnings to grow along with the economy is very logical. Believing that corporate earnings can grow faster than the overall economy leads to the conclusion that corporate profits will eventually consume the entire economic pie—leaving no returns to labor, interest, and other recipients of national income. Obviously this is a nonsensical conclusion, straining not only credibility but also the evidence. From 1950 to 1980, pretax corporate profits rarely wandered much beyond 8% to 12% of GNP. Over the past 40 years pretax corporate profits have rarely wandered much beyond 6% to 10% of GNP.

It is important for investors to understand that it is the shifts in interest rates, the equity risk premium, and expectations of corporate profits that account for the volatility of the market. The way these factors impact the market has proven to be virtually unpredictable, particularly in the short term (otherwise we would see active managers outperforming simple benchmarks). For example, all other things being equal, rising interest rates should negatively impact stock prices as the risk-free rate drives down the value of future earnings. However, all other things are never equal. There exists a very complex relationship between the 3 factors.

For example, rising interest rates should negatively impact stock prices as the risk-free rate rises. However, rising rates might reflect a stronger economy, leading investors to become more confident. The result is a fall in the equity risk premium, increasing the value of future earnings. Rising productivity also leads to rising interest rates (through an increase in the demand for capital), and rising productivity leads to rising corporate earnings. Once again, this could also lead to a falling risk premium.

To summarize, equity prices in the long term must reflect the overall growth in the economy. Equity prices can rise faster than the economy for some period of time as interest rates and risk premiums fall and earnings grow faster than the overall economy. However, this process must end at some point. It is very important for investors to understand that if either or both the risk-free rate and the equity premium fall for an extended period of time, there will be two results, not one. First, investors will receive very large capital gains. However, these are onetime gains, and future expected returns would be dramatically lower.

Unfortunately, it appears that recent experience has raised investor expectations to unreasonable levels. With about 90% of all the wealth that is now invested in the market having been accumulated after the 1987 crash, several recent surveys show that investors now expect to earn about 25% per annum, far in excess of the economy's ability to grow.

Given these expectations, investors are not only likely to be disappointed, they are likely to make poor investment decisions. First, if they have a goal of achieving a certain amount of funds for retirement, their overestimated returns could cause them to dramatically underestimate the amount of savings required. Second, the performance of the U.S. equity markets since the crash of 1987 appears to have caused investors to underestimate the risks of equity investing. While we experienced almost no market correction of any real magnitude and duration during the succeeding 13 years, historically the market has experienced a major bear market (where prices fall at least 10%, and on average fall almost 20%) 1 out of every 3 or 4 years. Thus, by underestimating the risks of equity investing, investors may be committing too high a percentage of their overall portfolio to equities and not enough to the risk-reducing asset class of fixed income. This is particularly dangerous. When the almost inevitable bear markets actually occur, if an investor is not fully prepared to accept the consequences (such as the 30% to 40% drop in values we saw in 1973 through 1974), then she is likely to lose the discipline required of long-term investors. The result is likely to be that she will panic and sell at the worst possible time.

Investors need to focus on long-term historical results when they make investment decisions. If they fail to "take off the blinders" of their recent experience, they are likely to make poor investment decisions.

Investment Insights

- The longer the investment horizon, the more likely it is that the expected will occur.
- The shorter the investment horizon, the more likely it is that the unexpected will occur.
- If stocks outperformed fixed income investments every year, investors would not really be taking any risk. The equity, size, and value risk premiums reflect the increased risks to investors.
- The longer an investor's investment horizon, the greater should be the willingness to accept risk.
- If investors want exposure to the higher returning asset classes, they should have a long-term investment horizon. In addition, they must be prepared to accept high volatility

and possibly long periods of underperformance as the "price" for investing in higher expected returning assets.

- The volatility of the equity markets is evidence of the frequency with which the expected fails to occur. That is why equities carry a risk premium.
- We only know after the fact whether the market is under- or overvalued. Just because something hasn't occurred before doesn't mean the market is either under- or overvalued.
- Bull markets have inevitably followed bear markets, and vice versa.
- When the investment horizon is very long, fixed income assets become the riskier asset class in terms of maintaining purchasing power.
- Asset classes move in and out of favor over unpredictable time frames. This is why diversification and the discipline to stay the course are keys to the winning strategy.
- It is very important for investors to not only be aware of the benefits of diversification, but also what risks you accept to obtain those benefits.
- The dramatic returns of the late 1990s created unrealistic expectations regarding both the risk of equity investing and likely future returns.

CHAPTER 8

◆

Active Management Imposes a Large Negative Impact on After-Tax Returns

The power to tax involves the power to destroy.
—John Marshall

If index funds look great before taxes, their performance is almost unbeatable after taxes, thanks to their low turnover and thus slow realization of capital gains.
—Jonathan Clements, *Wall Street Journal*,
December 22, 1998

For all long-term investors, there is only one objective—maximum total real return after taxes.
—John Templeton

Mutual funds are required to provide historical return data for investors. The successful funds will usually advertise in big bold print their historical returns. Unfortunately for investors, the return figures are pretax results.

Whenever a fund realizes gains it must distribute those gains to investors. Shareholders then owe taxes on those distributions. This chapter explores the impact that taxes on fund distributions have on returns, as well as the implications of that impact on developing the winning investment strategy. I believe that most investors will be surprised to learn that taxes are probably the largest expense they incur, far greater than even the operating expenses of their funds.

You will learn that when the investment horizon is long enough (25 to 30 years), taxes and the "black magic of decompounding" can reduce pretax returns by as much as 60%. The average turnover of actively managed funds is approximately 90% per annum. Yet studies have found that in order to materially reduce the negative impact of taxes on returns, turnover must be reduced to 20% or less. Investors are suffering from a case of "taxation without representation." *What Wall Street doesn't want investors to know* is that in order for active managers to continue to collect their large fees they need investors to continue to ignore the tax implications of active management.

After concluding this chapter, hopefully you will agree with the conclusion drawn by one study on the retail mutual fund industry: "The preponderance of evidence is so convincing we conclude that the typical approach of managing taxable portfolios as if they were tax-exempt is inherently irresponsible, even though doing so is the industry standard."[1] It is worth noting that in 2000 Vanguard announced that it would begin reporting mutual fund returns on both a pre- and after-tax basis.

Stealth Attack on Returns

The SEC requires mutual fund prospectuses to provide a great deal of information so that investors can make educated decisions. Among the information required are investment philosophy, expenses, and past performance. Unfortunately, information regarding the impact of taxes on returns is not required. However, because dividend and realized capital gains distributions are subject to state, local, and federal taxation, for taxable accounts, the after-tax returns are the only returns that matter. Several academic studies have all reached the same conclusion: taxes are the biggest expense most investors face—greater than management fees or commissions. These studies also conclude that mutual fund returns are far more dependent on the risks assumed (asset class allocation) and taxes than on the stock selection or market timing skills of the fund managers.

Although the effect of paying current income taxes may be minimal (and therefore insidious) in any one year, it becomes substantial over a protracted period of time. A study commissioned by Charles Schwab and conducted by John Shoven, a Stanford University professor of economics, and Joel Dickson, a Stanford Ph.D. candidate, demonstrated just how great an impact this stealth attack had on returns. The study measured the performance of 62 equity funds for the 30-year period 1963 through 1992. It found that while each dollar invested in this group of funds would have grown to $21.89 in a tax-deferred account, the same amount of money invested in a taxable account would have produced only $9.87 for a high tax bracket investor. Amazingly, and painfully, taxes cut returns by 57.5%.[2] For high tax bracket investors, the study also found that for the 10-year period ending December 1992, Vanguard's 500 Index fund would have outperformed 92% of the funds in the study.[3]

A simulated study covering the 25-year period ending in 1995 examined the effects of expenses and taxes on investor returns. This study assumed that a mutual fund (1) matched the performance of the S&P 500 Index (during this period the average actively managed fund underperformed by almost 2% per annum); (2) had average turnover of 80%; and (3) incurred expenses of 1% (the average fund today has expenses of about 1.5%). The study's results were amazingly similar to those of the Schwab study. It found that the typical investor received only 41% of the pre-expense, pretax returns of the Index. The government took 47% of the returns, a figure that would have been even higher if state and local taxes were considered or if the investor were subject to the highest tax brackets. The fund manager received 12% of the pretax, pre-expense returns. This study also found that reducing expenses to as low as 0.3% would have only raised the investor's share of returns from 41% to 45%. The study also examined the effect of reducing the turnover rate, and therefore the amount of realized gains, to the same turnover as the S&P 500 Index. By reducing turnover to 3%, the share of returns actually realized by the investor would have increased to 64%, increasing investor returns by 56%.[4]

The investment horizon doesn't have to be 25 to 30 years for the negative impact of taxes to be large. Let's look at several studies that cover progressively shorter time frames. Robert Jeffrey and Robert Arnott demonstrated the large impact of taxes on returns when they studied the performance of 72 actively managed funds for the 10-year period 1982 through 1991. They found that while 15 of the 72 funds beat a passively managed fund on a pretax basis, only 5 did so on an after-tax basis.[5]

Morningstar studied the 5-year period 1992 through 1996 and found that diversified U.S. stock funds gained an average of 91.9%. Morningstar then assumed that income and short-term gains were taxed at 39.6% and long-term capital gains at 28%. The result was that after-tax returns dwindled to 71.5%, a loss of 22% of the returns in just 5 years.[6] As this study demonstrates, while the impact of taxes is great over even short time frames, because of the power of "decompounding," the longer the time frame, the larger the impact of taxes on returns.

In light of all of the evidence, the only logical conclusion for investors is that for taxable accounts the already low probability of actively managed funds outperforming a passive alternative is dramatically reduced.

Tax Efficiency: A Major Determinant of Wealth Creation

The Schwab Center for Investment Research provided compelling evidence on the importance of taxes on after-tax returns. They examined the historical tax efficiency of 576 large-cap actively managed funds and 44 large-cap index funds for the 3-year period ending December 1997. The study calculated the tax efficiency of each fund by dividing its pretax return by its after-tax return. The study assumed a $10,000 investment at the beginning of the period. The study also assumed that the cash to pay the taxes was generated by selling shares. Tax rates of 39.6% for short-term gains and ordinary income and 28% for long-term gains were assumed. The study concluded:

- The average large-cap fund was approximately 86% tax efficient, losing 14% of its returns to taxes.
- The average large-cap index fund was approximately 94% tax efficient, losing only 6% of its returns to taxes.

It is important to note, especially for investors residing in high-tax areas, that state and local taxes were not considered. If they were, the results would have been even more compelling.

The study also examined the amount of dollars that would have been lost to taxes over 5-, 10-, and 15-year holding periods.

Dollars Lost to Taxes, Assuming a $10,000 Initial Investment and a 10% Pretax Return

Holding Period	Actively Managed Fund	Index Funds
5 years	$ 999	$ 434
10 years	$3,118	$1,381
15 years	$7,302	$3,290

When Schwab examined small-cap funds they found that while small-cap index funds were more tax efficient than their actively managed counterparts, the difference was much smaller. This is due to the greater turnover in small-cap indices, as small-caps often grow into large-caps, causing passively managed and index funds to sell as the stock no longer fits the asset class or drops out of the index.

As investors awaken to the impact of taxes, the fund industry has responded by developing tax-managed funds. These funds seek to minimize distributions by minimizing turnover, increasing holding periods to take advantage of the lower long-term capital gains tax rates, and harvesting losses. Schwab found that for their very brief history tax-managed funds produced tax-efficiency rates of 98 to 99%. The impact of this improvement in tax efficiency can be seen by looking at a 15-year holding period. The dollars lost to taxes for actively managed large-cap funds was $7,302 and for large-cap index funds was $3,290. A tax-managed fund would only have lost $1,125.[7]

As promising as this sounds, investors should be careful, because strategies to reduce taxes may negatively impact *pre*tax returns. For example, the need to harvest losses will increase transaction costs. However, as can be seen in the example, the dramatic improvement in tax efficiency is likely to be the more important factor.

Investors should draw the following conclusions:

- Since actively managed funds have underperformed their passively managed (index) benchmarks even before taxes, it is highly unlikely that they will be able to outperform once the burden of taxes is taken into account. Investors persisting in their belief in active management should do so only in a tax-deferred account.
- For taxable accounts, investors should investigate the use of funds that are both passive and tax managed. Their use will probably result in an increase in after-tax returns.

Tax-Wise Investing

Academic studies have demonstrated that passively managed funds provide superior pretax returns. One reason is their low turnover. This produces not only relatively low taxable distributions but also a higher percentage of distributions that are taxed at the lower long-term capital gains rates. The result is an even greater advantage for passively managed funds over actively managed ones in terms of after-tax performance.

State Street Research examined how turnover impacts after-tax performance. They made the following assumptions:

- The investor makes a $25,000 investment for a 30-year period.
- Both funds earn 10% pretax.
- The high-turnover fund had a turnover rate of 81% (typical of an actively managed fund), and the low-turnover one had a turnover rate of 8% (typical of a passively managed fund).

- Fifty percent of the distributions would be taxed as ordinary income at 39.6%, and 50% taxed as long-term capital gains at 20%. State taxes were ignored.
- Taxes due were paid out of distribution proceeds and the remainder reinvested.
- All shares were sold at the end of 30 years.

The high-turnover fund turned the $25,000 original investment into $187,888. The low-turnover fund grew to $335,930. The benefit of low turnover and resulting lower current taxes produced 79% more after-tax dollars. This is why Kennard "Pete" Woodworth, portfolio manager of the State Street Research Legacy Fund, stated: "Taxable investors can no longer afford to overlook how taxes are affecting their investment performance."[8]

The awakening of individual investors to the important role that fund distributions play in after-tax performance has been one of the driving forces behind the rapid growth of index and other passively managed funds. Recently many fund families, including DFA, NationsBank, Charles Schwab, and the Vanguard Group, have taken this issue to the next level by creating passively managed funds that are also tax managed. These tax-managed funds strive to both minimize fund distributions and to maximize the percentage of distributions that will be in the form of long-term capital gains. They accomplish this by implementing the following strategies:

- Maintaining low turnover.
- Attempting to avoid realization of any short-term gains.
- Harvesting losses by selling stocks that are below cost, in order to offset gains in other securities.
- Selling the appreciated shares with the highest cost basis.

KPMG Peat Marwick studied the benefit that such a tax-managed fund might provide. To understand the impact of taxes on returns, they examined the hypothetical performance of $10,000 invested in 2 funds, 1 a tax-managed fund and the other an actively managed fund, both having pretax returns of 10%. The example assumed short-term gains and ordinary income would be taxed at 39.6% and long-term gains at 20%, and the funds would be liquidated after 20 years. The table lists the study's other assumptions.

	Tax-Managed Fund	Actively Managed Fund
Income and short-term distributions	0.0%	3.0%
Long-term distributions	1.0%	4.0%
Price appreciation (unrealized gains)	9.0%	3.0%
Total annual returns	10.0%	10.0%

After 20 years the tax-managed fund would grow to $54,792, or 25% greater than the $43,941 produced by the actively managed fund. The difference in after-tax returns was 8.9% versus 7.7%. Taxes cost the tax-managed fund 11% of its pretax returns, compared to 23% for the actively managed fund. Another way to look at it is that the pretax return of the actively managed fund would have had to be 11.6% (or 16% greater) just to match the after-tax return of the tax-managed fund. Given that the average actively managed fund has underperformed its benchmark on a *pretax* basis by almost 2% per annum, the extra burden of taxes would seem to create an almost insurmountable hurdle.

KPMG took their study one step further. They considered what would happen if instead of liquidating the funds after 20 years, the investor either transfers them to his estate at death or gifts them to a charitable institution. In either case, the capital gains taxes that were otherwise due on sale could now be avoided. In this case the $10,000 would have grown to $64,870 in the tax-managed fund, 39% greater than the $46,690 produced by the actively managed fund. The after-tax returns were 9.8% and 8.0%, respectively. The actively managed fund would have had to generate almost 23% per annum better pretax returns in order to match the after-tax returns of the tax-managed fund. Once again, given the evidence on the performance of actively managed funds, that seems a highly unlikely outcome.

Using data from Morningstar, KPMG found that over a 10-year period the median actively managed fund lost 16% of its pretax returns to taxes on an annual basis, with some funds losing as much as 40% of their pretax returns to taxes. This result was not all that different from the hypothetical example they created. Thus KPMG's examples are reasonably good approximations of the real world.[9]

The conclusions for taxable investors:

- Taxes create an almost insurmountable hurdle for active managers to overcome.
- For taxable accounts, investors should utilize funds that are both passive and tax managed.

The Tax Man Takes a Big Bite

Investors in the Berger 100 fund received an unpleasant surprise when the fund distributed its 1997 dividend and capital gains, a negative surprise that came on top of the fund's poor performance. In 1997 the fund returned just 13.6%, almost 10% below the return of small-cap benchmarks such as the Russell

2000. On top of this poor performance, the fund's capital gains distribution produced a tax bill that was about two-thirds of the pretax return. The fund distributed $6.95 a share in capital gains, or 33% of the fund's value of $20.94, as of the record date of December 1.

Berger 100 fund investors learned that one of the negative consequences of investing with active managers is that their high turnover rates can dramatically reduce pretax returns. The pain to investors in this fund was increased by the fact that over one-third ($2.37) of the distribution was in the form of short-term capital gains, which are taxed at much higher ordinary income tax rates. Assuming tax rates of 31% for short-term and 20% for long-term capital gains, this distribution produced a tax bill of about 9% of the fund's year-end value. And that's without even considering state taxes or the higher rates of a high-income bracket investor.

Another lesson learned by Berger fund investors is that, just as the track record of active managers is not a good predictor of future pretax returns, a fund's tax efficiency record is not a good predictor of future tax efficiency. In fact, from 1992 through 1994 this fund made no capital gain distributions. Investors relying on that track record received an unpleasant surprise.

It's also worth noting that Berger fund investors weren't alone in their agony: in the same year, both the Alliance Global Environmental Fund and the Prudential Global Genesis Fund paid out distributions that were an even larger percentage of assets. The negative consequences of high and unpredictable turnover rates of active managers were heightened by the 1997 Tax Act, which further widened the spread between ordinary income and long-term capital gains. This is why John Bogle suggests that all actively managed funds carry the following disclosure:

The fund is managed without regard to tax considerations, and given its expected rate of portfolio turnover, is likely to realize and distribute a high portion of its capital return in the form of capital gains which are taxable annually, a substantial portion of which are likely to be realized in the form of short-term gains subject to full income tax rates.[10]

The goal of achieving the highest *after-tax* returns is one of the major reasons why passive asset class funds should be your investment vehicle of choice.

Tax Hell

Investors in the actively managed Invesco Asian Growth Fund received a double dose of bad news in 1997. According to Morningstar, the fund lost 38.5% for the year. A hypothetical investor who had put $10,000 into the fund at the start of the year would have had just $6,150 by year-end. Unfortunately for investors in this fund, the bad news did not end there.

In December 1997, the fund made a taxable distribution of 21% of its net asset value. Our hypothetical $10,000 investor would have had to pay taxes on about $1,300 of income. The net result is that after-tax losses (the only kind that matter) were probably about 43% (even before state taxes are considered).

Investors in the Artisan Small Cap Fund had a similar experience. By the end of the third quarter of 1998 the fund had produced a negative return of about 23%. This was significantly worse than their small-cap benchmarks, such as the Russell 2000, which was down about 16%. But that wasn't the only bad news. The fund announced a distribution of nearly 9% of its net asset value. Investors in the Artisan Small Cap fund were taken for a ride to tax hell.

Another trip to tax hell was endured by the owners of the closed-end Emerging Markets Fund, which distributed $4.53 to shareholders of record on October 30, 1998. On the date the distribution was announced, the current price was $12 15/16, down about 32% from its opening price. In addition to that loss, the fund owners would now have to pay taxes on a distribution equal to 35% of assets.[11]

The best way to avoid unexpectedly facing the double whammy that Invesco Asian Growth, Artisan Small Cap, and Emerging Market Fund investors experienced is to invest in passively managed funds. These funds, by their very nature, minimize turnover and taxable distributions.

Taxes Do Matter

The rapid growth of index and other passive asset class funds is strong evidence that investors are awakening to the poor and inconsistent performance of actively managed funds. The failure of active managers to outperform their benchmarks, be it the S&P 500, the Russell 2000, or any other index, is not the only cause for investor discontent. The market's spectacular gains beginning in 1995 led to the largest distributions in mutual fund history. Morningstar estimated that in 1997 alone mutual fund investors turned over to Uncle Sam more than $150 billion of their investment gains.

Investors have reason to gripe about their tax bills, as tax inefficiency further reduces the already poor performance statistics of active managers. The following illustration compares the performance of one of the few funds that beat the S&P 500

Index for the 3-year period ending in 1997, at least before taxes. Using the Morningstar database, the Gabelli Growth Fund, with a return of 32.95%, outperformed the DFA Large-cap Fund (an S&P 500 Index fund), which returned 30.85%. However, these returns are prior to adjusting for the then current long-term capital gains rate. The Gabelli fund lost 15% of its return to taxes, reducing after-tax returns to 28.03%, while the passively managed DFA fund lost only 3.4% to taxes, producing an after-tax return of 29.80%. The impact of taxes turned the Gabelli fund's 6% advantage into a 6% disadvantage. Even calculating the after-tax return using today's 20% rate, the DFA fund still produces higher after-tax returns by 29.83% to 29.42%.

Joel Dickson, who wrote his doctoral dissertation on mutual fund taxes, made the following recommendation for individuals considering investment choices: "Taxes and expense ratios are probably the most important things, after a well-diversified portfolio."[12]

Investors face problems when evaluating the tax efficiency of actively managed funds. First, just as past performance of an actively managed fund is not a good predictor of its future performance, neither is past tax efficiency. Another problem for investors in actively managed funds is that short-term performance success attracts new investors. This creates the illusion of tax efficiency as the fund's distributions are spread out over an increasing number of shareholders. These fund inflows often depart as rapidly as they came in when the "hot" fund's performance begins to lag. The shrinking asset base leads to asset sales (to meet redemptions) and realized gains, which then must be distributed. The shrinking shareholder base means the remaining shareholders bear the full tax burden of the distributed gains.

In this light, a market downturn has the potential to really hit investors with a huge tax bill, probably when they least expect it. Investors would then be faced with negative investment performance and taxes to pay at the same time.

The simple lesson for investors is that not only do taxes matter, they matter a lot.

A Conflict of Interest

File this tale under the heading: "I thought I had seen it all." At year-end 1997, the Stagecoach Strategic Growth Fund made a capital gains distribution of 27% of assets. This large distribution was made despite the fund returning just 7.7% for the year, dramatically underperforming both the market and the average mutual fund.

Actively managed funds have enough hurdles to overcome in order to outperform their respective passive benchmarks: greater expenses, greater trading costs, and less tax efficiency. As if this isn't enough, the Stagecoach Strategic Growth Fund just provided another: a conflict of interest, one Wall Street certainly doesn't want investors to know about. The main reason given for the large distribution was that the fund's large unrealized gains were scaring away potential new investors. The fund's manager found a convenient solution. In order to attract new investors, the fund would sell the stocks in which it had large unrealized gains and immediately buy them back. Not only did existing shareholders end up with a big tax bill, but they also had to absorb the trading costs (bid/offer spreads, market impact costs, and commissions) that were incurred. While the fund *may* have become more attractive to new investors, the existing shareholders were handed a big bill without any benefits. Clearly, existing shareholders' interests were sacrificed for the interests of the fund. If investors act rationally, the fund's strategy should backfire. First, under the "fool me once" principle, existing shareholders should flee. Second, why would any potential investor consider this fund, given its history of ignoring shareholder's interests?

There was another reason for the large distribution from the Stagecoach Strategic Growth Fund: a market timing money manager pulled out $20 million in order to switch asset classes. In order to meet the redemption request, the fund had to sell securities with previously unrealized gains. Of course, the remaining shareholders had to foot the tax bill.[13] This example provides a clear demonstration of why investing in passively managed funds is a necessary, but not sufficient, condition of the winning investment strategy. Investors should insist that the passively managed fund only accept investments from investors or advisors that are committed to a passive strategy. DFA provides a family of such funds. While not a guarantee, this condition provides the greatest likelihood that the fund will remain consistently tax efficient. Another good strategy is to look for passively managed funds that impose reimbursement fees. Vanguard and others have instituted reimbursement fees for many of their funds. Unlike loads, which are really commissions paid to third parties, reimbursement fees are paid directly into the fund. These fees are meant to *reimburse* either existing shareholders for the transactions costs imposed on the fund by new investors whose cash must be put to work or remaining shareholders when exiting shareholders cause the fund to sell shares and generate trading costs. Remember that these trading costs are incurred by the fund whether or not reimbursement fees are imposed. The only issue is which shareholders bear those costs, the passive or the active ones. The imposition of reimbursement fees goes a long way towards discouraging short-term trading activity.

The Really Dirty Secret

Aronson + Partners is an institutional fund that, as the plus sign in its name suggests, uses a quantitative (mathematically based rules as opposed to subjective judgment) approach to stock selection. The main variables they use to select stocks are value driven: price-to-book, price-to-earnings, and price-to-sales ratios. They then use a factor for momentum (the tendency for a stock to continue to move in the same direction) and management (Is management buying its own stock?). Their strategy leads to annual turnover of about 100 to 120% per annum.

In an interview in the June 15, 1998, issue of *Barron's*, Theodore Aronson made some very interesting statements.

- "I never forget that the devil sitting on my shoulder [is the] low-cost passive funds. They win because they lose less."
- "None of my clients are taxable. Because, once you introduce taxes . . . *active management probably has an insurmountable hurdle*. We have been asked to run taxable money—and declined. The costs of our active strategies are high enough without paying Uncle Sam."
- "Capital gains taxes, when combined with transactions costs and fees, *make indexing profoundly advantaged*, I am sorry to say."
- "All of the partners are in the same situation—our retirement dough (tax-deferred accounts) are here. But not our taxable investments."
- "If you crunch the numbers, turnover has to come down, not low, but to super-low, like 15–20%, or taxes kill you. That's *the real dirty secret in our business. Mutual funds are bought with and sold with virtually no attention to tax efficiency.*"

- "My wife, three children and I have taxable money in eight of the Vanguard index funds."

Investors can learn from Aronson, whose honesty is refreshing in an industry known for its focus on self-interest. Aronson could generate increased fees by just doing what his clients ask him to do—manage their taxable accounts. He refuses to do that because he doesn't believe that for taxable accounts he can out-perform passive asset class funds of similar style. In other words, he is putting his clients' interests ahead of his own.

Investment Insights

- Taxes are probably the largest expense investors incur, even greater than management fees or commissions.
- The typical approach of managing taxable accounts as if they were tax-exempt is inherently irresponsible, even though doing so is the industry standard. This has begun to change with the introduction of tax-managed funds.
- Although the effect of paying current income taxes may be minimal (and therefore insidious) in any one year, it is dramatic over protracted periods of time.
- Past tax efficiency of active managers is not a predictor of future tax efficiency.
- Investors in actively managed funds can receive taxable distributions even during years when the values of their funds fall.
- Investors should look for passively managed funds that only accept investments from investors or advisors who are com-

mitted to a passive strategy or that at least impose reimbursement fees.

- Once the impact of taxes on returns is considered, active managers probably have an insurmountable hurdle in their attempts to outperform their benchmarks.

CHAPTER 9

◆

Understanding and Controlling Human Behavior Is an Important Determinant of Investment Performance

It ain't what a man don't know as makes him a fool, but what he does know as ain't so.
—Josh Billings

Of all the words of tongue and pen, the saddest are these: It might have been.
—John Greenleaf Whittier, "Maud Muller"

Fear has a far greater grasp on human action than does the impressive weight of historical evidence.
—Jeremy Siegel, *Stocks for the Long Run*

The investor's chief problem—and even his worst enemy—is likely to be himself.
—Benjamin Graham

One of the hottest fields in the academic investment community is behavioral finance. Behavioral economists provide psychologically based explanations for what appears to be irrational behavior by investors. For example, the September 9, 1998, edition of the *Wall Street Journal* reported that the average investor believed that she would earn a rate of return on her investments of 12.9%. This compared to the rate of return she expected the market to provide of just 10.5%. In other words, the average investor thinks that she will outperform all other investors by almost 2.5% per annum. Obviously it is impossible for all investors to outperform the market—since they are the market.

A February 1998 survey by Montgomery Asset Management found that 74% of investors interviewed expected their funds to consistently outperform the market.[1] This overconfidence allows investors to ignore the seemingly overwhelming odds of choosing the few active managers who will manage to beat the market in any given year and then picking the new group that will beat the market the next year.

I believe that there are other behavioral reasons why investors choose active managers. Investors feel that by choosing an index fund they give up the chance of being above average, and the vast majority think they can at least do better than that. Individuals also like to be able to blame active managers when they underperform yet be able to take credit for choosing the active managers who happen to outperform their benchmark.

Professor Richard Thaler of the University of Chicago and Robert J. Shiller, an economics professor at Yale, note that "individual investors and money managers persist in their belief that they are endowed with more and better information than others, and that they can profit by picking stocks. If you ask people a question like, how do you rate your ability to get along with people? ninety percent think they're above average. Ninety percent of all investors also think that they're above average at picking money managers. While sobering experiences sometimes help those who delude themselves, the tendency to overconfidence is apparently just one of the limitations of the human mind."[2] This insight helps explain why individual investors think they can identify the few active managers who will beat their respective benchmarks. On the other hand, all fund managers must think they're above-average money managers; otherwise they would have no reason for existing.

Behavioral studies have found the following patterns and resulting mistakes.[3]

- Investors see order where it doesn't exist and interpret accidental success to be a result of skill, either their own or their advisor's.
- Overconfidence and confusing luck with skill leads to trading too often. Investors are guided by the courage of their *misguided* convictions. Trading increases costs and taxes, resulting in reduced after-tax returns.
- Investors see other people's decisions as the result of mood and temperament but their own as the result of objective and rational thought.
- Investors treat the highly probable as certain and the improbable as impossible.
- Investors give too much weight to recent experience, so that recent gains lead to overconfidence and recent losses to excessive caution.
- Investors are reluctant to revise long-held opinions, like the idea that active management outperforms a passive strategy, even in the face of overwhelming new information.
- Investors are biased by their hindsight. They perceive events to have been more predictable after the fact than was the case before the fact. They also recall their successes but not their failures. They rarely compare their own returns to benchmarks in order to protect their illusions and their belief that they are right to be optimistic.

- Investors seek only confirming evidence and ignore "disconfirming" evidence.
- Investors are influenced by the herd mentality.
- Regret avoidance, resulting in holding on to losers, instead of selling them to obtain the tax benefit of capital losses.
- Chasing the action, letting media attention as well as greed and fear dominate decisions, investors tend to buy yesterday's winners (greed) and sell yesterday's losers (fear). This generally results in buying high and selling low—not exactly the prescription for investment success.

This chapter discusses why human behavior may be the most important variable in determining the outcomes of investment strategies. You will learn that investment outcomes may be less dependent on the returns of the investments than on the behavior of the investors. Hopefully you will be able to put the insights provided in this chapter to use in developing the winning investment strategy. Forewarned is forearmed.

Emotions Impact Fund Returns

Despite conventional wisdom, many studies have confirmed that value (distressed) stocks outperform growth stocks. Studies have also found that the value asset class and value index funds outperform their actively managed counterparts. For the 5- and 10-year periods ending June 30, 1997:

- Actively managed small-cap value funds underperformed their benchmark by 17.85% to 19.95%, and 11.6% to 12.8% per annum, respectively.

- Actively managed mid-cap value funds trailed their benchmarks by 18.1% to 19.5%.
- Actively managed large-cap value funds trailed their benchmarks by 12.9% to 14.3%.[4]

There are several obvious reasons for this phenomenon.

- Academics would say that because markets are efficient, active managers cannot consistently identify "mispriced" securities.
- Active managers incur greater expenses, both in terms of salaries and research.
- Active managers incur greater trading costs because of their greater portfolio turnover.

There may be yet another reason for underperformance of active managers: human emotion. Despite academic evidence demonstrating that the more distressed (riskier) the company, the greater the returns, fund managers are afraid to purchase the stocks of the most distressed companies because they don't want to be perceived as "stupid" if the stocks of these obviously poorly run companies fall even further. Since the most distressed stocks have been shown to provide the highest returns, by avoiding the most distressed companies active managers are prevented from reaping the greater returns these companies provide. This behavior is one reason why active managers in value stocks underperform their benchmarks.

Investment Memory

As we age, our long-term memory skills tend to remain strong but our short-term memory skills erode. Unfortunately, individuals don't benefit from that tendency when it comes to investing. The historical evidence demonstrates that investors tend to ignore long-term historical evidence and invest according to the most recent headlines—they chase the action. This leads to buying yesterday's winners and selling yesterday's losers. While most financial publications give lip service to the premise that a buy-and-hold strategy is likely to produce the best results, their headlines generally scream at their audience advice like "Buy Large-caps NOW!" Wall Street and the media encourage this behavior. Unfortunately it has produced inferior investment results, especially after expenses and taxes.

The latest version of long-term memory loss and chasing recent returns is the current tendency toward large-cap investing. From 1995 to 1998 the S&P 500 outperformed the smallest 20% of market cap stocks (as represented by the DFA 9–10 fund) by 30.5% to 15.8%. The outperformance was greatest in 1998, +28.6% to −7.3%. With this outperformance have come such claims as "large-caps are the only place to invest and small-caps never really did provide greater returns anyway." Let's examine the facts.

Sherman Hanna, professor at Ohio State University, and Peng Chen, a research consultant at Ibbotson Associates, conducted a study on the comparative performance of large-caps (S&P 500) and small-caps (bottom 20% of NYSE stocks as ranked by market-cap). They looked at real (after-inflation) returns for all possible holding periods from 1926 to 1996. Here are their findings.[5]

- The average terminal value for small-caps was greater than the terminal value for large-caps for all possible holding periods. For holding periods of one, 5, 10, and 20 years, small-caps outperformed large caps 56%, 58%, 68%, and 92% of the time, respectively. For holding periods longer than 25 years they outperformed 100% of the time.
- The advantage for small-caps increased as the holding period lengthened—and was very substantial for long holding periods. For example, for holding periods of 5, 10, and 20 years, the real growth of each dollar invested in small-caps compared to large-caps was $7.48 to $6.34, $20.24 to $15.92, and $79.08 to $51.01. At 40 years the numbers were $652.18 compared to $218.53.
- When the holding periods were relatively short, the greater average returns for small-caps were accompanied by more risk. Greater risk was determined by looking at the worst case results for each holding period. For example, for one-, 5-, and 10-year periods the worst case for small-caps and large-caps was $0.41 and $0.63, $1.66 and $3.06, and $5.28 and $6.21. When the holding period was 15 years or longer, the worst case for small-caps was always better than the worst case for large-caps.

There is no way for investors to know whether the past performance of small-caps compared to large-caps is prologue. It is worth noting, however, that small-caps (using as a benchmark the DFA Small-cap 9–10 Fund) outperformed large-caps (as represented by the S&P 500) by about 9% in 1999 and again by about 10% in the first half of 2000. Mr. Spock (the Vulcan not the doctor), who never let his emotions get in the way of his logical thought process, would advise that ignoring 70 years of historical evidence in favor of following the "flavor of the moment" is likely to prove to be a loser's strategy. Seventy years of data presents a compelling case that the recent outperformance of large-caps is nothing more than a random event, one that is likely to be repeated over various future short time periods. The far greater likelihood seems to be that if the investment horizon is long term, small-caps will outperform large-caps. (Oh yes, and we have heard the story that this time it's somehow different.) While including 1997 through 1998 data would have improved the case for large-caps somewhat, the data suggests that owning small-caps as part of a diversified portfolio and having the discipline to ignore the "noise" created by recent returns and hype of the media is likely to prove to be the winning strategy.

Before concluding, there is one important point to make. Some investors may view the preceding data and remark: "But I don't have 25 years to invest. I can't afford to wait that long for small-caps to perform." Even if this statement of time horizon is true (in my experience, it usually is not), it makes the mistaken assumption that evidence of long-run patterns is only useful if one has an equally long-term investment horizon. The notion that relying on these long-run estimates as the best estimate of short-term results appears to escape many investors.

The Reliability of Conclusions

People often draw faulty conclusions from information. Sometimes they mistakenly trust their intuition. Other times the information may be complicated. When information involves investment decisions, mistakes in judgment can be very costly. A

Hebrew University psychologist, Amos Tversky, tried the following experiment in human behavior.[6]

Imagine that 2 bags are filled—out of sight—with the same number of poker chips. Bag A has two-thirds chips that are white and one-third that are red. In bag B the proportions are reversed. Your task is to guess which is the bag with mostly red chips. From bag A you are allowed to withdraw only 5 chips, 4 of which turn out to be red. From bag B you are allowed to withdraw 30 chips, 20 of which turn out to be red. Which bag would you guess has the most red chips?

If you are like most people, you would probably guess bag A, since 80% of the chips you withdrew were red, versus just 67% from bag B. However, statistics tell us that you are more likely to be right if you had chosen bag B. The reason is that because the sample size from bag B is much larger, you have more confidence in the result. Statistical theory tells us that the 20/30 bag is much more likely than the 4/5 bag to be the bag with more red chips.

What does this have to do with investing? Investors often make decisions based on very small samples. For example, from 1996 through 1998, growth stocks outperformed value stocks and large-cap stocks outperformed small-cap stocks. The press and airwaves have been filled with gurus stating that investors should avoid those "lousy" small-cap and value stocks, as they are obviously poor investments. Small-cap and value funds (and emerging market funds, among others) experienced outflows of funds, and large-cap growth funds experienced inflows.

Think of the period from 1996 to 1998 as bag A, from which you were only able to draw a few samples. Think of the 73 years of data for which information on equity markets is available as bag B. While large-cap and growth stocks have outperformed over the very recent past, over the longer term we know that small-cap stocks have outperformed large-cap stocks and value stocks have outperformed growth stocks. Investors who ignore the much larger data set are making the same mistake as those who chose bag A on the basis of a very small sample. The only difference between the two is that choosing bag A didn't cause you to lose any money. Basing investment decisions on very small samples can lead to very costly outcomes, particularly if a small (recent) data series causes investors to abandon a well-thought-out investment strategy.

The best illustration of incorrectly basing investment decisions on small data sets is the following tale. Every investor knows that stocks provide higher returns than bank certificates of deposits. However, for the 19-year period 1966 through 1984, an investment in the S&P 500 underperformed 1-month bank CDs by almost 1% per annum. If after 19 long years you abandoned your strategy of investing in the higher expected returning asset class of equities and switched to bank CDs, you would have missed the greatest bull market in history. Despite that lesson, investors are all too willing to abandon their investment strategies based on much shorter term results—often on just a few months of data, let alone just a few years. It appears that making irrational decisions based on short-term results is just an all too human pattern of behavior.

The lesson for the investor: make sure that your decisions are based on long-term historical evidence and not on short-term data, which is probably a random outcome by its very nature.

Index Funds May Be Boring, But . . .

What do "good news, bad news" stories have to do with investing? Behavioral economists would find the following story quite revealing of investor behavior.

Rex Sinquefield, co-chairman of DFA, tells this tale. A woman went to her doctor because she wasn't feeling well. The doctor examined her and said: "I have good news and bad news for you." The woman asked: "What's the bad news?" The doctor responded: "You have only 30 days to live." The woman asked: "Oh my gosh, what's the good news?" The doctor responded: "You could hire an index fund manager and it will seem like 30 years."[7]

This tale is illustrative of why, despite an overwhelming body of evidence supporting the view that passive investing is the winning investment strategy, only about 10% of individual investors' dollars are invested in this manner. Simply put, index funds are boring. They lack the excitement of trying to pick individual stocks that somehow everyone else has mispriced. Indexing doesn't provide the great stories to tell about the great stock picks investors make. Of course you never hear about the losing picks. Individuals also like to pick active managers. If the manager succeeds in beating the market, the investor takes the credit for being smart enough to find one of the few winners who actually outperformed his benchmark. On the other hand, if the manager underperformed, and virtually all invariably do, the individual gets to blame the manager and promptly fires him.

Individuals also don't like being average. They listen to brokers and active managers who tell them that if they index their portfolio, they will just get average returns. The problem with this statement is that the benchmark is wrong. While it is true that investors who own index funds will "only" earn market rates of return, the fact is that the average actively managed fund has underperformed its style benchmark by almost 2% per annum, even before loads and taxes are considered. Add in these 2 factors, and the performance only gets worse. Index fund investors win the game by assuring themselves of "average" or, more correctly, *market* returns. By attempting to beat an efficient market, believers in active management end up playing a loser's game.

Before attempting to pick stocks, time the market, or choose an active manager, investors should be asking the question: Do I want excitement or superior performance from my portfolio? If the answer is superior performance, choosing the right strategy is simple.

The following is the conclusion reached by Gary Belsky, a writer at *Money* magazine from 1991 to 1998, and Thomas Gilovich, a psychology professor at Cornell University, in their excellent book *Why Smart People Make Big Money Mistakes—Lessons to Be Learned from the New Science of Behavioral Finance*:

> Any individual who is not professionally occupied in the financial services industry (and even most of those who are) and who in any way attempts to actively manage an investment portfolio is probably suffering from overconfidence. That is, anyone who has confidence enough in his or her abilities and knowledge to invest in a particular stock or bond (or actively managed mutual fund or real estate investment trust or limited partnership) is most likely fooling himself.
>
> In fact, most such people—probably you—have no business at all trying to pick investments, except as sport. Such people— again, probably you—should probably divide their money among several index funds and turn off CNBC.

Mutual Funds: Reported *versus* Realized Returns

In 1994, Dalbar released a study that showed that "do-it-yourself" investors (using no-load mutual funds) realized lower returns than investors using the services of "financial advisors" (using load funds).[8] Although it is denied by Dalbar, the rumor is that Merrill Lynch funded the study. The story goes that Merrill's intention was to demonstrate that the load fees investors paid was justified by the higher returns those investors received. Unfortunately, the results of the study could be used in a way that could allow an investor to come to the wrong conclusion. The following is an example of a misleading interpretation of the Dalbar study.

Dalbar found that the do-it-yourselfers using no-load funds during the period studied (1984 through 1995) earned a total return of 80% versus the 96% that was earned by investors purchasing load funds through brokers or other financial advisors. The "obvious" conclusion was that the commissioned advisors more than compensated for their expenses.

However, it should be noted that the reason for the higher returns was not that the funds the advisors chose had better returns. Instead, the reason for the better returns was that the do-it-yourself no-load investors had very short holding periods (only about 3 years). These short term–oriented investors kept chasing yesterday's winners and selling yesterday's losers. Investors purchasing load funds, having paid those heavy load fees, tended to hold on longer. The longer average holding period, not better returning funds, was the source of the greater returns.

What Merrill Lynch (and other brokerage firms) would never tell you was that for the same period the S&P 500 Index was up 385%, large value stocks were up 443%, small value stocks were up 410%, and international large value stocks were up 912%. The key to getting those great returns was twofold. First, believe that passive (vs. active) investing was the winning strategy. Second, have the discipline to stay the course. Unfortunately, too few investors have the needed discipline. An important observation is that good financial advisors can more than earn their fees simply by helping investors keep disciplined.

Dalbar updated its study to include data from 1984 to 1997. The study now focused on "the average equity fund investor" and a "buy-and-hold" indexed investor. Once again, Dalbar concluded that mutual fund investors earn far less than reported returns. While the S&P 500 Index returned over 17% per annum, equity fund investors realized returns of less than 7% per year. This gap of over 10% was again explained by the short term–oriented behavior of equity fund investors. Individual investors, as a group, simply do not have the discipline to buy and hold. Despite all the evidence that trying to time the market is a loser's game, individuals continue to invest in what is called a convex manner—buying yesterday's winners (too late and at high prices) and selling yesterday's losers (too late and at low prices). By not remaining fully invested for the entire period, investors miss out on the majority of the returns that are available simply by buying and holding. Another amazing statistic Dalbar found is that the average individual equity investor (despite the great returns that were available) would have been better off simply holding bonds. The total return to government bond fund holders far surpassed the returns to the average individual equity mutual fund investor—*but was only about one-half of the returns available to the passive equity investor*.

While the 10% per year gap in returns (greater than 17% vs. less than 7%) cited by Dalbar is huge, on a total return basis, the numbers look even more impressive: average individual investor, 148%; S&P 500 Index, 820%. The importance of Dalbar's work is that it quantified the difficulty individual investors have in keeping the discipline to stick with a long-term asset allocation. All too often investors fall prey to emotion (fear or greed) and become tempted by the prognostications of the "guru" of the moment.

Long-Term Earnings Forecasts and the Growth *versus* Value Conundrum

Value stocks have provided investors with significantly higher returns than growth stocks. However, there is a great debate about the source of the outperformance. Most financial economists favor the explanation that the high book-to-market ratios of value stocks reflect the risky nature of these distressed securities. The higher returns have thus been compensation for greater risk. On the other hand, the fact that value stocks have provided these higher returns with lower volatility (one measure of risk) is offered as proof that the market is inefficient. The argument is that higher returns have been a free lunch: there was less risk—at least as defined by standard deviation (volatility).

Financial economists argue that the markets are efficient and that the greater risk is just not being captured by a volatility measure. Behavioral economists argue that the markets are inefficient and that investors consistently overestimate the returns of growth stocks and overestimate the distress of value stocks. The result is that growth stocks become overvalued and produce low future returns and value stocks become undervalued and produce high future returns. The debate rages on. While the financial economist's argument has more intellectual appeal (the behaviorists argue that markets are irrational), it always pays to keep an open mind.

Richard Harris, in his study "The Accuracy, Bias and Efficiency of Analysts' Long Run Earnings Growth Forecasts" (*Journal of Business Finance and Accounting*, June/July 1999), sought to determine a possible cause of any persistent "over-valuation" of securities. His study covered 6,660 5-year earnings forecasts of NYSE, AMEX, and NASDAQ firms in the IBES (Institutional Brokers Estimate System) database for the period beginning in 1982. He then compared the forecasts to actual profits using the S&P and Compustat databases. Here is what he found:

- The earnings forecasts were extremely biased, with actual profits overestimated by 7% per annum. A simple forecast of no change in earnings would have produced more accurate results. An even better forecast would have been to assume that a firm's earnings would grow in line with the overall economy.
- The errors were highly correlated with themselves. Low-profit forecasts had low errors, and high-profit forecasts had high errors. Thus, high-growth forecasts had the worst errors. Large companies with high book-to-market ratios (value stocks) had the fewest errors.
- The forecasting errors were not from having overestimated the growth of the overall economy. Most errors were from individual company forecasts, with a small contribution from overestimating industry profits.

Harris hypothesized that the source of the errors might easily be explained by the following:

- The sell side of investment banking firms might want to hype the stock they follow in order to help with the sale of securities.
- Analysts are afraid to publish negative reports for fear they will lose access to management as a source of information.
- Analysts hype the stock to win favor with company management in the hope that they will win more investment banking business for their respective firms.

All these explanations have appeal, though they do not explain why the errors are worse for growth stocks than for value stocks. However, the following observation seems quite interesting. From 1964 to 1998 large value stocks outperformed large growth stocks by about 4% per annum (15.1% vs. 11.4%) and small value stocks outperformed small growth stocks by over 5% (17.7% vs.12.1%). With the average error found by Harris being 7%, and the error being larger for growth than value stocks, it would seem that the outperformance by value stocks is very similar to the magnitude of the forecasting error. Maybe a coincidence, maybe not.

A study published in the summer 1999 issue of the *Journal of Portfolio Management* looked at international markets and came to the same conclusion as Harris. The study covered the 11-year period 1986 through 1996 and 20 developed country markets. The authors found that earnings forecasts for growth stocks were consistently too high, thus creating "overvalued" stocks. The actual earnings announcements disappointed growth investors the most, and their stocks (since they had the greatest expectations) were punished. The overestimation of earnings fully explained the value effect.[9]

The belief that value stocks provide higher returns than growth stocks as compensation for greater risk has great intellectual appeal. The alternative is to believe that investors have been systematically stupid in setting prices for growth stocks for 70 years and that they never learn from their mistakes. This alternative explanation seems far less likely. However, it is worth considering this alternative explanation because of its potential consequences. If analysts continue to overestimate earnings (possibly for the reasons Harris cited), it seems likely that 1 of 2 scenarios will unfold. First, the market will continue to ignore the excess enthusiasm—and growth stocks will ultimately deliver disappointing earnings and therefore disappointing returns relative to value stocks. Alternatively, investors will wake up to the problem of overestimation of earnings, and growth stocks will experience a massive one-time selloff to reflect the currently too-high valuations. Not a good scenario for growth stocks in either case.

Confusing Strategy and Outcome

One of the biggest mistakes investors make is confusing strategy (ex-ante decisions) with outcomes (ex-post results). The following example is illustrative of this point. Imagine that it is January 1999 and your best friend just inherited $10 million of Exxon stock. Being of modest means up to this point, your friend's inheritance constitutes virtually 100% of her assets. Your friend tells you that she plans on holding the stock, as she thinks that not only is Exxon a great company but also that oil prices will rise in 1999. She then asks your opinion on her strategy.

Giving sound counsel, you advise her that putting all her eggs in one basket is a very risky strategy. Your advice is to diversify. Your friend agrees and states that she will sell $5 million of

Exxon stock and with the proceeds buy $5 million of Shell Oil. You laugh. You tell her that while owning two companies instead of one is diversification, because both Exxon and Shell are likely to move up and down together (in response to the rising and falling of oil prices), she hasn't achieved effective diversification. The price movement of these two stocks is likely to be highly correlated; thus she really hasn't reduced the risk of her portfolio.

You suggest that in order to achieve effective diversification, instead of buying Shell, she buy something that would benefit if oil prices fell (something with low correlation). You therefore recommend that she purchase United Airlines. If oil prices rise, Exxon will do well. On the other hand, if oil prices fall, United Airlines will do well, as its largest expense after labor costs falls. Now, because Exxon and United Airlines have low correlation, the portfolio is effectively diversified—at least against the risk of changing oil prices. The portfolio's risk has certainly been reduced.

Your friend agrees that the strategy is correct, and she makes her trades the very next day. Fast-forward to the end of the year. Your friend is very angry with you. Why? Oil prices have risen dramatically, resulting in Exxon's price rising sharply and United's price falling sharply. You rightly point out that your friend agreed at the beginning with the strategy of protecting against oil price changes. You also point out that back at the start of the year you knew with certainty that over the next 20 years there would be periods when oil prices did well and Exxon would do well and United poorly. However, you also knew with certainty that there would also be periods when oil prices would fall and Exxon would do poorly and United would do well. Since your friend did not have a crystal ball that would allow her to predict oil prices—thus knowing when to only own Exxon and only own United—the correct strategy (ex-ante) was to diversify.

You then point out that the strategy was working exactly as expected. Your friend just didn't like the results (ex-post). You also point out that she would have been very happy if oil prices had fallen.

The lesson: keep your opinions to yourself. Just kidding. The lesson of course is that because investors do not have crystal balls, a strategy is correct ex-ante, whatever the outcome. As proof I offer the following. Do you know of any person who complains at the end of the year that he "wasted" his life insurance premium? Was buying life insurance the wrong strategy? Diversification is the correct strategy, whatever the outcome. So why are so many investors with diversified portfolios unhappy, many to the point that they abandon the strategy of building a diversified portfolio and instead chase the latest hot asset class (the equivalent of not renewing your life insurance policy)?

The biggest problem for investors is that they confuse ex-ante strategy with ex-post results. Investors understand that the winning strategy is to build a diversified portfolio of low correlating asset classes. However, many investors then focus on the performance of the individual components instead of on the performance of the portfolio.

Diversification also creates a "tracking error" problem. Investors know that devoting a substantial allocation to international stocks is an effective way to reduce risk. As in the Exxon and United Airlines example, investors know in advance that there will be periods, probably even long ones, when U.S. stocks outperform foreign stocks. They also know that the reverse will also be true. Since neither they nor anyone else has shown the consistent ability to predict which will do well when, the winning strategy is to buy and hold both in a proportion you are comfortable with. However, when international stocks do poorly (fail to track) relative to a benchmark of U.S. stocks (i.e., the S&P 500), investors experience "tracking error" regret. Some will even abandon the winning strategy, despite having known ahead of time that they would experience such periods.

The final problem created by diversification is similar to the tracking error problem. It is called a frame-of-reference problem. Investors are bombarded daily with financial news. In 1999 the headlines were dominated by the performance of the technology-loaded NASDAQ, which had its greatest performance ever. Thus the frame of reference for many investors is comparing the performance of their portfolio to that of the NASDAQ and to technology stocks in general. While investors know that owning only technology stocks wouldn't be much different from only owning Exxon (in terms of diversification), their daily experience is telling them that their portfolio (and therefore their strategy) is performing poorly. Again, they may be tempted to stray from what they know is the winning strategy.

A perfect example is that for the past 5 years non-U.S. investors have been very happy if they diversified and owned U.S. stocks, which have generally far outperformed international stocks. On the other hand, U.S. investors who diversified and owned foreign stocks might have been very unhappy. In both cases the strategy to diversify was the same. Either the strategy is correct or it isn't—ex-ante, of course. Unfortunately we live in an ex-ante world.

The bottom line is that in order to benefit from the advantages of a globally diversified portfolio of low correlating asset classes, investors must have patience and discipline and remember the following:

- Don't confuse ex-ante strategy with ex-post results.
- Ignore tracking error. Since each investor's portfolio should reflect her unique investment horizon, risk tolerance, and financial goals, the only benchmark should be one's own portfolio (assuming, of course, the exclusive use of passive asset class or index funds).
- Turn off the television and radio and stop checking daily, monthly, and even annual stock prices and portfolio performance. Constant monitoring can only lead to frame-of-reference and tracking error problems, leading one to stray from the winning strategy.

The first task of an advisor is to educate a client about the winning strategy of passive asset class investing. The next step is to provide knowledge on the benefits of diversification and how it can be used to improve risk-adjusted returns. The third step is to help clients define the right mix of asset class funds for their unique situations. Last but certainly not least, advisors should help clients remain disciplined by reminding them regularly why they adopted their strategy in the first place. When clients' portfolios are doing "well" (outperforming their frame of reference benchmark) the advisor should remind them that they expected that there would be periods like this. However they also know with certainty that there will be periods when the reverse will be true. When a client's portfolio is doing "poorly," the advisor reminds them of the same thing—that they expected that there would be periods like this, but that they knew with certainty that there will also be periods when the reverse will be true. Remember that diversification is always working. Sometimes you like the results, and sometimes you don't. But the strategy is always correct.

There Is Nothing New—Only the History You Don't Know

The financial markets in 1999 witnessed some truly amazing phenomena. Among them were the astronomical and seemingly inexplicable rise of Internet stocks; the "birth" of day trading, with thousands of otherwise normal individuals abandoning their chosen professions to speculate on minute-to-minute pricing of securities; and the push for extended trading hours. New technology, especially the growth of the Internet, provided the fuel for all of them. Are these all new phenomena, or have we already *been there and done that*?

Let's take them one at a time, beginning with the Internet craze. Internet stock prices have risen to levels that could not be justified by any traditional valuation measure. Analysts were forced to come up with new ways to properly value these stocks (to justify the unjustifiable). Longtime professionals and academics cried that this was just another in the long line of financial bubbles that would eventually burst. And the history of financial markets is filled with financial bubbles that eventually burst. The most famous bubble is, of course, the tulip bulb mania that occurred in Holland in the 1630s. "Tulip prices rose as much as 1,000% over a three-year period. At a time when the average annual wage was between 200 and 400 guilders and a small house cost about 300 guilders, tulip bulb prices reached as high as 6,000 guilders for the most prized bulb."[10] Prices went up because they were going up. Speculators bought on the assumption that there would always be a greater fool to buy at ever higher prices. Unfortunately for some investors, the greater fool was staring at them in the mirror when prices suddenly collapsed and there were no buyers to be found at any price. It is worth noting that the fad of momentum investing is just another version of the greater fool theory—buy because the price has gone up. More recent examples of bubbles are the conglomerate craze of the 1960s, the biotech craze of the late 1980s, and the casino stock craze of the early 1990s. All of these bubbles eventually burst. (It is important to point out that it is easy to say that they are all bubbles after the fact and much harder before the fact. In case you doubt that, just recall the irrational exuberance declared by Alan Greenspan when the Dow was below 7,000.)

Let's turn to the "birth" of day trading. Another financial bubble appeared in the early 1700s when the South Seas Company, an English company that received a monopoly on the trade with the Spanish colonies of Latin America, was formed. When the king of England personally invested in its stock, the price of its shares bloomed in a manner strikingly similar to the rise of tulip bulb prices. Speculation ran rampant. A Dutch newspaper reported that the level of speculation soared to such a level that "trade has completely slowed down, that more than 100 ships moored along the river Thames are for sale, and that the *owners of capital prefer to speculate on shares than to return to work at their normal business.*"[11] Sir Isaac Newton was reported to have said: "I can calculate the motions of heavenly bodies, but not the madness of people."[12] In due course prices collapsed and everyone went back to business (at least those who still had businesses to go back to).

Let's now turn to the latest craze for extended trading, another new phenomenon—NOT. A combination of events led to a burst of speculative activity in the 1860s: the expansion of the rail system; the advent of the telegraph, allowing information to travel at previously unimaginable speeds (sounds familiar); and the Civil War. The prices of gold and silver mining stocks rose and eventually crashed in true tulip bulb fashion. Speculation on the price of that new commodity, oil, was so rampant that the price of crude rose ninefold in just a few months, reaching a level in real terms that it has never again reached.[13] By 1864 trading had reached such a feverish peak that after-hours trading was moved from the Exchange to the basement of the Fifth Avenue Hotel, where it continued until 9 o'clock in the evening.[14] The introduction of the "ticker" in 1867 further fueled the frenzy of speculation. It got so bad that ordinary clerks formed investment clubs to pool their limited resources (the Beardstown Ladies had nothing on these folks).[15]

Another new phenomenon related to the Internet craze is the trend to bringing public only a very small offering. The idea is to create a scarcity value for the shares of newly public companies. The scarcity of shares is also intended to prevent short-sellers from speculating in "overvalued" stock in fear that they might not be able to buy shares back. In the 1840s British railway companies were being created with about as great a frequency as Internet stocks are now created. Each offering was for only a very few shares, with the issuers retaining a large allocation for themselves. The stock would be hyped to speculators. When the stocks rose, on very thin trading, of course, the promoters would sell their retained stock at a big profit, and, of course, the stocks would collapse.[16]

The only thing you don't know is the history you don't know. Investors unaware of the history of financial follies are doomed to repeat the same mistakes. Too many investors are so overcome by emotions of greed and the noise of the moment that they ignore the lessons of history. Here are 2 such lessons. In June 1929, just 4 months before the crash, *Forbes* magazine stated: "For the last five years we have been in a new industrial era in this country. We are making progress industrially and economically not even by leaps and bounds, but on a perfectly heroic scale." In October 1968, just before the onset of a slump that knocked prices down 60% in real terms, *Forbes* noted: "As a result of all that has been happening in the economy during the last decade, we are in a different—if not new—era and traditional thinking, the standard approach to the market, is no longer in synchronization with the real world."[17]

Does history repeat itself? Are we experiencing another "tulip craze"? The following data might provide some perspective. By the start of the year 2000 there were over 500 auction sites, 50 beauty sites, and 1,500 e-commerce shoe sites. From 1855 to 1861 the number of telegraph companies shrank 88%, from 50 to 6. From 1894 to 1903 an estimated 20,000 telephone companies were started.[18] Are we at the beginning of the Internet Revolution or the beginning of the end of just another bubble? When considering this question investors would do well to remember that the 4 most dangerous words in the English language are THIS TIME IT'S DIFFERENT.

Bubble or New Paradigm?

Without question the topic of greatest debate among investors, including investment professionals, and financial economists, as we entered the twenty-first century, is whether or not the market, and the technology sector in particular, is overvalued. There are 2 very strong conflicting views regarding not only the current valuation of technology stocks but also the valuation of the entire asset class of large-cap growth stocks. One side I'll call the "new paradigm" or "it's different this time" school. The other side I'll call the "been there, done that" school; its theme is that those who don't learn from the past are doomed to repeat the same mistakes. No 2 sides could have more different viewpoints.

To understand each side, let's imagine a dialogue between the 2 schools.

NEW PARADIGM: It's a new world order. It's the new new thing. Investors should own great companies at any price. Never discard the right company just because the price is too high.

BEEN THERE, DONE THAT: That is exactly what investors were saying in the late 1960s. There was a group of stocks called the Nifty-Fifty—roughly 50 large-cap growth stocks with P/E ratios of about 50 or more. They were mostly high-tech stocks like IBM, Sperry Rand, NCR, Control Data, Xerox, Honeywell, Polaroid, and so on. Like today's Ciscos, they were called one-decision-just buy-at-any-price-and-hold-forever stocks. Within 2 years many of them had fallen by 80% to 95%. And not a single stock of that Nifty-Fifty group that sold above a 50 price-to-earnings ratio was able to match the performance of the S&P 500 over the next 25 years.[19] The only differences are that today investors are buying at even higher price-to-earnings or price-to-sales ratios and they are buying anything that is Internet related. Then it was anything electronics related. Now if it has an e- prefix, it gets billion-dollar valuations from investors who can't even tell you what the company does, let alone how it is going to make money doing it. Back then, investors bought anything with the suffix "tronics" or "onics." Just like today, the IPO market was hot, and companies were changing names just to have the correct suffix. Been there, done that.

NEW PARADIGM: But it's different this time. The Internet is changing the world. It's a great revolution, supercharging the economy.

BEEN THERE, DONE THAT: The story is the same. In the sixties it was the same technology story. Many companies eventually succeeded, and many failed. But most failed to justify the valuations placed on them. We also see no reason to think that this revolution will have any bigger impact than the previous society-changing inventions such as the automobile, air travel, TV and radio (RCA hit 114 in 1929 and it took almost sixty years for it to recover to that level—how's that for a sure thing?), or the electronics and computer revolution. Remember that technology benefits everyone. In fact, it often benefits the users more than the inventors and eventual industry winners—even if you can somehow identify them ahead of time. Besides, even if you are right about technology's great future, are you the only one who knows this? If not, the market has already incorporated your great future into current prices (maybe that is why prices are very high now). The only way to outperform the market is to exploit pricing mistakes by others. With investment professionals determining prices (they do about 80% of all dollar-weighted trading), are you sure they have undervalued these stocks? And remember that the evidence is very clear that great earnings do not necessarily translate into great returns. Low-earning value companies have historically provided much higher investment returns (as compensation for their greater risk) than high-earning growth companies.

NEW PARADIGM: You just don't get it. For 5 years now, tech and large-cap growth stocks have led the way. It's so obvious, why can't you see it? I pity you.

BEEN THERE, DONE THAT: It's always obvious after the fact. Unfortunately, our before-the-fact crystal ball isn't that clear. At the end of the 1970s the obvious asset classes to own were oil companies (6 of the 10 largest cap stocks by market cap were oil companies), gold, other commodities, collectibles, and hard assets in general. These all proved to be very poor investments over the next 20 years. Sure I wish I had owned more technology over the past few years, but I didn't have your crystal ball.

NEW PARADIGM: But this is different. The United States clearly is the leader in technology. We dominate the Internet and biotech and financial services sectors. That is where the future is. Besides, the U.S. free enterprise system has proven it's the best model. Others have to now catch up.

BEEN THERE, DONE THAT: At the end of 1989 Japan was at the top of the world. The Nikkei approached 40,000, having soared almost 500% for the decade (sounds familiar). Their "managed economy" system was the envy of the world. Their model of giant interlocking companies was clearly superior to our model. Their technology was dominating ours. Tokyo was sure to become the financial center of the world. The Japanese had even bought up such important U.S. symbols as Rockefeller Center and the Pebble Beach Golf Course. Financial publications were saying, "You ain't seen nothing yet." We were reading such scary books as *The Land of the Rising Sun*. The United States was headed the way of the Roman and British empires. With all that certainty, within 3 months the Nikkei fell 23%, finishing the year down almost 40%—and it kept falling. A decade later it is still over 50% below its peak of over 11 years ago. Sure thing?

NEW PARADIGM: Just look at returns over the last few years. The opportunity is enormous. You can't afford to miss out.

BEEN THERE, DONE THAT: What investors can't afford is to be caught at the tail end of a bubble. When bubbles burst, they burst very quickly, affording little opportunity to exit. Liquidity, which once seemed infinite, virtually dries up—buyers disappear and prices collapse. This is what happened to tulip bulbs, South Seas shares, in the stock market in 1929 . . . and may happen again. Investors in those bubbles were not making investment decisions based on traditional valuation methods. Instead, they were relying on faith and momentum—the ability to sell to somebody at a higher price. In fact, because market prices couldn't be justified, new metrics were invented to justify them. In the Japanese bubble's case, something called the Q-ratio was invented. Ever hear of the Q-ratio since?

NEW PARADIGM: Don't you get it? United States productivity is improving, growing at the fastest rate.

BEEN THERE, DONE THAT: United States productivity is growing rapidly. However, it grew even faster in the 1920s.

NEW PARADIGM: You just don't get it. The future for New Age companies like AOL, Amazon, Cisco, and the like is so bright and obvious, how can you possibly go wrong?

BEEN THERE, DONE THAT: First, the future is never perfectly clear. Second, even if the future turns out like you believe, that doesn't guarantee great investment returns. Take the RCA example. Every positive thing that was priced into RCA actually occurred. And some positive things that no one could have envisioned also occurred. For example, radio exploded as a medium, radio listenership increased for decades at a rapid pace, RCA remained a major player with a dominant market share, and new forms of entertainment specific to radio (example: the soap opera) were created that brought in advertising money far in excess of what the newspapers generated. Nonetheless, investing in RCA was a financial disaster. The "crystal ball" was clear, yet that was not enough to compensate for the "bubble" valuations.

LARRY SWEDROE: It is impossible without the benefit of a rear-view mirror to tell whether a market or a sector is overvalued. In fact, the EMT tells us that the market's price is the one most likely to be the correct one. What we do know is that high valuations reflect great expectations. Great expectations mean low perception of risk. In turn, the result is low future expected returns. In addition, since we can't determine if it's a bubble, the winning investment strategy is to build a globally diversified portfolio that reflects your risk profile, financial objectives, and investment horizon. Then have the discipline to regularly rebalance; selling some of that supernova sector when it's hot to buy something that is currently relatively cheaper. Trying to guess whether a bubble is building (which you can take advantage of by jumping on the bandwagon) or about to burst (which you could take advantage of by shorting) is a loser's game. It may be exciting, but it's speculating, not investing.

Investment Insights

- Human behavior can have a major impact on portfolio returns.
- Despite sobering experiences, individual investors and money managers persist in their belief that they are endowed with more and better information than others, and that they can profit by picking stocks and timing the market.
- Overconfidence leads to increased trading and lower returns.
- Investors chase the action, leading to buying high and selling low. They thus earn lower returns than the reported returns of the funds in which they invest.

- Investors feel that by not selecting an actively managed fund they give up the chance of being above average, and the vast majority think they can do better than that. They fail to understand that by just accepting market (average) returns they will outperform most investors (be above average).
- Individuals like to be able to blame active managers when they underperform yet be able to take credit for choosing the active managers who happen to outperform the market.
- Investors treat the highly probable as certain and the improbable as impossible.
- Investors give too much weight to recent experience, so that recent gains lead to overconfidence and recent losses to excessive caution.
- Indexing and passive investing may be boring, but it is the winning strategy. Investors should either seek entertainment elsewhere, or establish a small entertainment account.
- Investors need filters (knowledge) to screen misinformation.
- Earnings forecasts for growth companies are generally far too optimistic, leading to poor investment performance.
- Never confuse ex-ante strategy with ex-post results.
- There is nothing really new in investing, just the history you don't know.
- The four most dangerous words in the English language are: it's different this time.

CHAPTER 10

◆

Play the Winner's Game and Invest the Way "Really Smart Money" Invests Today

The beginning is the most important part of the work.
—Plato

Indexing is a wonderful strategy. It's a shame most folks do it wrong.
—Jonathan Clements, *Wall Street Journal*,
June 17, 1997

A rising tide lifts all boats. It's not until the tide goes out that you realize who's swimming naked.
—Warren Buffett

As with any undertaking, an investment strategy should begin with the development of a business plan. Each individual must carefully consider his or her:

- Investment horizon (ability to take risk)
- Tolerance for risk (willingness to take risk)
- Financial goals (need to take risk)

Investors should formalize their conclusions by writing and signing an investment policy statement (IPS). It is my experience that while it is easy for investors to have discipline when things are going according to plan, it is much more difficult to do so when the unexpected occurs. Formally signing an IPS helps remove emotion from the decision-making process. It also makes it far more likely that investors will have the discipline to stick with their plan during the inevitable, and *anticipated*, bad times.

This chapter focuses specifically on helping you profit from the indexing revolution. You will learn how to develop an IPS, one that specifically addresses your unique situation. You will also learn how to:

- Determine the appropriate equity and fixed income allocations.
- Determine the specific allocations to the various equity and fixed income asset classes.
- Establish a systematic rebalancing program.

In summary, you will learn how to invest the way the most sophisticated institutions invest. You will learn how the "really smart money" plays the winner's game of passive asset class investing using the principles of MPT.

Investing Internationally: Risky or Not?

Many investors avoid adding international investments to their portfolios because they believe international investing is too risky. Academics, however, recommend that investors add international assets to their portfolios because they actually reduce risk. International equities have low correlation (their prices do not rise or fall at the same time and/or at the same rate) with domestic equities. Therefore, the addition of international stocks to a portfolio reduces the volatility (risk) of the *overall* portfolio. A study published in the fall 1998 issue of the *Journal of Investing* sought to determine whether international equity diversification actually provided that theoretical risk reduction benefit.

The study covered the period 1970 through 1996. David Laster examined the performance of portfolios with varying allocations to the S&P 500 Index (representing large-cap domestic equities) and the EAFE Index. The study looked at portfolios with allocations of 10% S&P 500 and 90% EAFE, 20% S&P 500 and 80% EAFE, and so on. At the end of each year each portfolio was rebalanced (correcting for market movements) to its original allocations. Using a statistical method called "bootstrapping" (creating a series of monthly returns using randomly selected subperiods from the entire period), the study was able to effectively examine far more 5-year holding periods than its 27-year period contained. Before reviewing the results of the study, it is important to note that during this period the S&P 500 Index outperformed the EAFE Index by 12.29% to 12.03% per annum. In addition, the coefficient of correlation of returns between the 2 indices was 0.48, a fairly low figure.

The study concluded the following:

- A combination of the S&P 500 Index and the EAFE Index outperformed either index individually—a result of the low correlation.
- Increasing the international allocation to as much as 40% increased returns and reduced risk as measured by standard deviation (volatility).
- An allocation of 40% international produced the highest

Sharpe ratio—a measure of the amount of return for a given level of risk.

* Increasing the international allocation from 0% to just 20% reduced the likelihood of negative returns by one-third.
* Investors with a 10% international allocation could be 98% certain that they would reduce risk by raising the international allocation.
* Investors with even a 22% allocation could be 90% certain that they would reduce risk by raising their international allocation.

What may surprise some investors is that adding international assets to a portfolio during a period when they underperformed actually resulted in higher returns and lower risk. This study provides a powerful argument for including significant exposure to "risky" international equities to reduce overall portfolio risk and improve returns.

Asset Class Contributions to Incremental Returns from Portfolio Diversification

One of the first mathematical theorems we learn is that the sum of the parts must equal the whole. Fortunately, when it comes to investment portfolios, this isn't true. The compound return for a portfolio with a fixed percentage invested in various asset classes is greater than the sum of the weighted average of the compound returns of the individual asset classes. This will hold true if the portfolio's asset allocation is kept relatively constant through a program of regular rebalancing. The fact that the "whole"—the compound return of the portfolio—is greater than the sum of its parts—the weighted average compound return of the individual components of the portfolio—is one of the major tenets of MPT. MPT has demonstrated that there is in fact a "free lunch": you can actually reduce risk without a commensurate reduction in returns by *effectively* diversifying a portfolio. Conversely, you can increase returns without a commensurate increase in risk. The effectiveness of the diversification (the incremental returns) depends on the degree of the correlation of returns (the degree to which prices rise and fall at the same time and by the same amount) between the various asset classes chosen to construct the portfolio.

David G. Booth and Eugene F. Fama made a major contribution to understanding how asset class returns affect portfolio returns when they demonstrated that "the compound return of an asset class is a misleading measure of the contribution of that asset class to the compound return of the portfolio." Their conclusion: "The contribution of each asset class to the portfolio's return is greater than the asset's compound return." The incremental return is the result of the beneficial impact of portfolio diversification.[1]

This conclusion has profound implications for investors. In order to determine which asset classes (or mutual funds) to include in a portfolio, the investor must first determine the expected returns of each asset class. The next step is to determine the degree to which each asset class is expected to contribute to the returns of the overall portfolio. The second step is important, because while you might have 2 asset classes with similar expected returns, if one has a lower correlation of returns with the other components of the portfolio, it will have a greater expected contribution to the portfolio's return than the other.

The following example will clarify the issue. Booth and Fama examined the returns for the 50-year period 1941–1990 of a simple 2 asset-class portfolio—50% S&P 500/50% 20-year Treasury bonds. Here is a summary of what they found:

- The S&P 500 produced an annualized return of 11.31%.
- The Treasury bonds produced an annualized return of 4.36%.
- The average of the two compound returns was 7.84%.
- A constant 50%/50% portfolio, achieved by regularly re-balancing the portfolio, produced a compound return of 8.11%.
- Diversification thus added 0.28% (8.11% to 7.84%) to the portfolio's return.

Booth and Fama developed a formula that allows investors to calculate the estimated diversification benefit from each asset class within a portfolio. This represented a significant advance in investment decision-making because it allows investors to create the most efficient portfolio (highest expected return) for the amount of risk they are willing to accept.

With their formula the authors were able to calculate what they called the "return contribution" of each asset class. It also enabled them to specifically calculate how much of the return contribution was related to the benefit of diversification. In the preceding example:

- The return contribution for the S&P 500 was 11.79%. Portfolio diversification accounted for an incremental return contribution of 0.48%.
- The return contribution for the 20-year Treasury bond was 4.44%, or 0.08% greater than its compound return.

Booth and Fama then looked at the benefit of adding the asset class of small-cap stocks to a portfolio. The table shows the results for the same 1941 through 1990 period for a 60% equity/ 40% fixed income portfolio. Two different small-cap asset classes were used; the smallest half (deciles 6 to 10) of all equities as ranked by CRSP, and the smallest 20% (deciles 9 to 10). The fixed income allocation was also divided equally between 20-year Treasuries and 1-month Treasury bills. The illustration shows the portfolio with deciles 6 to 10 as P1 and the portfolio with deciles 9 to 10 as P2. The purpose of this example is to examine the impact of diversification of 2 asset classes with different correlations to the other components of the portfolio. Deciles 9 to 10 have a lower correlation to the S&P 500 (0.638 for the period 1/1926 to 3/1998) than do deciles 6 to 10 (0.774 for the same period). Here is what they found (note some of the columns do not total due to rounding): See chart page 272.

The results demonstrated a few key points:

- Small-cap stocks provided greater incremental returns than did other asset classes.
- Deciles 9 to 10 provided higher returns than deciles 6 to 10 by 14.06% to 12.96%, or 1.10%.
- The incremental contribution from deciles 9 to 10 at 1.36% was 0.37% greater (1.36 to 0.99) than the incremental return of deciles 6 to 10. This difference was due to the lower correlation of the asset class to the other components of the portfolio.

Through this example, Booth and Fama provided investors with a very important insight: "Measuring the contribution of assets to portfolio returns, rather than the compound returns on the assets, substantially increases the premium for small-cap

Portfolios with Small-Caps 1941–1990

	S&P 500, P1 and P2	U.S. Small-Cap, 6–10, P1	U.S. Small-Cap, 9–10, P2	20-Year Treasuries, P1 and P2	One-Month Treasury Bills, P1 and P2	Portfolios, P1/P2
Portfolio weights	50%	10%	10%	20%	20%	100%
Compound portfolio return						9.02%/9.17%
Compound return of each asset class and average asset class return	11.31%	12.96%	14.06%	4.36%	4.3%	8.68%/8.79%
Diversification return	0.41%	0.99%	1.36%	0.16%	0.0%	0.33%/0.37%
Return contribution	11.72%	13.96%	15.42%	4.52%	4.29%	9.02%/9.17%

stocks" from 1.10% (14.06 to 12.96) to 1.46% (15.42 to 13.96). The reason is that while small-cap stocks have high return variances (high volatility), their low correlation to other assets in a diversified portfolio makes their risk in a portfolio much lower than their risk as a stand-alone asset.

Booth and Fama found similar results when they looked at adding international equities to a portfolio. Using data from the period 1971 through 1990 (international data does not go back as far as domestic data) they built a 60% equity/40% fixed income portfolio with the following allocations:

S&P 500 15%	International small 15%
U.S. small 6–10 15%	20-year Treasury bonds 20%
International large 15%	One-month Treasury bills 20%

With the addition of the 2 international equity asset classes to the portfolio, the incremental returns resulting from diversification increased even further. The compound annual returns for each asset class understated the incremental return of the asset class to the portfolio by the following amounts:

S&P 500	0.56%
U.S. small-cap 6–10	1.31%
International large-cap	1.30%
International small-cap	1.23%

This study also found that the U.S. small-cap and the international large- and small-cap premiums over the S&P 500 were all understated by about 0.75% (due to diversification benefits). The benefits of investing in small and international equities cannot be determined by looking solely at the compound returns of the individual asset classes. Instead, investors should examine the expected impact of the diversification created by adding these asset classes to a portfolio.

Booth and Fama demonstrated that the incremental returns over compound returns are very large for both small-cap and international equities. These large incremental returns are a result of the low correlations these asset classes have with the other components of a portfolio. Diversification benefits these asset classes (enhances their returns) the most, and that is why investors should include these asset classes in their portfolios.

Why Bond Funds Should Not Be the Vehicle of Choice for Fixed Income Investing

Many investors utilize bond mutual funds for the fixed income portion of their portfolio. This section explores both why that decision may not be in their best interest and provides alternative strategies that are likely to produce superior results.

Let's begin this discussion by examining the role that fixed income assets play in a portfolio. Are fixed income assets expected to generate income that is needed to meet living expenses? Or are fixed income assets being used to reduce the risks of an equity portfolio? It is my experience that for the vast majority of investors (with the exception of retired individuals), the overriding motivation for including fixed income assets is risk reduction. Assuming that current income is not the primary reason for holding fixed income assets, we can determine the strategy that is most likely to produce the desired results.

We begin with the following facts.

- Academic research has determined that fixed income markets are just as efficient as, and possibly even more than, the equity markets. Far fewer fixed income fund managers have demonstrated the ability to outperform the market (by guessing the direction of interest rates) than would be randomly expected. In fact, the most comprehensive study on bond mutual funds found that they underperformed their benchmark index by 0.85% per annum.[2] Furthermore, a Vanguard study found that the performance of bond funds was correlated with only one thing: expenses. The lower the expenses, the higher the returns. Managers were unable to add value by guessing the direction of interest rates.[3] Fund managers charge Georgia O'Keeffe prices and deliver paint-by-numbers results. The obvious conclusion is: if you are going to use a mutual fund for fixed income investing, buy the one that matches the risk (credit and maturity) profile you seek and has the lowest expenses for that category.

- Academic research has determined that over long periods of time, while investors are compensated for accepting the risk of owning longer maturity fixed income assets, this relationship breaks down beyond 2 to 3 years. Therefore, if a fixed income investor is seeking the highest expected return over a 30-year period, he should buy a 2- to 3-year note and continually roll it over (instead of buying a 30-year bond).[4] Research on the relationship between risk and return has shown that:

- Holding very short-term U.S. Treasury bills provides a risk-free rate of return (historically about 6.5%) and has a standard deviation of just over 1% per annum.

- Extending the maturity to one year increases returns above the risk-free rate by about 1% while increasing the standard deviation to about 2%. The Sharpe ratio (a measure of the amount of return earned for the level of risk accepted) is about 0.5.

- Extending the maturity to 5 years adds only another 0.3% (total above the risk-free rate of about 1.3%) to expected returns, yet the standard deviation more than *triples* to over 6.5%. The Sharpe ratio falls to less than 0.2.

- Extending the maturity to 20 years causes returns to *fall* almost 0.5% (total premium above the risk-free rate of about 0.8%), yet the standard deviation almost *doubles* again to 11.5%. The Sharpe ratio falls to less than 0.1.

The fact that riskier long-term bonds have provided lower returns than safer shorter-term instruments conflicts with the EMT. There is, however, a logical explanation. There is a very strong preference among institutional investors for long-term maturities, since they match the long-term nature of their pension liabilities. The demand for longer term assets exceeds the supply of bonds, driving up their price. These institutional investors are purchasing maturities that are within what is known as their preferred habitat. These investors are unconcerned about the riskiness of the assets from a maturity perspective. By eliminating any mismatch between the maturity of their assets and the maturity of their liabilities, they are actually reducing the risk of their portfolio.

With the preceding information, we can now determine the winning strategy for the fixed income portion of our portfolio. For the vast majority of investors using fixed income assets to reduce the risk of an equity portfolio, the winning strategy seems obvious: own only very short-term fixed income assets. Here's why.

- Since the main purpose of fixed income assets is to reduce the volatility of the overall portfolio, investors should include fixed income assets that have low volatility. Short-term fixed income assets have both low volatility and low correlation with the equity portion of the portfolio.

- By limiting the maturity of the fixed income portion of the portfolio to just one year, we get most of the yield benefit and accept only moderate risk (a standard deviation of only 2%). The combined benefit of lower volatility of the asset class itself, and the reduced volatility of the overall portfolio, seems a small price to pay for giving up the extra 0.3% that could be gained by extending the maturity of the fixed income assets to 5 years. Remember, in a 60% equity/ 40% fixed income portfolio, that extra 0.3% becomes only a 0.12% (0.3% $\times$ 40%) added return on the overall portfolio.

We can further improve on this scenario by including international short-term fixed income assets within the fixed income allocation, as long as these assets are fully hedged against currency risk. The reason is that their inclusion should further reduce volatility, since not all international fixed income markets fluctuate in the same direction at the same time and/or by the same amount. The lack of perfect correlation will reduce the overall volatility of the fixed income portion of the portfolio.

These conclusions are supported by studies that have demonstrated that portfolios that are 60% S&P 500 Index/40% Lehman Bond Index have historically provided lower returns, with the same degree of risk, than 70% S&P 500 Index/30% cash portfolios. Moving the bond portion of the portfolio to cash may have reduced the portfolio's return. However, this was more than offset by the higher returns provided by the 10% greater equity allocation. In addition, the reduced volatility of the cash position itself (as compared to the volatility of previously held bonds) and the lower correlation (reducing overall portfolio volatility) of the cash portion of the portfolio to the equity portion served to offset the risk incurred by raising the equity allocation 10%.

We can now explore other reasons why bond funds should not be the investment vehicle of choice for fixed income investors.

- A primary reason to exclude bond funds is they have no effective maturity. If you buy a bond fund that has an average maturity of 20 years, it will probably always have a maturity of about that level. If you happen to buy a bond fund and interest rates go up, you may never recoup the loss of principal, because the bond fund never matures. If, however, you buy an individual bond, in order to recoup your principal, you need only wait for the bond to mature. With very short-term fixed income funds the standard deviation is very low, which limits risk. In addition, individual issues within a short-term fund are rolling over so quickly to current rates that risk is further reduced.

- Another reason to exclude bond funds is that it is very hard to see how they can add value if they cannot correctly forecast interest rates. And there is no such evidence that this can be done. You certainly don't need to pay a bond fund 0.5% or more to simply buy government bonds. Individuals can buy these directly from the government or very cost effectively from a discount broker. And since there is no credit risk in owning government bonds, there is no benefit to diversifying credit risk across various issues. Just buy the bond that matches the maturity you seek. If you seek higher yields available from corporate bonds, there is plenty of good public information available on credit quality by rating agencies such as Moody's and S&P. You don't need to pay a fund to get that information. Once you determine the amount of credit and maturity risk you are willing to accept, you can buy the appropriate bonds directly from a discount broker. It is also worth noting that the extra yield you are likely to gain by buying a corporate bond fund, instead of individual government bonds, is likely to be offset by the fund's expenses. Any extra yield probably is not worth the credit risk accepted.

The evidence seems to present a very compelling case that today's investors have far too great an allocation of bonds in their portfolios. Investors would benefit greatly from reducing or eliminating their allocations to long-term fixed income assets and replacing them with very short-term fixed income assets.

Inflation Protected Securities

Fortunately for investors, two new and highly attractive fixed income investment vehicles have recently been introduced. Both of them offer the attractive feature of inflation protection not present in bonds or bond funds. The first is the Treasury Inflation Protected Security (TIPS). TIPS are bonds, sold at auction, that receive a fixed stated rate of return but whose principal is also increased by the changes in the nonseasonally adjusted U.S. city average all items consumer price index for all urban consumers (CPI-U), published monthly by the Bureau of Labor Statistics. The fixed interest payment is calculated on the inflated principal, which is eventually repaid at maturity. For example, if a $1,000 TIP had a stated (real) interest rate of 4% and the CPI-U rose 2% during the year, the investor would have received $40 ($1,000 × 4%) in interest and seen the principal of the note increased from $1,000 to $1,020. Next year the investor would receive $40.80 ($1,020 × 4%) interest. (In practice, the adjustment is done on a semiannual basis.) This gives an investor the ability to protect against inflation while providing a certain "real" return over a predetermined investment horizon. Interest is paid (the real rate) and accrued (the inflation adjustment) semiannually. At maturity the bondholder will receive the greater of the inflation-adjusted value or par. The bonds are available in both 10- and 30-year maturities. They can be bought either electronically directly from the Treasury or through a local broker/dealer. A further benefit of TIPS is that they are exempt from state and local taxes (except when held in tax-deferred accounts, as states tax distributions).

Investors should note that TIPS, like most fixed income instruments with a long maturity, are subject to price risk. The following is a good example. In April 1999 the 30-year TIP (maturity 2029) was trading at par (100) and yielding 3.9%. By January 2000 the real yield had risen to 4.4%. This caused the price of the 2029 TIP to fall from 100 to 92. Of course, the reverse is true. Using the same example, by March 2000 the real yield on the 2029 TIP had fallen back to almost 4%, and the price of the TIP had risen to about 97. Another potential negative for TIP investors is their relatively lower level of liquidity, which increases trading costs. The volatility and the relatively lower levels of liquidity associated with TIPS may result in their not being the appropriate instrument for either investors with short investment horizons (not able to hold to maturity) or investors not willing to accept significant principal risk.

Another negative is that an investor must pay the federal tax on both the real and the "unrealized" income (the amount of each year's inflated principal). Thus the best place to hold a TIP is in a tax-deferred account (despite the loss of state tax exemption).

The other inflation-protected vehicle is called an I Bond. An I Bond works like a TIP in that it provides a fixed real rate of return and an inflation protection component. There are, however, significant differences. The fixed rate over the entire life of an I Bond is announced by the Treasury in May and November and applies to all I Bonds issued during the following 6 months. Like zero coupon bonds, they accrue in value by their total return (fixed rate plus inflation adjustment). I Bonds increase in value on the first of each month and compound semi-annually. They pay interest for up to 30 years. They can be bought and redeemed at most financial institutions. An important feature of I Bonds is that they can never decrease in value. All income is deferred for tax purposes until funds are withdrawn from the account holding the bond. The tax deferral feature makes an I Bond a more attractive candidate than a TIPS for a taxable account. As with TIPS, a further benefit of I Bonds is that they are exempt from state and local taxes (again with the exception that all distributions from tax-deferred accounts are taxed).

The maximum amount of I Bonds that can be purchased annually is $30,000 per individual or $60,000 per married couple. They can be bought in denominations of $50, $75, $100, $200, $500, $1,000, $5,000, and $10,000. Although they can be redeemed at any time after 6 months of issuance, they are meant to serve as long-term investments. Therefore, there is a prepayment penalty of 3 months' interest if not held for a minimum of 5 years.

It is important to note that the fixed (or real) rate of return on both TIPS and I Bonds changes regularly. Investors should, therefore, evaluate the decision on which is the preferred vehicle on the basis of current rates, their current tax situation, and whether the investment is for their taxable or tax-deferred account. These investments should also be compared to the yields on short-term fixed income choices as well. Keep in mind that while traditional short-term fixed income vehicles do not contain a specific inflation protection component, their short-term nature offers similar protection. If inflation picks up, interest rates will rise, and their short maturity structure will allow these vehicles to quickly capture the new higher rates.

REITs, Your Home, and the
Asset Allocation Decision

Diversification across asset classes is an important component of an investment plan. Put simply, diversification reduces risk by not putting all your eggs in one basket. It is also important to diversify across asset classes that have low correlation. Real estate is an asset class that not only has its own risk and reward characteristics but also has a relatively low correlation with other U.S. equity asset classes. It is, therefore, a good diversifier of risk and should be considered when constructing an asset allocation plan.

For the period 1975 through 1999, REITs (Real Estate Investment Trusts) provided a rate of return of 16.0%. This compares to a return of 17.2% for the S&P 500 Index. It is worth noting that all of the outperformance by the S&P 500 Index occurred during just the last 2 years. Looking only at the period 1975 through 1997, REITs outperformed the S&P 500 by 18.5% to 16.6%. It is also worth noting that in 1977 when the S&P 500 Index was down 7.2%, REITs were up 18.0%. In 1981, the next year of negative performance by the S&P 500 Index (it fell by 4.9%), REITs were up 6.1%. In 1984 and 1992, when the S&P 500 Index rose just 6.3% and 7.7%, REITs returned 21.8%

and 28.3%. Of course, there are also periods when the S&P 500 Index outperformed REITs. For example, from 1998 to 1999 the S&P 500 Index outperformed REITs by 24.7% per annum to −8.9% per annum. The combination of the lack of predictability of returns and the low correlation makes a strong case for including REITs as an asset class in an investment portfolio.

Once a homeowning investor decides to include real estate in a portfolio, he must decide how to view his home in the asset allocation process. In addition, if the home is financed, the nature of the mortgage should be considered in terms of its risk implications for the portfolio. Let's first address the home itself.

A home is clearly real estate. However, it is very undiversified real estate. First, it is undiversified by type. There are many types of real estate: office, warehouse, industrial, multifamily residential, hotel, and so on. Owning a home gives an investor exposure to just the residential component of the larger asset class of real estate. Even then, by excluding multifamily residences, it is only exposure to the single-family component. Of course, the best way to gain exposure to the broad equity real estate asset class is to own an index or passively managed REIT fund that invests in all equity REITs. Vanguard and DFA both offer such a fund.

Another problem is that a home is undiversified geographically. Home prices might be rising in one part of the country and falling in another.

Another problem is that home prices may be more related to an exposure to an industry than to real estate in general. For example, in the 1980s home prices in Texas, and in oil-producing regions in general, collapsed when oil prices collapsed. In the late 1990s home prices in Silicon Valley skyrocketed, riding the technology boom (and, of course, could reverse if the boom turns to bust). Homes in other areas of the same state experienced a totally different pricing environment. This creates another problem in that often your employment prospects are highly correlated with the value of your home. This problem would be further compounded if your investment portfolio is loaded with assets with exposure to the same industry to which your home is exposed. This is often true of executives who own stock in their company and/or have stock options. It is also true of employees who invest in their employer's stock through retirement plans. A good example of the problem I am describing is the following situation.

Seattle used to be considered a one-company (Boeing) town. Accordingly, this example might have been very typical. A senior executive at Boeing owns an expensive home in Seattle. She has the vast percentage of her financial assets invested in Boeing stock. She contributes to Boeing's retirement plan, purchasing more Boeing stock. She also has stock options. She thought she had some diversification of assets because her home was considered real estate exposure (not Seattle, nor Boeing, nor airline, nor even oil price exposure). There were several periods when Boeing was impacted by a recession in the airline industry. The company's stock, reflecting those troubles, fell sharply. Strike 1 for our investor. Boeing reacted by laying off employees. Being one of those laid off, strike 2 for our investor. With so many unemployed, Seattle home prices collapsed. Strike 3 for our unlucky investor. The problem was that all of the risks (employment, equity, home) our investor incurred were highly correlated.

The bottom line is that owning a home and considering it exposure to real estate might be similar to being a senior executive with lots of stock and options in Microsoft and thinking you have exposure to large growth stocks. The correlation of any one stock to the overall asset class of equities, or large growth stocks, might turn out to be very low. Stocks might be up overall, but your stock might be down. Similarly, real estate might be up, but the price of your home might be down. Therefore, as a general rule, investors should not consider their homes exposure to real estate. About the only real protection a home provides is against inflation in construction costs. And since in many parts of the country land is by far a more important component of home prices than the cost of construction, it may not be much protection at all.

Let's now turn to how a home is financed. If a home is financed with a fixed rate mortgage, that mortgage effectively is a short (negative) bond position, and should be considered so when looking at the overall portfolio. The fixed rate on the mortgage does provide inflation protection. A fixed rate mortgage also has a put feature. If interest rates decline, the put (putting the mortgage back to the lender by paying it off) allows the borrower to refinance the mortgage at the then current rate. This provides protection against falling interest rates (for those on fixed incomes) and deflation. If a home were financed with an adjustable rate mortgage, the risk picture would be considerably different. Therefore, it is very important that investors consider how a home is financed in developing an asset allocation strategy.

As always, a good financial advisor can help you sort through these complex issues.

A Problem with S&P 500 Index and Total Market Funds

One of the biggest and most common mistakes investors make is to confuse indexing, or passive investing, with the exclusive use of an S&P 500 Index fund. Investors building a portfolio of only an S&P 500 Index fund are not getting sufficient diversification. This is despite the fact that through such a single fund they are getting ownership in 500 companies. The lack of diversification arises both from how the stocks are selected by Standard & Poors for inclusion in the index and also from the market-cap weighting mechanism used to calculate the index. The result is that an S&P 500 Index fund is almost by definition a large-cap growth fund. I am sure most investors will be surprised at just how skewed the index is toward the largest-cap stocks. As of year-end 1999 the S&P 500 weightings were:[5]

- The largest 50 stocks: 60%
- The largest 100 stocks: 75%
- The largest 200 stocks: 88%
- The largest 300 stocks: 95%

Here is another interesting statistic. As we began the second quarter of 2000, the average market cap of the S&P 500 stocks was $143 billion, yet only 16 stocks were larger than the average! If the 500 stocks in the index were equally weighted, the average market cap would have been just $24 billion, or one-sixth of the actual average.[6]

Investors in an S&P 500 Index fund lack the diversification benefits possible through exposure to small-cap and value stocks. To solve this problem, total market cap funds, or Wilshire 5000 funds, have been created. While total market funds provide better diversification than an S&P 500 fund, the improvement is marginal. It's similar to diversifying a portfolio consisting solely of stock in Exxon by adding Shell Oil. Yes, it is more diversified, but not by much. While all your eggs aren't in one basket (Exxon), you still own only oil stocks. Let's see how this relates to the S&P 500.

The S&P 500 has a weighted average market cap of $143 billion. Thus it is a first (largest cap) decile fund. When considering the value versus growth question, we look to the btm ratio as our measure. The lowest btm stocks (first 3 deciles) are considered growth stocks, and the highest btm stocks (last 3 deciles) are considered value stocks. The btm of the S&P 500 placed it in the first or most "growthy" decile. So an S&P 500 Index fund is very large-cap, and very growth-oriented. Even though you own 500 stocks, you haven't achieved effective diversification because they are all mostly large-cap growth stocks.

Total market-cap funds were created to help investors achieve greater diversification than just an S&P 500 Index fund can achieve. The appeal of owning the entire market is intuitively attractive from a diversification perspective. However, the market-cap weighting mechanism that is used to make index funds easy to manage provides a far different outcome from what one would expect. Market-cap weighting means that equal dollars are not invested in all shares. Instead, the weighting in an index is based on the percent of the total market cap of the individual stock as it relates to the total market cap of all the stocks contained in the index. For example, as I wrote this, the 2 largest stocks in the S&P 500 Index, GE and Microsoft, made up about 10% of the entire Index by market-cap weighting. An examination of the CRSP data reveals that a total market portfolio (CRSP 1 to 10) has a weighting of 94% large-cap (deciles 1 to 5 by market cap) and a weighting of just 8% of value (deciles 8 to 10 by btm). Almost 70% of the portfolio is large-cap growth stocks (deciles 1 to 5 by size and 1 to 3 by btm). A total market fund is not inherently bad. It is not, however, a well diversified portfolio in terms of asset class diversification. You should only want to own a total market fund if that is the asset allocation (almost all large-cap growth) you seek.

Let's now look at 2 views of the world. The first is the "Fama-French" view of the world. Their belief is that the small-cap and value asset classes are riskier than their large-cap and growth counterparts. Investors receive a *risk premium* in the form of higher expected returns by investing in small-cap and value stocks. Therefore, investors wanting greater than market returns need to "tilt" their portfolios to those asset classes. Thus a portfolio must hold more than the 6% small-caps and the 8% value stocks that a total market fund provides.

An alternative view of the world is that growth stocks and value stocks have the same expected returns, as do small- and large-cap stocks. If you accept this view, it seems illogical to place so large an allocation to large growth without the expectation of greater reward for taking the risk of owning such an undiversified portfolio. Since you expect equal returns, why not equally weight the 4 asset classes of large value, large growth, small value, and small growth? That would provide much better diversification.

Either view of the world leaves you with the conclusion that while S&P 500 Index and total market funds make for effective pieces of an investment pie, they should be only slices, not the whole pie. They just don't provide sufficient diversification as stand-alone vehicles.

Ultimately, there is no correct asset allocation. Each investor should determine the amount of exposure he or she wants to each of the 4 major asset classes. Having said that, as a general rule, diversification is the winning strategy. The strategy of diversification should also be implemented in the international portion of a portfolio. International assets provide diversification benefits to an all-domestic portfolio. Many investors use an EAFE Index fund to accomplish this objective. However, the EAFE Index fund is similar to an S&P 500 Index fund in that it is effectively a large-cap growth fund. To achieve more effective diversification, investors should consider including in their portfolio funds that cover the asset classes of international large value, international small, international small value, and emerging markets.

The Investment Policy Statement

No traveler would begin a trip to a place he or she had never been without a road map. For investors, a road map is an investment policy statement. Investors should not make any investments until they have addressed 3 important issues.

1. How long is my investment horizon? This helps define the *ability* to take risk.
2. What is my tolerance for risk? This helps define the *willingness* to take risk.
3. What are my financial objectives? This helps define the *need* to take risk.

Let's begin with the investment horizon. The length of your investment horizon is important because of the nature of the risks of equity investing. Equity investors must be aware that the longer the investment horizon, the more likely it is that the expected will occur (i.e., stocks will significantly outperform both money market funds and bonds). Conversely, the shorter the horizon, the more likely it is that the unexpected will occur (i.e., stocks will generate negative returns). Therefore, investors with long investment horizons have a greater *ability to take risk* and can therefore allocate a greater percentage of their portfolios to equities than investors with shorter investment horizons. The table suggests a reasonable guideline for an investor's maximum equity exposure.

Investment Horizon	Maximum Equity Allocation
0–3 Years	0%
4 Years	10%
5 Years	20%
6 Years	30%
7 Years	40%
8 Years	50%
9 Years	60%
10 Years	70%
11–14 Years	80%
15–19 Years	90%
20 Years or longer	100%

Because I believe that most investors are generally not risk neutral and are in fact risk averse, the table is probably more conservative than historical evidence would require. Accordingly, investors with a high tolerance for risk might want to be more aggressive.

Turning to the issue of risk tolerance, investors must ask themselves how much they can see their portfolios lose in value without losing sleep. No investor should take on so much risk that she is likely to lose sleep worrying about her portfolio. In addition, investors must ask themselves how much of a loss they think they could absorb without panicking and selling. These questions help define the investor's *willingness to accept risk* and play an important role in determining the percent of equity assets allocated to a portfolio. The following are 2 very good reasons why understanding your "threshold for pain" is important to successful investing.

1. "Fear leads to panic, panic breeds the inability to distinguish between temporary declines and permanent losses. That, in turn, leads to the well-documented propensity to be massive sellers of good investments near market bottoms."
2. "Success is purely a function of two things. First, a recognition of the inevitability of major market declines. Second, an emotional/behavioral preparation to regard such declines as . . . nonevents."[7]

Investment advisor and columnist Nick Murray put it this way: "The governing variable in investment success is not the 'performance' of investments, but the behavior of investors." He continued: "The great enemy of long-term investment success isn't ignorance. It's fear."[8] I would add: the antidotes to fear are a well-thought-out written investment plan, preparation for the inevitable bad times, and the knowledge that bear markets are temporary and bull markets permanent.

The role that emotions play in the success of an investment strategy cannot be overemphasized. Its importance is summarized by this quotation: "Successful investment management depends to a large extent on the emotional stability of the individual, particularly during periods of strain and stress, and on his ability to overcome the severe psychological hurdles present during crucial periods."[9]

I suggest that a reasonable guideline for investors is that the maximum equity exposure should be no greater than indicated in the table.

Maximum Tolerable Loss	Maximum Equity Exposure
5%	20%
10%	30%
15%	40%
20%	50%
25%	60%
30%	70%
35%	80%
40%	90%
50%	100%

Again, because I believe that most investors are risk averse, these guidelines are more conservative than historical evidence might suggest.

Investors should compare the results from the investment horizon question with the results from the risk tolerance question. The equity allocation should be the *lower* of the two numbers. For example, if you have a high tolerance for risk but a short investment horizon, the short investment horizon should determine the equity allocation. Conversely, if you have a long investment horizon but a low risk tolerance, the risk tolerance should determine the equity allocation.

Finally, we turn to the question of financial objectives (*the need to take risk*). The table serves as a general guideline to help investors match their financial goals with their equity allocation. The financial goal is expressed in terms of rate of return needed to achieve this goal. The return numbers in the table are based on a balanced portfolio including exposure to small-cap and value asset classes. Please keep in mind that for 2 investors with the same equity allocation, the one with the greater allocation to the higher returning asset classes of size and value will have greater expected returns. Also remember that when we speak of returns on equities we are always speaking of *expected* returns, not *guaranteed* returns.

Financial Goal	Equity Allocation
5.0%	0%
6.5%	20%
8.0%	40%
9.5%	60%
11.0%	80%
12.5%	100%

Please note the following in regard to this table. First, the 5% figure for an all-fixed-income portfolio is based on the prevailing rate on short-term Treasury bills. Investors should adjust these figures to reflect current rates. All other return figures should be raised or lowered by the same amount. For example, if the current rate on short-term treasuries is 4%, all return figures should be lowered by 1%. The reason is that equity investors receive an expected return *premium* above the risk-free rate. Note that if investors are willing to lengthen the maturity of their fixed income allocation to 1 to 5 years, then another 1 to 1.5% can be added to expected returns for that portion of the portfolio that is fixed income. All return figures would have to be adjusted to reflect the higher return of the fixed income component. Third, the equity returns are based on the type of allocations suggested in the section hereafter entitled "Constructing the Portfolio."

The returns are based on a portfolio that is two-thirds value (one-third growth) and equal weighting of large and small (see section Constructing the Portfolio for specific allocations). A lower allocation to value and small would result in lower expected returns. Finally, the preceding return figures are intentionally lower than the actual expected return figures for the suggested portfolio. The suggested all-equity portfolio actually has an expected return of about 14%. However, since that is the expected return, there is a 50% probability of the actual returns falling below the objective. (Actually, the probability of achieving the returns is even a bit worse—but the math is too complicated to go into.) I believe that investors would prefer a much greater probability than the equivalent of a coin toss. Therefore, I have lowered the return figures to provide a greater likelihood of success. Finally, these returns are all pretax and pre-advisor fees. And taxes and fees must be considered.

Returning to the importance of the individual's financial objectives in determining the appropriate equity allocation, it can best be illustrated by using the following examples.

The first tale involves a discussion with a new client, a 55-year-old investor. During our initial discussion I learned the following:

- He currently had $2.5 million of net assets.
- He wanted to retire in 10 years.
- He was a long-term investor with a high tolerance for risk, evidenced by his current portfolio's equity allocation of almost 100%.

When asked how much money he felt he would need to comfortably retire, he responded: "$4 million." I then asked him whether his lifestyle would change much if instead of $4 million he ended up with $6 million. He said: "No." I then asked him if his lifestyle would change if he ended up with just $3 million. He said: "Yes, I would have to keep working." Clearly the reward of his ending up with more dollars than his goal was far less than the pain of ending up with less. In other words, he was clearly risk averse. I then showed him that to achieve his $4 million goal in 10 years, including the savings from his salary over that period, he would need to earn less than the rate of return on a money market account. He didn't *need to take the risk* of an all-equity portfolio to achieve his objective. He ultimately decided to reduce his equity allocation to 60%.

The second tale involves Philip, a good friend and client. Philip is an extremely nervous investor. His risk tolerance produces an equity allocation of close to 0. He knows, however, that a very low equity allocation is apt to produce very little, if any, growth in the real value of his portfolio and directly conflicts with his personal objective, which was to retire within 10 years.

Together we calculated that Philip needed an equity allocation of at least 80% to have a good chance of meeting his retirement objective. To attain his objective, Philip understood that he would have to accept more risk than he was comfortable with. His equity allocation decision became a choice between sleeping well and working longer or losing sleep worrying about his portfolio but probably being able to retire early. The lower the equity allocation, the longer he would have to continue in the workforce. The greater the equity allocation, the more likely it was that he would be able to retire early. The results of the risk tolerance test proved to be in direct conflict with his personal goals. I told Philip there was no correct answer to his conundrum. He had to choose which one of his objectives had the greater priority, the need to sleep well or his desire for early retirement. Ultimately, Philip decided that his early retirement objective should take priority. He realized that this decision was apt to produce many sleepless nights and that his ability and willingness to stay the course might be sorely tested. Accordingly, Philip immediately purchased a 10-year supply of Extra-Strength Maalox. He had carefully thought through the process and understood the risks. Having anticipated the inevitable bad days, Philip was now more likely to stick with his investment strategy than he otherwise would have been.

These 2 examples illustrate why investors need to carefully address the 3 issues of investment horizon, risk tolerance, and financial goals. Determining the correct allocation is simple when the results lead to the same conclusion. It becomes more complex when the conclusions are in conflict. In those cases there are no right answers. Investors must weigh the risks and potential rewards of each strategy and then decide on the appropriate one. Having made the decision that is most appropriate for them, investors should formalize a written plan and then sign it. The plan should be reviewed each year to see if it still conforms to what are likely to be changing circumstances. First, time always marches on. Second, personal situations may arise that cause an investor to be able to accept either more or less risk. Finally, if the market rises dramatically in a short period (as it did from 1995 to 1998), an investor might be able to lower her equity allocation, as she no longer needs to achieve as high a rate of return to achieve her objective. She can now sleep better and still expect to reach her goals.

The Retirement Calculator

One of the key questions when approaching retirement is: What should my portfolio value be in order to provide a high level of confidence that the principal will not be exhausted during my life? A retiree must address the following issues:

- What is my (and my spouse's, if any) life expectancy?
- What will be the level of inflation?

- What will be the portfolio's investment returns?
- What pretax dollars do I want to be able to withdraw to maintain my desired lifestyle?

Time, inflation, and expected returns take on greater significance in retirement. During your working life, a few bad years of high inflation or negative investment returns can be overcome. You can add savings or work longer to make up for any portfolio shortfall. In retirement, however, money is being withdrawn all the time, both in good and bad years.

Let's first address the issue of life expectancy. The investment time frame is longer than most people think. First, it is my experience that most individuals underestimate their life expectancy. For example, the average 65-year-old couple has a second-to-die life expectancy of well over 20 years. In addition, when determining how long you'll need your assets to last in retirement, you should not simply take average life expectancies as your guide. An average results in approximately a 50% chance of living longer. This table, a safer benchmark, is based on a probability of only a 20% chance of outliving the expected time frame. For example, a 60-year-old male has only a 20% chance of living beyond 27 years.

Years You Should Plan to Live
When Calculating a Retirement Plan

At Age	Female	Male
55	36	32
60	31	27
65	27	22
70	22	18

Source: National Center for Health Statistics

Note that a married couple's second-to-die life expectancy is greater than the longest of the 2 individual life expectancies.

Turning to the issue of investment returns and inflation, when projecting returns, a common investor mistake is the singular use of averages. A useful analogy is the case of a man drowning in a lake that has an average depth of 6 inches. The man didn't realize that he jumped into the part of the lake that was 10 feet deep. Investors planning retirement need to be sure they don't unexpectedly drown in the deep part of the lake. Let's see how that might happen.

For the period 1926 through 1997, a portfolio consisting of 75% S&P 500 Index and 25% U.S. Government bonds returned an average of 10%. During the same time period, the inflation rate was 3%. Therefore, the real (inflation adjusted) rate of return for this 75/25 portfolio was 7%. You might conclude that you could withdraw $70,000 per year from a $1 million portfolio and maintain the same real income in the long term, increasing the $70,000 by the future rate of inflation. The problem with this approach is that inflation rates and investment returns vary each year, and using averages may cause unexpected and unpleasant surprises. If you retire before the start of a bull market, it is likely that you could withdraw 7% per year and maintain a portfolio in excess of $1 million. Retiring at the beginning of a bear market, however, can produce very different results. For example, had you retired in 1972 and withdrawn 7% of your original principal every year, you would have run out of funds within 10 years, by the end of 1982! This is because the S&P 500 Index declined by approximately 40% in the 1973 through 1974 bear market.

Systematic withdrawals during bear markets exacerbate the effects of the market's decline, causing portfolio values to fall to levels from which they may never recover. For example, if an investor withdraws 7% in a year when the portfolio declines by 20%, the result is a decline in the portfolio of 27% in that year. A 37% increase is now required in the next year just to get even, plus another 7% for the annual withdrawal (a total of 44%) to make up for the prior year's decline.

Given the possibility of a market decline occurring at the very early stages of retirement, investors need to determine how much money they can withdraw annually and still have only a minimal risk that they might outlive their assets. On the basis of historical evidence, I believe that investors with a 20-year or longer investment horizon should not withdraw more than 4% of the starting value of a portfolio.[10] This amount can be increased every year by the previous year's inflation rate, thereby maintaining the same level of real purchasing power. With at least a 50% allocation to equities, the historical evidence suggests that you will have less than a 5% chance of outliving your assets with this strategy. Note that even a 75-year-old investor has an investment horizon of about 15 years. At 15 years the maximum suggested withdrawal rate is still just 6%. Using a 4% withdrawal rate, it is easy to calculate the portfolio size needed to feel comfortable about retirement. Investors can estimate the amount of pretax income desired (after subtracting any social security and pension income) and then multiply that figure by 25 (inverse of 4%). For example, investors needing $50,000 a year in income after taking into account social security and so on need to achieve a portfolio of $1,250,000 ($50,000 × 25). Using the 6% withdrawal rate, the multiplier would be about 17.

It is important for investors to remember that if they have a long investment horizon they need to include a substantial allocation to equities as protection against the damage of inflation to fixed incomes. For example, investors with a 30-year horizon and an equity allocation of just 25% had only a 71% chance of not outliving their assets. Reducing the equity allocation to 0% lowers the odds of success to just 20%. Equities may be *risky* when the investment horizon is *short*, but fixed income assets become the *riskier* asset class when investment horizons are *long*.

Constructing the Portfolio

Portfolio construction is not a science. There is no one right portfolio. However, there are a few good rules to follow:

- Regardless of the asset class, use only index or passive asset class funds. Active management is a loser's game.
- Diversify across many asset classes. This will reduce portfolio risk and probably increase returns as well.
- International investing is less risky than using only U.S. asset classes.
- If you seek higher returns, tilt your portfolio to the higher risk, higher returning asset classes of small-cap and value.
- Since value is a stronger and more persistent risk factor than size, tilt more to value than small. A value tilt while staying size neutral (equal allocations to large and small) is a good option. For taxable accounts, whenever possible, use index and passively managed funds that are also tax-managed.
- Generally avoid bonds and always avoid bond funds. For the fixed income portion of a portfolio use only short-term fixed income instruments or very short-term fixed income funds, with an average maturity of no more than 2–3 years. As noted earlier, TIPS and I Bonds are also good choices to consider. Since the main purpose of the fixed income

allocation is usually risk reduction (not higher yield), investors should choose only the lowest cost, highest quality fixed income funds.

The following portfolio example, covering the equity portion of a portfolio, is just a suggestion. On completion of your investment policy statement (determined by your investment horizon, risk tolerance, and financial goals) you can then multiply the following suggested asset class allocations by your equity allocation to determine your specific asset class allocations. For example, if an asset class has a suggested allocation of 20%, and your equity allocation is 60%, then you should have a 12% (20% × 60%) exposure to that asset class. The following portfolio also contains a 30% exposure to international markets. Again, this is not a science. If you are not comfortable with this degree of exposure to international equity markets, make it 25%, or 20%. If you can't sleep well owning an emerging market fund, don't own one. The anxiety isn't worth it.

Equities

Domestic 70%	International 30%
Large 10%	Large value 10%
Large value 20%	Small 5%
Small 10%	Small value 10%
Small value 20%	Emerging markets 5%
Real estate 10%	

The specific asset class allocations you make should become part of your investment policy statement. The following list of recommended asset class funds can be used to build your portfolio. Funds with an asterisk are *tax-managed* (TM) and, therefore, are strongly recommended for taxable accounts. Two asterisks mean the fund is appropriate for only nontaxable accounts. Numbers following a fund name generally represent the CRSP deciles from which the fund buys its securities. Also note that if an ETF (see chapter 3) exists for an asset class, it should also be considered. You should compare both the possible tax advantages of the ETF and its operating expenses and trading costs against similar passively managed or passive and tax-managed mutual funds.

Domestic Equities	**International Equities**
Large-Cap (S & P 500)	**Large**
Bridgeway Ultra Large 35*	DFA Int'l Large
DFA Large Cap	Fidelity Spartan Int'l
Dreyfus Basic	Vanguard Developed
Fidelity Spartan	Foreign Markets
SSGA S & P 500	
USAA 500	
Vanguard 500 Index	
DFA Enhanced Large**	
Large-Cap Value (LV)	**Large-Cap Value (LV)**
DFA LV	DFA Int'l LV
DFA TM Marketwide Value*	DFA TM Int'l LV*
Vanguard LV	
Small-Cap	**Small-Cap**
Bridgeway Ultra Small-Cap*	DFA Int'l Small-Cap
DFA 6–10	
DFA TM 6–10*	
DFA 9–10	
Vanguard Small-Cap	
Vanguard Small-Cap*	
Small-Cap Value (SV)	**Small-Cap Value (SV)**
DFA 6–10 Value	DFA Int'l SV
DFA TM 5–10 Value*	
Vanguard Small-Cap Value	

Real Estate	*Emerging Markets (EM)*
DFA Real Estate	DFA EM
Vanguard REIT Index	DFA EM Small
	DFA EM Value
	Vanguard EM

Fixed Income
DFA 1-year
DFA 2-year
DFA 5-year
DFA Global Bond
Vanguard Short-Term

Investors need to be aware that the DFA funds are only available through approved financial advisors. There are several hundred such advisors around the country.

Rebalancing and Style Drift

Rebalancing is the process of restoring a portfolio to its desired asset allocation. It is an integral part of the winner's game, because each asset class is likely to change in value by a different percentage during any specific time period. Without rebalancing, market movements will cause your portfolio to *style drift* away from your desired risk profile.

A simple example will illustrate this point. Assume an investor starting out with $100,000 to invest chooses an asset allocation of 80% equities ($80,000) and 20% fixed income ($20,000). If the value of the equity portion of the portfolio increases 40% while the fixed income portion increases 5%, the investor would then have $112,000 in equities and $21,000 in fixed income assets—a total portfolio worth $133,000. The difference in performance of the 2 asset classes causes the asset allocation to change from 80%/20% to 84%/16%. The portfolio now has different risk and return characteristics from those of the original portfolio; its expected return is greater, but so is its risk.

	Original Portfolio		*New Portfolio*	
Equity allocation	80%	$ 80,000	84%	$112,000
Fixed income allocation	20%	$ 20,000	16%	$ 21,000
Total portfolio	100%	$100,000	100%	$133,000

Two methods may be used to rebalance the portfolio and re-store the desired 80/20 asset allocation. The first is to reallocate. A portfolio of $133,000 with an 80%/20% asset allocation would have $106,400 in equities and $26,600 in fixed income assets. The investor would have to sell $5,600 of equities and buy an equal amount of fixed income assets to restore the port-folio to the original (80/20) level of risk. Unfortunately, this method of rebalancing may incur transaction fees. And unless the rebalancing occurs in a nontaxable account, taxes will be due on the capital gain realized on the sale of $5,600 of equities. Fortunately, the impact will not be great because the investor only sold a small portion of the equity portfolio. Taxes, however, should be avoided or deferred whenever possible because they reduce long-term returns. Therefore, an investor must exercise judgment when weighing the benefits of rebalancing against the taxes generated. If taxes are not an issue, as with a tax-deferred account such as an IRA, there is no reason not to undertake regular rebalancing.

Fortunately, there is a more tax-friendly way of rebalancing a portfolio. If an investor has generated additional investable funds, these funds can be added to the fixed income portion of the portfolio to restore the original 80%/20% allocation. With a current equity portfolio of $112,000, one needs a total portfolio of $140,000 ($112,000/80% = $140,000) to restore the desired allocation. With a portfolio currently valued at $133,000, one would need to purchase $7,000 of fixed income assets to rebalance the portfolio. By adding new funds one avoids a taxable event, and with fewer trades (only purchases, no sales), transaction costs may be reduced. If there is insufficient new cash to fully accomplish the desired rebalancing, a combination of the 2 strategies can be used.

		End of Period Portfolio		Rebalanced Portfolio
Equity allocation	84%	$112,000	80%	$112,000
Fixed income allocation	16%	$21,000	20%	$ 28,000
Total portfolio	100%	$133,000	100%	$140,000

Rebalancing: The 5%/25% Rule

Because rebalancing generally incurs transaction fees and may have tax implications, it should only be done when new investment funds are available or when your asset allocation has shifted substantially out of alignment. I suggest using a 5%/25% rule in an asset class's allocation before rebalancing. That is, rebalancing should only occur if the change in an asset class's allocation is greater than either an absolute 5% or 25% of the original percentage allocation.

For example, let's look at an asset class with an allocation of *10%*. One would not rebalance, applying the 5% rule, unless that asset class's allocation had either risen to 15% (*10%* + 5%) or fallen to 5% (*10%* − 5%). Using the 25% rule one would, however, rebalance if it had risen or fallen by just 2.5% (*10%* × 25%) to either 12.5% (*10%* + 2.5%) or 7.5% (*10%* − 2.5%). In this case, the 25% figure was the governing factor. If one had a 50% asset class allocation, the 5%/25% rule would cause the 5% figure to be the governing factor, since 5% is less than 25% of 50%, which is 12.5%. In other words, one rebalances if either the 5% or the 25% test indicates the need to do so.

The portfolio should undergo the 5%/25% test on a quarterly basis, and the test should be applied at 3 levels:

1. At the broad level of equities and fixed income.
2. At the level of domestic and international asset classes.
3. At the more narrowly defined individual asset class level.

For example, suppose one had 6 equity asset classes, each with an allocation of 10%, resulting in an equity allocation of 60%. If each equity class appreciated so that it then constituted 11% of the portfolio, no rebalancing would be required if one only looked at the individual asset class level (the 5%/25% rule was not triggered). However, looking at the broader equity class level, one can see that rebalancing is required. With 6 equity asset classes each constituting 11% of the portfolio, the equity asset class as a whole is now at 66%. The equity allocation increasing from 60% to 66% would trigger the 5%/25% rule. The reverse situation may occur, where the broad asset classes remain within guidelines but the individual classes do not. Once again, the 5%/25% test is just a guideline. You can create your own rebalancing guideline. The discipline this process provides is far more important than the ratios used.

If we now return to the portfolio recommendations made in the previous section (constructing the portfolio), we can construct a portfolio rebalancing table that incorporates the 5%/25% rule.

Asset Class	Minimum Allocation	Target Allocation	Maximum Allocation
U.S. large	7.5%	10%	12.5%
U.S. large value	16%	20%	24%
U.S. small	7.5%	10%	12.5%
U.S. small value	16%	20%	24%
Real estate	7.5%	10%	12.5%
Total U.S.	65%	70%	75%
Int'l large value	7.5%	10%	12.5%
Int'l small	3.75%	5%	6.25%
Int'l small value	7.5%	10%	12.5%
Emerging Markets	3.75%	5%	6.25%
Total Int'l	25%	30%	35%

Remember to include any fixed income allocation when you calculate your target, minimum, and maximum allocations.

In summary, rebalancing:

- Should be incorporated into your investment policy statement.
- Should be done regularly, using a disciplined approach, such as the 5%/25% rule.
- Should be done whenever new investment dollars are available.
- Adds discipline to the investment process and maintains control of the most important investment decision, asset allocation.
- Allows investors to avoid style drift.

To Hedge or Not to Hedge, That Is the Question

Should a mutual fund hedge its foreign currency risk? The answer is yes and no. Confused? The answer is no when the assets are equities and yes when the assets are debt instruments (fixed income assets). The different conclusions are due to the different roles equities and fixed income assets play in a portfolio.

An important part of the winning investment strategy is to build a globally diversified portfolio. To best accomplish this objective for the equity portion of a portfolio, investors might include the international asset classes of large, large value, small, small value, and emerging markets. When buying funds that invest in these asset classes, investors have the choice of buying mutual funds that hedge currency risk or those that do not. The choice should be to buy equity funds that do not hedge.

First, hedging currency risk adds costs. But since currencies have zero expected return, there is no expected return for the increased costs. Second, one advantage of diversifying internationally is the risk reduction (lowering of standard deviation) obtained by adding low correlating asset classes. The currency risk incurred with international equities is one of the reasons for the low correlation. By hedging currency risk, a fund will increase the correlation of that asset class to the domestic portion of the portfolio. While seeming to reduce risk by hedging the currency risk, the fund manager actually increases the risk of the investor's portfolio, while incurring additional costs at the same time.

Let's now turn to the fixed income portion of the portfolio. For most investors the main role of their fixed income allocation is to be the anchor, or risk-minimizing, portion of their portfolio.

Choosing an equity-to-fixed income allocation that allows the investor to sleep well and stay disciplined is an important part of the winning strategy.

Some fixed income funds invest solely in U.S. debt instruments, while others invest globally. As long as credit risks are similar (investment grade, meaning government or AA—or better—rated) a fund may be able to find more attractive investments in global markets than if limited solely to the domestic market. In addition, by including international assets in a fixed income allocation, an investor gains some diversification benefit. For example, while U.S. fixed income markets may be falling, Germany's markets may be rising. Please note, however, that when you purchase foreign debt instruments you take on currency risk, which increases the volatility of the asset class. Since the main purpose of fixed income assets is to minimize risk, we do not want to increase the volatility of this portion of the portfolio. Therefore, for fixed income assets it makes sense to hedge the currency risk.

To summarize, when considering international *equity* funds, select only those that do not hedge. When considering international *fixed income* funds, choose only those that hedge.

Too Many Eggs in One Basket

Every investor knows that putting too many eggs in one basket is a risky investment decision that can easily be avoided by building a diversified portfolio. Yet many executives and long-term corporate employees end up with a very substantial portion of their assets in the stock of the company for which they work. I have seen many cases where employees have as much as 80% or even 90% of their entire net worth in their employer's stock.

WHAT WALL STREET DOESN'T WANT YOU TO KNOW

The unusually large share is usually the result of stock options and savings plans that encourage ownership of corporate stock. My experience has been that in the vast majority of cases no actual decision was made to hold such a risky portfolio. The person just ended up with the portfolio without thinking about the risks incurred. In addition, in many cases people believe that because they work for the company they "*know* just how good an investment they have." Let's examine why holding such an undiversified portfolio is really a poor decision, no matter how good the prospects for the company look. In fact, if the investor had taken the time to think about the decision in a rational manner, he would, in all likelihood, never have ended up holding the vast majority of his assets in his own company's (or any other company's) stock.

Whenever I meet with a client who has a large percentage of her assets in her own company's stock, I ask her to put herself in the following situation. I point out that she needs to think of the situation as a real-life one. I tell her that she is the single greatest blackjack player in the world. She knows that she never makes a mistake counting cards. A casino has offered her a challenge match in which only one deck of cards will be used. On any individual hand she can bet any amount she likes, from 1 cent to her entire net worth (for the purpose of this example, let us assume it is $2 million). She can also quit the game at any time. She accepts the challenge and proceeds to bet 1 cent on every hand. Finally, the perfect situation arises. The dealer is down to only 4 cards left, all of them kings. The dealer can only deal 3 cards (because the last one is face up) and then must shuffle and deal himself one more card. The client is then left with the following situation. She will have 20 points and the dealer will have 10, with one more card to be dealt. With only 49 cards remaining, the client will have:

- A 12.5% chance to lose (the 4 aces and other combinations which add to 21).
- A 30% chance to tie.
- A 57.5% chance of winning.

In all likelihood, this will be the best bet (investment) the client will ever have a chance to make. The odds of winning are 4.6 times (12.5/57.5) greater than the odds of losing, and there is only a 1 in 8 chance of losing. Now, with her spouse looking over her shoulder, I ask: How much of your $2 million net worth would you bet? Very rarely do I get an answer that even approaches 10% of the client's net worth. Most people say something like $5,000 or $10,000. I then ask the client if she believes that the odds that her company's stock will outperform the market are as good as that blackjack bet. Most will admit that it isn't.

What do we learn from the blackjack example? We learn that when the cost of losing (being wrong) is high, people become risk averse. Even with the odds greatly in their favor they avoid risk. Other examples of this behavior are the purchase of home owner's or life insurance. No one expects either to have their home destroyed or to die in the near future. Yet virtually everyone buys insurance because the cost of being wrong is high. Again, when the cost of losing is high, investors become risk averse. They do so because while it is *highly unlikely* that if they went uninsured they would suffer a loss, it is *not impossible*. Conversely, when the cost of losing is low, people become risk takers (even when the odds are greatly against them). Examples of this type of behavior are the purchase of lottery tickets. All purchasers know that they are likely to lose; yet they all buy because the cost of losing is low.

We can apply the blackjack lesson to the example of investors with the vast majority of their assets in their own company's stock. First, investors who are also employees are actually making a double bet, one part of which they may not even be conscious of: if the outlook for the company turns negative, the company may lay off staff to reduce costs, so their jobs may be in danger at the same time their investments may come under pressure.

Second, there is really no logical reason for investors to believe that their own stock will outperform similar stocks. Obviously, not all investors' stocks can outperform the average. Some will do better and some will do worse. However, since investors are risk averse when they might lose a large amount, it doesn't make sense to own only one stock, especially when higher returns are not expected (let alone when the odds of losing are only 1 in 8). Even if it were logical to believe that an investor would get higher returns, are the odds against being wrong as great as they are in the blackjack example? If investors wouldn't bet a large amount at the blackjack table with odds as stacked in their favor as they are in the hypothetical example, why should they make a large bet when the odds are far less favorable? It is my experience that unlike the insurance decision, where investors treat the highly unlikely as possible, when it comes to their company's stock they treat the highly unlikely—a sharp drop in their company's stock—as impossible. I usually point out that the many employees of once high fliers such as E-Loan and Silicon Graphics watched the vast majority of their net worth evaporate because they made the mistake of treating the *highly unlikely as impossible*. The following are some good examples of how investors in great companies ended up with very poor investment results:

- Black & Decker. The shares of the "do-it-yourself" tool-maker had risen 500-fold in 15 years. The 1972 peak was not revisited until 1998.
- Campbell Soup. The 1961 price was not regained until 1982, 21 years later.
- Digital Equipment. The shares of this minicomputer maker, which had skyrocketed a thousandfold from 1967 to 1987, lost 85% of their value over the next 5 years.
- Polaroid. The stock price in 1998 was only a third of its price 30 years earlier.

There are of course many more examples of investors being burned by placing too many eggs in one basket. They are also good examples of why investors should never treat what may seem highly unlikely to them as impossible.

It has been my experience that once investors take the blackjack test they become aware, for the first time, just how risky a decision they have made. At that point I ask them: "If you currently didn't own any of your employer's stock, how much would you buy?" I usually get an answer that is a small fraction of the amount currently held. I then point out that every day they own the stock, they are effectively buying that amount of stock—because, of course, they don't have to own it. It is at that point that they will usually agree to sell enough shares to bring their investment down to a more acceptable level. The proceeds can then be used to build a globally diversified portfolio that reflects their unique appetite for risk, investment horizon, and financial goals.

Take the Plunge, or
Drip by Drip

One of the issues most frequently faced by investors goes something like this: "I just received a large lump sum of money. Should I invest it all at once or spread the investment out over time?" From one perspective the answer appears simple. Since the market rises a significant majority of the time, common sense tells us to invest all at once. To do otherwise will probably cause an investor to eventually buy at higher and higher prices? Unfortunately, investors do not always base decisions on logic. In fact, the stomach (emotions such as fear) often plays a far greater role in decision-making than the head (logic).

It is my experience that almost all investors are often sure that if they were to take the plunge and invest all at one time, that day would turn out to be an all-time high, not to be exceeded until the next millenium. This causes them to delay the decision altogether, with often paralyzing results. If the market rises after they delay, they feel that if they couldn't buy at what they felt was too high a price, how can they buy now at even higher prices? If the market falls, they feel that they can't buy now because the bear market they feared has now arrived. Once a decision has been made to not buy, exactly how do you make the decision to buy?

I believe that there is a good solution to this dilemma, one that addresses both the logic and the emotional issues. I recommend that an investor write down a business plan for his or her lump sum. The plan should lay out a schedule with regularly planned investments. The plan might look something like one of these alternatives:

- Invest one-third of the investment immediately and invest the remainder one-third at a time during the next 2 months or next 2 quarters.
- Invest one-quarter today and invest the remainder spread equally over the next 3 quarters.
- Invest one-sixth each month for 6 months or every other month.

With one caveat, the important issue is writing down and adhering to the schedule, not the specific schedule itself. The caveat is that investors should not make the schedule too long. I suggest a maximum of one year. Keep in mind that the longer the schedule, the more likely it is that the investor will miss out on market gains.

Once an investor has written up the schedule, he or she should sign it. If the investor has an advisor, he or she should instruct the advisor to implement the plan, regardless of how the market performs. This is the only way an investor can be sure that the plan will actually be implemented. Otherwise, the latest headlines or guru forecasts might tempt the investor

Having accomplished these objectives, I suggest that the investor should adopt the following "glass is half-full" perspective. If the market rises after the initial investment, the investor can feel good about how her portfolio has performed. The investor can also feel good about how smart she was not to delay investing. If, on the other hand, the market has fallen, the investor can feel good about the opportunity to now buy at lower prices. The investor can also feel good about being smart enough not to have put all of her money in at one time. Either way the investor wins, at least from a psychological perspective. Since we know that emotions play an important role in how individuals view outcomes, this is an important consideration.

Once an investor is convinced that a gradualist approach is the correct one, I believe that it is important to ask the following question. "Having made your initial partial investment, do you now want to see the market rise or fall?" Unless one has an extremely short investment horizon (in which case one probably shouldn't be in equities at all) the clear logical answer is that one should root for the market to fall so that one gets to make their future investments at lower prices. Aren't we all taught to buy low and sell high?

Choosing an Investment Advisory Firm

If you don't know where you are going you will probably end up someplace else.
—Laurence J. Peter

You now have the knowledge and tools to successfully implement the winner's game. However, even though you have the necessary information to do so, you may not be comfortable enough to go it alone. Even Pete Sampras has a coach with him at every match. There are a variety of reasons to consider hiring a financial advisor.

These are questions you should ask when interviewing prospective firms about ways they can add value to your portfolio:

- Do you provide continuing access to the latest academic research on the financial markets? A good advisory firm will continue to educate its clients through conferences, seminars, and/or newsletters.

- Do you integrate an investment strategy into an overall financial plan? At the very least, an advisory firm should be able to act as quarterback for your financial services team, which might include, among others, your accountant, attorney, and life insurance agent.
- Do you establish an investment policy that incorporates my unique personal circumstances and personality (i.e., tolerance for risk)?
- Do you develop an individually tailored portfolio and appropriate asset allocation, ask the appropriate "devil's advocate" questions, and help select the specific investment vehicles? Or do you have a cookie-cutter approach with each client having the same asset allocation?
- Will you meet with me on an ongoing basis to discuss whether the investment policy remains appropriate over time and as personal circumstances change?
- Do you provide access to institutional-style passive asset class funds not available to the general public?
- Will you help provide the discipline, during both good and bad times, to help me stick with the strategy? An investment advisor should be able to help take the emotion out of the decision-making process. Will you share with me your own portfolio statements to verify that your actions match your words?
- Do you provide expertise over a broad range of financial issues, such as what type of mortgage to use when buying a home or whether a variable annuity is appropriate?
- Do you provide creative approaches to meeting cash flow needs and to developing solutions for financial problems?
- Will you track the performance of my portfolio and ensure that the rebalancing process is performed on a regular basis and in a cost- and tax-efficient manner?

- Do you provide regular reporting, at least on a quarterly basis, that clearly communicates the performance of the portfolio?
- Are you available at any time to discuss my portfolio and changing personal circumstances and market conditions?
- Do you build trust, get to personally know the client, and establish rapport along with a high level of comfort?
- Finally, do you put your money where your mouth is? In other words, do you invest in the same funds you recommend? (Personally, I would not invest with a firm whose principals do not invest according to the same strategy they recommend.)

The Checklist

If you hire an investment advisory firm, here is another checklist you will find useful:

- The investment philosophy of the advisory firm should be consistent with your own. The advisory firm should require, and specifically sign off on, a jointly developed investment policy statement.
- The only way to ensure that your advisor's interests are aligned with your own is for the investment advisory firm to be independent of any potential conflicts of interest, such as earning commissions from the sale of products it recommends. Therefore, I recommend working with a fee-only advisor.
- The firm should have a team with which you are comfortable. No one individual has all the knowledge and skills necessary to be able to assist over the entire financial spectrum. In addition, you may need advice at a time when one

particular individual is not available; and, unfortunately, one particular individual may not always be there. This is another reason why an investment policy statement is important. If your main contact is unavailable, by reviewing the investment policy statement any of the firm's advisors will quickly be able to understand your situation and provide the appropriate response. The firm should be committed to a team approach, and you should interview more than just one individual.

- You should perform a careful due diligence on the firm and its principals. You should do a thorough reference check and make sure that both the firm and its individual members have the appropriate licenses. Most importantly, this due diligence should include a careful review of a document called the Form ADV. This form is required by the Investment Advisors Act of 1940 and must be filed with the regulatory body with which a Registered Investment Advisor (RIA) has registered (either the SEC or his or her state). The ADV is basically a disclosure document that sets forth information about the RIA, including the investment strategy, fee schedules, conflicts of interest, regulatory incidents, and so on. All RIAs are required to furnish to new clients either a Form ADV or another document containing similar information in order to satisfy the "Brochure Rule" prescribed by the Act.

- The firm should be able to demonstrate to you that it can add value in a way that more than justifies its fees.

Sound financial advice is not expensive. An effective advisor can add value equal to many times his fee simply by preventing you from making some very poor investment decisions (like chasing yesterday's hot sector). The typical investment advisory firm charges between 1% and 2% per annum, based on the amount of assets under management. For large accounts, fees are generally negotiated to below 1%. In general, the greater the assets under management, the lower the fee. The reason is that firms generally have to spend almost as much time with smaller accounts as they do with larger accounts. This provides some economies of scale, allowing for somewhat lower fees for larger accounts. On the other hand, the opportunity for an advisor to add value generally increases as the size and complexity of the estate increases. In addition, in terms of returns on the portfolio, if an advisor can improve returns, the investor with the largest assets under management benefits the most in absolute terms (while paying the lowest percentage fee).

It is my experience that many investors view fee structures from an incorrect perspective. They concern themselves with either the amount of time an advisor spends with them personally (effort) or the size of the fee (looking for lowest cost). Instead, investors should be concerned with how much *value* the advisor adds *relative* to the *cost*. If the value added exceeds the fee charged, even if the fee seems high in absolute terms, you will have received value. On the other hand, if the value added does not exceed the fee, no matter how low the fee, it is still too high.

When comparing fees be sure you are comparing apples to apples, as some firms only provide investment advice, while others provide a broader array of services within their fee structure. Finally, remember that while good advice may not be cheap, it is far less expensive than bad advice.

Investment Insights

- Investors should begin the investment process with the development of an investment policy statement (IPS).
- The IPS should define the investor's investment horizon, risk tolerance, and financial goals.
- An IPS can help an investor minimize the impact of emotion in the investment process. While it is okay to be an optimist, it is important to be prepared for the worst.
- Investors should construct a broad globally diverse portfolio using index and/or passive asset class funds, and/or ETFs.
- The use of active managers to implement an investment strategy can lead to out-of-control outcomes as active managers "style drift." Investors should, therefore, choose passively managed funds to implement their investment strategies because they allow investors to get precise and consistent implementation of their asset allocation decisions. They never style drift.
- To *reduce* risk, investors should include in their portfolios a significant allocation to international asset classes.
- There is no one right portfolio.
- Investors seeking higher returns should increase the exposure to the small-cap and especially value asset classes.
- S&P 500 Index and total stock market funds do not offer broad diversification. They are very heavily weighted toward the single asset class of large-cap growth stocks. Therefore, they should generally be used as one component of a portfolio, not as the only fund.
- When choosing international equity funds, choose only those that do not hedge currency risk.
- The fixed income markets are just as efficient, and maybe

more so, than the equity markets. Thus passive management is the winning strategy.

- Bond funds should not be the investment vehicle of choice for fixed income investors. For the fixed income portion of a portfolio, investors should generally avoid maturities beyond 3 years (unless, of course, they are trying to match the maturity of their assets and their liabilities). Investors should also consider the new inflation protection securities, TIPS and I Bonds.
- Investors should consider including real estate as an asset class in their portfolios. The home, however, should not be considered part of the real estate exposure.
- Investors should include a rebalancing table in their IPS.
- Investors should rebalance regularly, and whenever new cash is available.
- Investors should never put too many eggs in one basket.
- When planning for retirement, investors need to be very conservative in their assumptions about withdrawal rates. One reason is that they underestimate their investment horizon. A good rule of thumb for 65-year-old investors is to withdraw no more than 4% of the assets each year (adjusted for inflation).
- Investment advisory firms can add significant value. However, investors should be very careful in choosing a firm. Choosing a fee-only advisor is the only way to ensure that your and your advisor's interests are always aligned.

Summary

Individuals begin their investment journey staring at a fork in the road. The arrow pointing to the left says active management. The arrow pointing to the right says passive management. Unfortunately for most investors, they base their decision on the investment propaganda put out by the Wall Street establishment and the financial press, neither of which has their interests at heart. The vast majority of investors have not been exposed to findings of financial economists. They probably don't know that a Nobel Prize was awarded in 1990 to 3 financial economists for their contributions to the body of work known as MPT. They are almost surely unaware that the American Law Institute rewrote the Prudent Investor Rule in 1992 recognizing that passive management, by definition, was the prudent investment approach. And they are probably unaware of the vast and compelling body of evidence supporting the view that markets work, that they are efficient, and that active management is a loser's game for all but the sellers of active management services.

Summary

Individuals are taking the left (active) fork of the road based on the fairy tales, legends, lies, myths, and what Jane Bryant Quinn calls the "investment pornography" of Wall Street and the financial press. William Sherden, author of *The Fortune Sellers*, provided the following insight:

"Despite recent innovations in information technology and decades of academic research, successful stock market prediction has remained an elusive goal. In fact, the market is getting more complex and unpredictable as global trading brings in many new investors from numerous countries, computerized exchanges speed up transactions, and investors think up clever schemes to try to beat the market. Overall, we have not made progress in predicting the stock market, but this has not stopped the investment business from continuing the quest, and making $100 billion annually doing so."

The truth is that the winning investment strategy is to take the right (passive) fork and invest using a passive asset class strategy. As Charles Ellis stated in his excellent book *Winning the Loser's Game*, "The real challenge in portfolio management is not how to increase *returns*—by buying low and selling high—but how to *manage risk* by deliberately taking appropriate risk or bets that lead predictably over time to increased returns."

The following is a brief summary of *what Wall Street doesn't want investors to know*:

* Markets are highly efficient.
* Even if market inefficiencies exist, the cost hurdles that must be overcome are so great that active management is a loser's game.
* Efforts to outperform the market are not only nonproduc-

tive, they are counterproductive because of the expenses and taxes incurred.

- Taxes dramatically reduce pretax returns. For most investors, taxes will be the greatest expense they face, even greater than the fees charged by the funds in which they are invested.

- Although there will always be some managers that outperform the market, far fewer will do so than would be randomly expected. In addition, since past performance has proven to be a poor predictor of future performance, investors have no reliable way to identify, in advance, which few active managers will be the future winners.

- Markets reward for taking risk. Investors demand excess returns, in the form of risk premiums, for accepting greater risk. The asset classes of small-cap and value stocks are riskier asset classes than large-cap and growth stocks; therefore, they provide expected higher returns.

- Virtually all of the returns (as much as 97%) from a portfolio are determined by asset allocation decisions. Stock selection and market timing account for less than 3% of returns.

- You should build a globally diversified portfolio with a significant allocation to international equities.

- You should avoid putting too many eggs in one basket.

- Behavioral economists have provided us with valuable insights into why investors appear to act in irrational ways, often ignoring powerful evidence that they are playing the loser's game. By understanding these behavior patterns, investors can avoid taking that left fork and play the winner's game instead.

- Investors considering adopting passive asset class strategies do not have to feel like investment pioneers. Institutional investors have traveled on the right fork for more than 20 years. Today, 40% of their investment funds are passively managed, and the trend is accelerating. Individuals have not totally ignored the trend. They have made the Vanguard S&P 500 Index the largest in the world.

As promised in the introduction, here are the 7 easy steps to help you play the winner's game.

Seven Easy Steps to Playing the Winner's Game

Step 1: Admit to yourself that while trying to time the market and pick stocks is exciting, it is a loser's game. Admit that passive investing, while possibly boring, is the winner's game, played by the most sophisticated institutions and individual investors. As *Fortune* magazine pointed out in its July 6, 1998, issue, it is the way the "really smart money" invests. *Fortune* posed the following question: "Suppose you made a list of the smartest people alive in finance—and those who have done the most to advance our understanding of how the stock market really works. . . . What would you give to know how these titans invest their own money?" As *Fortune* then pointed out, you don't have to give anything. Many of these economists either work for, are on the board of, or are associated with DFA, an institutional fund manager whose funds are available to the public through a select group of financial advisors. Among them are the leading proponents of the EMT, professors Eugene F. Fama of the University of Chicago and Kenneth R. French of MIT. Also included is Nobel laureate Myron Scholes. Add to that list Roger Ibbotson and Rex Sinquefield, who together have compiled the most comprehensive database of stock and bond market returns dating to 1926. All of them put their money where their mouths are, investing their money in DFA's funds. And what type of funds does DFA manage? Index and passive asset class funds!

Step 2: If you need or enjoy the excitement of active investing, set up an entertainment account with 5 to 10% of your assets and go ahead and *"play the market."* Then, prudently *invest* the rest of your assets. Life is too short to miss out on the fun. Besides, because the market is highly efficient, you will, in any case, probably earn about the same gross return as the market. However, you will probably do so with higher costs and, therefore, lower net returns. Of course, you will have the possibility of outperforming and having great stories to tell. On the other hand, if you underperform, no one need know. That can remain a secret between you and the mirror you look into each night.

Step 3: Use the tables provided in chapter 10 to help you determine your unique risk tolerance, need to take risk, investment horizon, and cash flow needs. The answers will help you determine your allocation between equities and fixed income assets. This is probably the most important decision you will make. Give these issues lots of thought and ask yourself many "devil's advocate" type questions to be sure you have thought through many scenarios (not just ones where the market keeps going up in a straight line at very high compound rates). Make sure that you are comfortable with your conclusions. This is an area where a financial advisor can add significant value. The conclusions you draw should be reviewed on at least an annual basis. These conclusions should also be reviewed whenever a significant event occurs that impacts your financial situation, either positively or negatively.

Step 4: Build a globally diversified portfolio consisting of multiple asset classes. For the equity portion you should strongly consider including such "risky" asset classes as small-caps, value stocks, real estate, international stocks, and even emerging markets. Remember that while these asset classes may be risky when viewed in isolation, their inclusion in the portfolio is highly likely to reduce the risk of the total portfolio. For those investors seeking higher expected returns and willing to accept the greater risk associated with those higher expected returns, allocate a greater percentage to the equity asset classes of value, small-caps, and even emerging markets. For the fixed income portion, generally long-term maturities should be avoided (and especially avoid long-term bond funds). The preferred fixed income vehicles are short-term investments (one- to two-year in maturity) and the new U.S. Treasury inflation protection instruments known as TIPS and I Bonds.

Step 5: Write and sign an IPS. Review it annually to remind yourself why you adopted the winner's game. Doing so will help you remain a disciplined and patient investor, one who avoids the siren song of the latest craze and does not end up crashing on the shoals, seduced by "investment pornography." The following analogy is worth remembering. Imagine that you had to drive from New York to L.A. You're hopelessly stuck in midtown Manhattan traffic. You observe bicycle messengers whizzing past. You jump out of your car, sell it, and buy a bicycle to continue your journey.[1]

As absurd as that sounds, investors make very similar mistakes when the investment "noise" that surrounds them on a daily basis causes them to abandon well-thought-out plans for a long-term journey.

As with your asset allocation, your IPS should also be reviewed whenever a significant event occurs that impacts your financial situation, either positively or negatively.

Step 6: Regularly rebalance your portfolio to its targeted asset allocation. Use the 5/25 rule from chapter 10 to assist in this process. You should perform a rebalancing check on a quarterly basis, although even annually would be acceptable. Whenever you have new cash to invest, take advantage of the opportunity to rebalance. It is the cheapest and most tax-efficient way to do so.

Step 7: In general, allocate your most tax-efficient asset classes to your taxable accounts, and your least tax-efficient to your tax-deferred accounts. Whenever possible use tax-managed funds for taxable accounts.

As promised, I will conclude the book with one of my favorite tales. I hope you find the message as important and relevant as I do.

One day, an expert in time management was speaking to a group of business students. As she stood in front of the group of high-powered overachievers she set on the table a large mason jar. She then produced some fist-sized rocks and carefully placed them, one at a time, into the jar. When no more rocks would fit inside, she asked, "Is this jar full?" Everyone yelled, "Yes." She replied, "Really?" She reached under the table, pulled out a bucket of gravel, dumped some in, and shook the jar. This caused pieces of gravel to work themselves down into the spaces between the big rocks. She then asked, "Is the jar full?" One student answered, "Probably not." She then reached under the table, brought out a bucket of sand, and started dumping the sand in the jar. It went into all of the spaces left between the rocks and the gravel. Once more she asked, "Is this jar full?" Everyone shouted, "No!" She then grabbed a pitcher of water and poured until the jar was filled to the brim. She then asked, "What is the point of this illustration?" One student raised his hand and said, "The point is, no matter how full your schedule is, you can always fit some more things in it!'' The speaker replied, ''That's not the point. The truth this illustration teaches us is: if you don't put the big rocks in first, you'll never get them in at all. What are the 'big rocks' in your life—time with your loved ones, your faith, your education, your dreams, a worthy cause, teaching or mentoring others? Remember to put these BIG ROCKS in first, or you'll never get them in at all.''

Individual investors following an active management strategy spend much of their precious leisure time watching the latest business news, studying the latest charts, scanning and posting on Internet investment discussion boards, reading financial trade publications and newsletters, and so on. They are focusing on the gravel, the sand, and the water. On the other hand, passive investors, ignoring all the ''noise,'' are playing the winner's game and focusing on the big rocks, the really important things in their lives.

Welcome to the winner's game.

Appendices

APPENDIX A:
EFFICIENT FRONTIER MODELS

NASCAR racing machines are very sophisticated, complex automobiles. In the hands of a Mario Andretti, they are capable of great feats. The same machine, however, in the hands of a drunk driver is a very dangerous vehicle. The financial equivalent of racing cars is an efficient frontier model. They are one of the most touted, yet misunderstood and therefore misused tools in the field of financial planning.

Harry Markowitz first coined the term "efficient frontier" almost 40 years ago. He used it to describe a portfolio that was most likely to deliver the greatest return for a given level of risk. Today, there are many efficient frontier programs available. They begin by having an individual investor answer questions about his or her risk profile. The program will then generate a portfolio consisting of various asset classes that will deliver the greatest expected return given the individual's risk tolerance. Sounds like a wonderful idea. So what's the problem? The problem is understanding the nature of an efficient frontier model and the assumptions on which it relies. As with a sophisticated racing car, a powerful tool in the wrong hands can be a very dangerous thing.

Efficient frontier models, in effect, attempt to turn investing into a science, which it is not. For example, it is very logical to believe that in the future stocks will outperform fixed income investments. The reason is that stocks are riskier than risk-free Treasury bills. Investors will demand an "equity risk premium" to compensate them for this risk. While the past may be a guide to the size of the "equity risk premium," it is not, however, a guarantee. For example, if we look at the period 1926 through 1990, the equity risk premium for the S&P 500 was 6.7%. Once we include the bull market of the 1990s, the risk premium jumps by well over 1% to about 8%. As you can see, the equity risk premium is not constant. We shall see why even this seemingly small change is very important when it comes to efficient frontier models.

Efficient frontier models rely on historical data and relationships to generate the "perfect" portfolio. Expected returns, correlations, and standard deviations (measure of volatility) must be provided for each asset class, or building block, that could be used in a portfolio. Let us begin with a simple portfolio that can potentially invest in just 5 asset classes: S&P 500 (U.S. large-cap); U.S. small-cap; one-year fixed income; EAFE (international large-cap); and international small-cap. The table shows our assumptions regarding historical data for returns, correlations, and standard deviations. Using standard deviation as the measure of risk, let us also assume that we have designated a 12% standard deviation as the level of portfolio risk we are willing to accept. An efficient frontier model will then generate the "correct" asset allocations.

Correlation (R)

	S&P 500	U.S. Small	One-Year Fixed Income	EAFE Index	Int'l Small
S&P 500 Index	1.0				
U.S. small	0.8	1.0			
One-year fixed income	0.0	0.0	1.0		
EAFE Index	0.6	0.4	0.0	1.0	
Int'l small	0.4	0.4*	0.0	0.8	1.0

	S&P 500	U.S. Small	One-Year Fixed Income	EAFE Index	Int'l Small Co.
Expected return (%)	12*	14	6	12	14
Standard deviation (%)	20	30	4	20*	30

The following is the recommended allocation generated by our efficient frontier model.

	Case 1
S&P 500 Index	22
U.S. small	9
One-year fixed income	38
EAFE Index	22
International small	9

We will now make a series of minor changes to expected returns, standard deviations, and correlations in order to see how sensitive the efficient frontier models are to assumptions. Each change, indicated by an asterisk in the preceding table, will be a minor one from our original base case. In case 2 we reduced the expected return of the S&P 500 from 12% (its return from 1934 to 1996) to 11% (its return from 1926 to 1996). In case 3 we increased the standard deviation of the EAFE Index from 20% to 22%. In case 4 we reduced the correlation between U.S. small-caps and international small-caps from 0.4 to 0.2. In each case the efficient frontier model generated a dramatically different asset allocation, in some cases entirely eliminating an asset class from the portfolio. This implies a precision that just does not exist in the field of financial economics.

	Case 1	Case 2	Case 3	Case 4
S&P 500 Index	22	0	36	15
U.S. small company	9	20	4	15
One-year fixed income	38	40	40	40
EAFE Index	22	36	0	15
International small company	9	4	20	15

Investing is not a science. It is foolish to pretend that we know in advance the exact levels for returns, correlations, and standard deviations. Yet that is the underlying assumption of any efficient frontier model. Experienced practitioners know that in order to come up with something intelligent, they generally impose constraints on efficient frontier models. Examples of constraints might be that no asset class can either exceed 30% or be less than 10% of a portfolio. Another constraint might be that international assets in aggregate cannot exceed 30% or 40% of the portfolio. The impact of constraints is similar to what a simple common-sense approach without modeling would end up with—a relatively balanced globally diversified portfolio with exposure to all the major asset classes. In other words, don't waste your time with efficient frontier models.

In summary, it is my experience that most investors using efficient frontier models are unaware of their pitfalls. These models are being marketed as solutions to the problem of portfolio construction; but they come without *instructions*. The models are marketed to individuals not only over the Internet but also by many large companies to their 401(k) and profit-sharing participants. These corporations may view this offering as a way to fulfill their fiduciary responsibility to educate their plan participants. That is a real problem, given the model's pitfalls (unless of course they come with the appropriate instructions and disclaimers).

Another problem is that the most popular efficient frontier model comes from William Sharpe (Nobel Prize recipient and a major contributor to MPT) and his Financial Engines advisory service. Sharpe's name and reputation provide instant credibility with investors. In addition to these problems with efficient frontier models, there are major problems with some of the assumptions in Sharpe's model. As of January 2000, Financial Engines was making some assumptions about returns that do not appear to make sense. For example, the real return assumption for long-term bonds was about 2.6%. At the same time the return on TIPS was in excess of 4% (in other words, just buy TIPS). Financial Engines also assumes that value stocks will provide the same returns as growth stocks, despite the overwhelming evidence both domestically and internationally that value stocks have provided substantially greater returns.

The model also assumes that Japanese small-cap stocks will provide almost no real return. Why would anyone invest in a risky asset class with virtually no expectation of reward? That makes no sense at all. Finally, the model assumes much lower returns for most international asset classes, including emerging markets, than for U.S. asset classes. Given the high degree of freedom of capital to move around the globe, there is no reason to expect any difference in returns over the long term. Remember that if there were expected differences, they would already be incorporated into current prices. And, again, why would anyone invest in the very risky asset class of emerging markets and accept lower expected returns? The only assumption one can make is that Financial Engines has chosen to look at the most recent data and ignore the long-term historical evidence.

Given the problems with efficient frontier models, perhaps investors should be required to show their "driver's license" before being able to use such a model.

APPENDIX B:
ENHANCED INDEXING, FIXED INCOME STRATEGIES, AND THE FUTURES MARKET

This appendix is an extension of chapter 4's "enhanced" indexing tale. What follows is a detailed explanation of how futures and cash markets interrelate and how arbitrageurs (arbs) work their magic. The explanation will provide insight into how enhanced index funds that focus on enhancing returns using fixed income (instead of equity) strategies attempt to add value.

HOW ENHANCED FUNDS WORK

What do fixed income markets have to do with an S&P 500 Index fund? The answer provides an understanding of how equity futures contracts and stock prices interrelate. There are actually 2 ways a fund can own the stocks of an index, such as the S&P 500. A fund can use its cash to buy actual securities in proportion to their market cap weighting within the Index. Or the fund can hold its cash and buy a futures contract that represents the stocks of the Index. (A futures contract, in this context, is an agreement to purchase or sell a specific collection of equity securities, representing ownership interest in the S&P 500 Index, at a specified price or yield for delivery on a specific date on a particular exchange.)

Logically, if it is cheaper to own the stocks, the fund will purchase stocks. With the stocks, the fund also earns dividend yields. However, it foregoes the income it would have earned by investing its cash elsewhere. This consideration must be added to the overall equation. If it is cheaper to own the futures contracts (if the fund can generate a rate of return on its available cash that is higher than the rate implied by the price of the futures contract), the fund will keep its cash and purchase the futures contract, tied to a specific maturity date and representing the value of the stocks. It foregoes equity dividends but is able to earn interest by investing its cash. Since most S&P 500 futures contracts used by professionals are very short term, a good proxy for the interest rate is the rate available on money market funds.

Thus, if an enhanced index fund can provide greater returns, it may be an attractive investment vehicle. However, there are 2 important caveats:

1. By using futures contracts, a fund converts all of its income into realized (taxable) short-term gains. Therefore, any index funds that attempt to enhance returns through fixed income investments combined with futures contracts should only be con-

sidered for tax-deferred or nontaxable accounts (or for those special situations where realized taxable current income is needed).

2. It should be noted that an enhanced fund could easily be expected to enhance returns by taking on increased risk. For example, a fund can assume credit risk or maturity (interest rate) risk by investing its cash in high-yield or junk bonds or by investing its cash in bonds with maturities longer than those of the futures contract. Some funds assume risk by investing their cash in mortgage-backed securities and other instruments with uncertain principal repayment schedules. In all of these scenarios, different types and varying amounts of risk are being assumed that have the potential to negatively impact total return. It is important to analyze each fund that is accomplishing its enhancements in this manner; this is an example of where an investment advisor capable of conducting the appropriate analysis can really add value.

Determining When to Enhance

Details follow on how arbitrageurs make their decisions to implement enhancement strategies. As described earlier, investors seeking an enhanced index fund should generally only consider one where the fund seeks its enhancement through the fixed income markets. A fund can use its cash to buy actual securities in proportion to their market cap weighting within the index. Or the fund can hold its cash and buy a futures contract that represents the stocks of the index. I believe this type of fund—which capitalizes on interest rates rather than equities—is worth consideration, particularly for tax-deferred or nontaxable accounts. A more detailed description follows of the analysis that fund managers use to determine when to purchase futures and hold cash, and when to use cash to purchase stocks.

The Role of Arbitrageurs

The process for determining the price of the futures contract is guided by what is known as arbitrage. Arbitrage ensures that the prices of our two alternatives (purchasing stocks or purchasing futures) rarely deviate far from "equilibrium," once transactions costs are taken into account. When prices do deviate, arbitrageurs exploit the price difference by simultaneously (thereby avoiding risk) buying one at a lower price and selling the other at a higher price. This action locks in a risk-free profit for the arbs and brings the prices back to equilibrium.

For example, consider that wheat is selling in Chicago for $2.50 per bushel and in Boston for $2.80 per bushel, and that it costs $0.10 per bushel to ship wheat from Chicago to Boston. A buyer can buy wheat in Boston at $2.80 per bushel or buy it in Chicago for $2.60 per bushel ($2.50 plus $0.10 for shipment). Spotting this opportunity, arbs buy in Chicago and sell in Boston, locking in a guaranteed profit of $0.20 per bushel. This action drives up the price in Chicago and down in Boston, until no further profit opportunities exist.

The prices of stocks and stock index futures interrelate in the same way. When it is cheaper to own stocks than to own the futures contracts (including all transaction costs), arbs buy stocks (have a long position) and sell futures (have an offsetting short position), locking in a profit. When it is cheaper to own futures, arbs take the reverse position—going long on futures and short on stocks.

Arbs in Action

Let's look at 2 examples. In both cases we will assume the following:

1. The current value of the S&P 500 Index is 100.
2. The interest rate for the period of the futures contract is 5% with a time frame of one year.
3. The dividend yield of the stocks in the Index is 2%.

From these figures, we can determine that the futures contract should be trading at approximately 103 (Futures = Index + Interest Rate − Dividend Yield, or 103 = 100 + 5 − 2).

First, let's assume that the futures contract is instead trading "expensive" at 107. Arbs would sell the futures contract at 107 (go short) and buy the stocks within the index (go long). The offsetting buys and sells leave the arbs with no net position, but they will have locked in a profit.

For example, let's say that, by the futures contract maturity date, the Index has risen from 100 to 105. On the futures side, an arb will have a profit of 2%, having sold at 107 and purchased back at 105. On the cash side, things are a bit more complicated. The arb would have earned the price appreciation from 100 to 105 on the stocks held. In addition, a financing cost of 5% (the cost of borrowing money to purchase stocks or alternatively using the cash to purchase stocks) would be offset by the dividend yield of 2%. The net financing cost would thus be 3%; when netted against the gain of 5% on the stocks, this would leave a net gain of 2%. Combining the futures gain of 2% and stock gain of 2% provides a total return of 4% to the arb. This 4% profit was earned without taking any risk on the movement of stock prices. Here is the same example in summary:

Futures and Cash/Interest Gains	
Futures contract profit (sold at 107 and purchased at 105)	2%
Stock Gains and Losses	
Stock price appreciation (from 100 to 105)	5%
Dividends on stock	2%
Financing cost (cost of using or borrowing cash)	−5%
Net stock gain	2%
Total Gain	4%

For our second example, let's assume the futures contract was trading "cheap" at 102. An arb would buy the futures contract (go long) and sell the stocks (go short). Again let's assume the Index rises to 105. The arb has a profit of 3% on the contract, having bought at 102 and watched the price rise to 105. In addition, the arb is able to earn 5% interest on the cash invested, resulting in a total 8% profit.

However, when the arb sells stocks, he or she forfeits the dividend and owes it to the buyer. Thus the total profit is reduced by the 2% dividend yield to 6%. In addition, the stocks the arb sold at 100 (the cash price at the beginning of the period) now must be repurchased at the current price of 105, for a loss of 5%. This reduces the profit to 1%. Again, it is a risk-free transaction, summarized as follows:

Futures and Cash/Interest Gains

Futures contract profit (purchased at 102 and sold at 105)	3%
Cash/interest gain	5%
Net gains	8%

Stock Gains and Losses

Loss of dividend	−2%
Stock purchase (sold at 100 and purchased at 105)	−5%
Net losses	−7%
Total Gain	1%

Computing Futures

Just as in the wheat example, if the prices in the 2 preceding examples did exist, then the actions of the arbs would drive the price back to approximately 103. It is at that point, once costs are considered, that the risk-free profit opportunity ceases to exist.

For those of you who watch CNBC, the fair value of the futures contract displayed represents this arbitrage "equalization" price. CNBC also displays prices for "buy programs" and "sell programs." The buy program reflects the price at which futures become so cheap, including transactions costs, that it pays to buy futures and sell stocks. Sell programs are triggered when futures become so expensive that, even including transaction costs, it pays to sell futures and buy stocks. The underlying expression that captures this cash/futures relationship is:

$$F = S[1 + (i - d)(t/360)]$$

F = Break-even futures price
S = Cash index price
i = Interest rate (expressed as a money market rate)
d = Projected dividend rate (expressed as a money market yield)
t = Number of days between today's index spot value date and the settlement date of the futures contract

Solve for F, and one can then determine a fair value number by subtracting S (the cash index price) from F (the theoretical futures value).

However, it is important to note that moving from the conceptual to the actual involves "slippages" and frictions; each market participant possesses unique economics that will drive him or her to action at different fair value levels. Participants across industrial and geographical regions will have different funding, investment rates, and transaction costs. Considerations such as accounting treatment and financial strategy also play a major role.

These differing firm dynamics result in market actions being taken across a range or zone of various fair-value levels, rather than one specific number. In other words, while market conditions may satisfy one participant, they may prove unsatisfactory for another. With this rather fluid backdrop, it is easy to see how what looks like a precise mathematical relationship in theory provides only a general guide in practice. It also indicates why investors (or their investment advisors on their behalf) should analyze closely each "enhanced" index fund prior to determining whether it is a suitable investment.

In conclusion, an investor seeking an enhanced index fund should generally only consider one where the "action" is *on the fixed income side* and not with equities. In addition, unless an investor wishes to take on significant interest rate or credit risk, he or she should seek enhanced funds that:

* Have very short maturity guidelines.
* Have known principal repayment schedules.
* Purchase only investment grade securities.
* Hedge their foreign currency exposure.

APPENDIX C:
THE IPO MYTH

One of the recurring themes of this book is that it is in Wall Street's interests to keep alive the myth that active management adds value. Another important myth that needs exposing is that Initial Public Offerings (IPOs) make great investments. Wall Street loves IPOs because they generate great fee income. The investment banker's fee is typically 7% of the offering price. Investors seem to love them as they desperately search for the next Microsoft, AOL, or Cisco. Let's look at the reality of actual performance.

A study covering the period 1970 through 1990 examined the returns from a strategy of buying every IPO at the end of the first day's closing price and then holding each investment for 5 years. The average return provided by this strategy would have been not only just 5% per annum but also 7% per annum less than a benchmark of an investment in companies with the same market capitalization that each IPO had on its first day of trading. It is worth noting that much of the poor performance of IPOs can be explained by the book-to-market (value) factor. IPOs tend to be low book-to-market (growth) stocks. Historically, the risk premium for value stocks (high book-to-market) over growth stocks has been in excess of 5%.[1]

University of Florida finance professor Jay Ritter found similar disappointing results for IPOs. Professor Ritter looked at 1,006 IPOs that raised at least $20 million from 1988 to 1993. He found that the median IPO underperformed the Russell 3000 by 30% in the 3 years after going public. He also found that 46% of IPOs produced negative returns.[2]

Another study examined the performance of 1993's IPOs through the period of mid-October 1998. The result was that the average IPO had returned just one-third as much as the S&P 500 Index. In addition, over one-half were trading below their offering price, and one-third were down over 50%![3]

A U.S. Bancorp Piper Jaffray study covering the period May 1988 through July 1998 and 4,900 IPOs found that by July 1998 less than one-third were above their IPO price. In addition, "almost a third weren't even trading any longer (having gone bankrupt, been acquired, or [being] off the active markets)."[4]

A study covering the period 1988 through 1995 and 1,232 IPOs found very similar results, with IPOs underperforming the market. This study did provide 2 additional insights. First, it found that 25% of all offerings actually closed the first day of trading below their offering price. The study also found that the IPOs they defined as "extra hot," meaning they rose 60% or more on the first day of trading, were the very worst performers from then on.[5] In fact, over the following year, the hottest IPOs underperformed the market by 2% to 3% PER MONTH.[6] This is very important information, because most individual investors cannot get access to the initial offering. These shares are usually reserved for big institutional clients. The only winners were the investment bankers and the institutional investors who "flipped" their stock (sold their shares on the day of, or shortly after, the offering).

The year 1999 was certainly a spectacular one for IPOs, with 555 companies raising a record $73.6 billion. The amount raised surpassed the previous record, set in 1996, by almost 50%. For all IPOs the median first day performance was 30%. However, investors who bought at the first day's closing price didn't do nearly as well. The median increase after 3 months was 0%, meaning that half of all issues lost money. The only investors who appear to benefit are the big investors who get allocated shares in the IPO.[7] Even more amazing, given the spectacular performance of any stock related to the Internet, is the following statistic. According to the February 26, 2000, issue of the *Economist*, nearly *three-fourths* of all U.S. Internet-related IPOs since mid-1995 were trading below their offering price at the time of publication. The first quarter of 2000 was not much better. According to Thompson Securities Data Company, the 146 companies that went public experienced an average first day rise of an incredible 98%. By April 6, 2000, however, almost 90% were trading below their opening day price and almost 30% were trading below their IPO price.[8]

In the face of this poor performance, why do investors continue to chase the latest IPO? I believe there are 2 explanations for this seemingly irrational behavior. First, unless an investor happens to read scholarly publications such as the *Journal of Finance*, he or she is unlikely to be aware of the facts. Second, even when informed, investors often act in what appear to be irrational ways. In this case I believe it to be another example of "the triumph of hope over experience." Investors seem to be willing to accept the high probability of low returns in exchange for the small chance of a home run or, possibly even more important, a great story to tell at the next cocktail party.

APPENDIX D:
SHIFTING FROM FUNDS TO STOCKS

This was the cover story of the March 2000 issue of Bloomberg's *Personal Finance* magazine. The article suggested that for higher net worth individuals, there are major advantages to owning individual stocks instead of mutual funds. The following is the article's summary of the advantages of owning stocks:

1. Put simply, stocks are more fun.
2. Investors are lured by the opportunity for the big kill and the opportunity to brag about it.
3. Mutual funds add another layer of expense.
4. Owning individual stocks gives you much greater control over taxes and thus is a more tax-efficient way to invest.
5. Investors only need to cover 10 basic industries to be fully diversified. This can be accomplished by owning as few as 20 stocks. "Your twenty-first stock won't cut your beta one iota," the author claims.
6. As global markets come together, the benefits of diversification are diminishing.
7. Asset allocation has in fact increased risk, not diminished it, over the past 10 years, as U.S. "small-cap stocks have been a disaster, and foreign stocks haven't helped."

Let's examine each one of these "advantages."

Owning Stocks Is More Fun

There is no doubt that owning stocks is more fun than owning mutual funds. However, investors should ask themselves if the objective is to have fun or to expect to earn the greatest risk-adjusted returns. If the answer is the latter, the academic evidence is very clear that very few professionals have been able to beat the market on a consistent basis by attempting to pick stocks or time the market. Indexing, or passive asset class investing, has proven to provide the average investor with far greater returns than the average mutual fund manager, especially after taxes. If professionals have generally been unable to beat the market by picking stocks, it certainly seems logical that the odds that an individual investor can are very low. This assumption is backed up by many studies showing that the average investor significantly underperforms the market over time. Investors who need or want the entertainment value that picking stocks or timing the market provides can set aside 5% to 10% of their assets in an entertainment account and in that way investors can have the best of both worlds. Investors can get the superior expected returns of passive investing from the vast majority of their portfolio, and they can play the market and have fun while taking the great risk of underperformance with only a small fraction of their assets.

The Thrill of the Kill

By owning mutual funds investors certainly give up the opportunity for the 10-bagger, as well as the opportunity for subsequent bragging rights. However, owning individual stocks also means assuming much greater risk of dramatic losses (of which, of course, no one will ever hear).

Mutual Funds Add Another Layer of Expense

Yes, mutual funds can add significantly to total expenses. However, that is only true of actively managed funds. Index and other passively managed funds are very efficient from a cost perspective. Not only are their operating expense ratios low but their low turnover results in low trading costs as well. An individual actively trading stocks will have much higher commissions and trading costs (and taxes as well) than an index fund.

There is one other potential advantage a mutual fund has over an individual investor. In the small-cap asset class, passively managed funds can act as sort of a market-maker of last resort for actively managed funds wishing to sell large amounts of stock quickly at one price. By engaging in what is known as a block trading strategy, some passively managed mutual funds have actually achieved negative trading costs, thus improving returns. The following is an example. Let us say that XYZ Inc. trades an average of about 25,000 shares a day. If an actively managed fund wants to sell 500,000 shares, it might take several days or even weeks to accomplish. Not wanting to take the risk of holding a stock it no longer wanted to own, the actively managed fund might seek a block buyer. Let us say that XYZ was trading at 16 ¾ bid and 16 ⅞ asked. A block buyer might bid 16 ⅛ for the whole amount. The seller might find that below-market price attractive, relative to the alternative of trying to sell small amounts of stock each day. Not only would the fund miss out on the opportunity to buy a stock it found more attractive, but by continuously selling into the market the fund runs the very real risk that selling a large amount of shares will substantially drive down the price of XYZ. Unless the seller had some "inside information," in all likelihood the stock will return to its original 16¾ bid after the transaction has been completed. Thus the passive buyer achieves a negative trading cost. An important point to note is that negative trading costs can only be achieved by passively managed funds if they are willing to accept the random tracking error that will occur, as their holdings will no longer exactly match their benchmark index. Small-cap passive fund managers such as Vanguard and DFA have been successful at converting the wider spreads (greater trading costs) of small-cap stocks into an advantage. Block trading strategies are not available to an individual.

Control over Taxes and Greater Tax Efficiency

Owning individual stocks does provide a greater degree of control over taxes. Mutual fund managers are generally concerned only about pretax, not after-tax, returns. For example, while a fund manager might be concerned only about pretax returns, an individual can harvest losses to offset gains he might have realized from other security sales. This can substantially improve after-tax returns. While this is true, the article fails to mention that there are now passively managed (or index) funds that are also tax managed (TM). The goal of TM funds is to achieve the greatest after-tax return. TM funds not only harvest losses, they also employ strategies such as never intentionally taking short-term gains and trading around dividend dates. An advantage that a mutual fund has over an individual is that the fund generally has a continuing inflow of new cash. This inflow creates the opportunity for greater harvesting of losses. For example, if an individual bought a stock at 20, then watched the stock rise to 30, then fall to 25, he would have no opportunity for loss harvesting. On the other hand, a mutual fund with new inflows would have bought some at 20, some at 30, and some at 25. The stock purchased at 30 would be available for loss harvesting. This is a significant advantage. In addition, a person holding maybe 20 stocks has far less opportunity to tax loss harvest than an index fund that might be holding hundreds, if not thousands, of stocks. The only advantage an individual has over a fund is that a mutual fund may only harvest losses to the extent it has gains. An individual might need to take losses in excess of gains to the extent she has gains outside of the individual stock portfolio (for example, there might be gains from the sale of real estate).

You Only Need 20 Stocks to Build a Diversified Portfolio

There are 2 major problems with this argument. First, it ignores the issue of tracking error (performing differently from the market). While it may be mathematically true that a portfolio of 20 large cap growth stocks can be expected to have the same volatility and returns as the S&P 500, it almost certainly will incur large tracking error from year to year. This could cause investors major problems in terms of keeping a disciplined approach. The second problem is that the 20-stock argument virtually ignores the benefits of diversification across asset classes. Even if you assume that with 20 large-cap U.S. stocks you can track the S&P 500, you will not have any exposure to small-caps or international stocks and almost no exposure to value stocks. For those investors believing in the benefits of global asset class diversification, a portfolio of about 8 to 10 asset classes might be needed and hundreds if not thousands of stocks. How would you decide on which ones to buy, and when to sell them?

Global Markets Are Coming Together

There is little evidence to support this statement. First, global trade today is no higher a percent of GNP than it was a century ago.[1] Second, anyone taking the time to look at actual returns can see the wide variation of returns between not only U.S. asset classes but also across the globe. The following are just some examples.

L = S&P 500; S = U.S. small (DFA 9–10); IL = Int'l large (EAFE); EM = Emerging Markets

- 1997 L +33%, S +23%, IL +2%, EM −19%
- 1998 L +29%, S −7%, IL +20%, EM −9%
- 1999 L +21%, S +30%, IL +27%, EM +72%
- 2000 (thru3/5) L −4%, S +37%, IL +2%, EM −1%

There doesn't appear to be any convergence of asset class returns.

Asset Allocation Has Increased Risk

This is "Monday morning quarterbacking" at its worst. The statement that "U.S. small-cap stocks have been a disaster, and foreign stocks haven't helped" is not only confusing well-researched and documented strategy with its short-term, recent outcome but, in my opinion, simply doesn't hold water.

First, since investing is not a science and we don't have a crystal ball, a strategy is correct before the fact, not after we get to look in the rearview mirror. Diversification is a strategy of not putting all your eggs in one basket (in this case U.S. large-cap growth stocks, as represented by the S&P 500). If investors could predict the future, they would only own the asset class that would be the best performing in the next time period and they would consistently switch asset classes each period. Since neither individual investors nor professional money managers have clear crystal balls, diversification is the common-sense strategy to reduce risk.

Second, since U.S. stocks have clearly outperformed foreign stocks over the past 10 years, non-U.S. investors have benefited from diversification (away from just owning their local stocks). The same strategy of diversification clearly worked for them. If we look back to the 1970s, the reverse would have been true. U.S. investors would have loved diversification, and foreign investors would have hated it. However, since neither had crystal balls, it was the correct strategy for both. I wonder what the author of the Bloomberg article would have advised in 1980 about diversification for U.S. investors (or Japanese investors taking the other side of the story) after watching Japanese large-caps outperform the S&P 500 by 11% per annum over the previous decade. During this period Japanese small-caps also beat U.S. small-caps (represented by the 9–10 deciles) by about 17% per annum and the S&P 500 by about 20% per annum.

Finally, the article is wrong on the facts, at least in regard to small-caps. Using the passively managed DFA 9–10 Small Company Fund as a proxy for small-cap stocks, small-cap stocks have not underperformed large-caps as measured by the S&P 500. For the period 1991 through 1994, the DFA 9–10 Small Company Fund outperformed the S&P 500 by about 10% per annum. (I wonder what the author of the article would have said about small-cap investing at that point.) Then from 1995 to 1998 the S&P 500 outperformed by about 15% per annum. The tables again turned (in unpredictable fashion) in 1999, when the DFA 9–10 fund outperformed the S&P 500 by about 9%. Then, through the first week in March 2000, the DFA 9–10 Small Company Fund outperformed by about 40%! This latest outperformance probably occurred right after the author wrote the article! The 10-year returns of the DFA 9–10 Fund were AHEAD of the S&P 500. Does that sound like a disaster? Obviously not. The author, unfortunately, was simply confusing short-term random noise with long-term historical results.

In summary, except for the excitement and the possible benefit of harvesting excess losses (to offset gains from other portfolio assets), mutual funds provide significant benefits over individual stock ownership in terms of diversification and risk reduction. If investors use passively managed TM funds to implement their portfolio strategy, mutual funds are still likely to be the superior choice for most investors.

APPENDIX E:
HOW TO ANALYZE THE HOLD OR SELL DECISION: TRAPPED BY A LOW TAX BASIS?

You are convinced that passive asset class investing is the way to invest the core, if not all, of your portfolio. Unfortunately, you are currently invested in actively managed funds. The only thing preventing you from selling these assets and investing the proceeds in a passively managed portfolio is that your current portfolio has a low tax basis, and you do not want to pay the capital gains tax. What to do? (Of course, if your funds are in a tax-advantaged account, like an IRA, this is not an issue.) The first thing you should do is check to see if you really have a tax problem. Many investors forget to add reinvested distributions (on which taxes have already been paid) into their cost basis. Once you have done so, the gain may not be as large as you thought. If you still have a big gain, I suggest that you investigate whether or not it is still advantageous to sell your actively managed funds, pay the requisite taxes, and reinvest the proceeds into a globally diversified and passively managed portfolio. The following example can be used as a guide.

Assume that you have a portfolio of actively managed funds with a current value of $200,000 and a tax basis of $150,000. If we assume a total state and federal capital gains tax of 30%, you would pay a tax of $15,000 ($50,000 x 30%), leaving you with only $185,000 to reinvest. Let us also assume that your actively managed funds are typical in that they will underperform their passive counterpart on a pretax basis by almost 2% per annum.

Now analyze the hold or switch decision. Since after-tax returns are the only ones that matter, assume that, conservatively, you lose only 1% per annum to taxes. If your fund has a high turnover rate, I would use a figure of 2% or 3%. Adding together the underperformance and the tax inefficiency, we can assume that your passive asset class portfolio will be expected to outperform your old actively managed portfolio by about 3% per annum (1% in tax efficiency and 2% in higher returns).

One can now estimate how long it will take to recoup the lost tax dollars. We take the $185,000 available for investment and multiply it by the 3% expected improvement in returns; the annual benefit is $5,500. Dividing this figure into $15,000, we arrive at a break-even point of just under 3 years. If our new $185,000 portfolio grew at a 13% rate over the next 3 years, it would increase to about $267,000. The $200,000 portfolio, growing at a 10% rate, would increase to about $266,000. Given the other benefits provided by the passive asset class strategy, including gaining control over the asset allocation decision, this decision should be easy.

Another important point to consider is that if you will be purchasing tax-managed funds, then I would suggest adding another 1% per annum in incremental value added (from the increased tax efficiency) to your hold or switch calculation.

The conclusion: you may not be as trapped as you think. I would suggest that the switch should be made at any break-even point of 7 years or less.

APPENDIX F:
VARIABLE ANNUITIES: A PRODUCT MEANT TO BE SOLD, NOT BOUGHT

Recent tax law changes, including the lowering of capital gains tax rates, should have wiped out sales of variable annuities (VAs). Unfortunately for investors, however, they are still being aggressively and successfully marketed. The reason: investors are not fully informed and they are being exploited by aggressive salesmen whose only interest is in collecting the large commissions these products offer.

A VA is a mutual fund-type account wrapped inside an insurance policy. The insurance component allows the investment earnings to be tax-deferred. Unfortunately, the tax deferral is just about the only good thing you can say about this investment product. Virtually everything else about them is not only bad, it is really bad. The negatives include:

- The generally high cost of the insurance wrapper.
- The high operating (investment account) expenses.
- The lack of passive, low cost investment choices inside the annuity wrapper.
- The lack of liquidity.
- The loss of the potential for a step-up in basis for the estate of the investor.
- Perhaps worst of all, the fact that the annuity converts low-taxed capital gains into highly taxed ordinary income.

The bottom line is that the tax deferral comes at a very high price. The 1997 Tax Act cut capital gains tax rates while leaving ordinary income tax rates high. Thus the benefit of wrapping an annuity around your equity portfolio vanished. That tax change should have stopped annuity sales cold. If that did not do the trick, the recent introduction of tax-managed mutual funds by such fund families as DFA and Vanguard should have. Tax-managed funds take one of the benefits of passive investing (tax-efficiency) to an even higher level. These new funds have basically eliminated any financial argument for purchasing a VA and using it as a vehicle for equity investing. (The one exception to this would be the asset class of real estate. Because of the requirement that Real Estate Investment Trusts have to distribute virtually all of their income, real estate is a very tax inefficient asset class. Of course, most investors don't need an annuity; they can simply hold their real estate assets inside an IRA, SEP, or tax-deferred plan.) Unfortunately for investors, because of the self-interest of sales people, there does not appear to be any slowdown in annuity sales. In fact, they continue strong. According to Michael Lane of Aegon, they exceeded $20 billion in 1999, and are likely to do so again in 2000.

Let's take a quick look at the insurance "benefit" that is touted. The insurance typically guarantees that when you die, the value of your account will be at least as great as the money you originally put in; unless you get a contract that steps up the insurance coverage over time, all you are insured for is the starting value. If the account has indeed grown, you still get only the value of the account. What is the economic value of that life insurance? It is safe to say that with the vast majority of annuities sold today, almost all the money you are assessed for "mortality and expenses" winds up in either the salesman's or the insurance company's pocket. Even if you get a periodic step-up in protection, the economic value of the insurance is negligible.

Put simply, annuities are costly to own. Expenses—portfolio management fees, plus that "mortality" charge—average in excess of 2% a year, but can range as high as 3%, or more. Surrender charges are common, starting out typically at 7% and reaching as high as 9% if you cash out in the first year and declining to 0% in the seventh year or even as long as the tenth year. Also, if you cash out before you reach 59½, you have to pay a tax penalty, except under certain narrow circumstances.

Consider the experience no-load fund giant T. Rowe Price had when it sent potential customers software to help them determine whether VAs were right for them. The program factored in the investor's age, income, tax bracket, and investment horizon—and it regularly told potential buyers that they would be better off in a plain old fund, let alone a low cost, tax efficient, passively and tax managed fund. An educated consumer, as it turned out, was not a good prospect for annuities.

There are a handful of exceptions to the high cost rule. They include Aegon (which provides access to DFA funds), Schwab, TIAA-CREF, and Vanguard. They are mostly sold to people with existing VAs through "Section 1035" *tax-free* exchanges. Existing holders of

VAs are looking to escape from their current high costs and poor investment choices. Unfortunately, the surrender charges often keep investors trapped for an extended period. The analysis to find out when and if a 1035 exchange makes sense is fairly straightforward. Your financial advisor/accountant can help you with the calculation.

If the terms of VAs are so bad, why do so many people buy them? The answer is that the tax deferral sales pitch mesmerizes them. Fortunately, the tax deferral comes much cheaper and more effectively through low cost, tax efficient mutual funds that are both passively and tax managed. A tax-managed mutual fund has another advantage over the supposedly tax-favored annuity. With mutual funds you may escape the capital gains tax altogether by either giving the fund shares to charity or leaving them in your estate (where you receive a step-up in basis upon death). No such option is available to an annuity holder. Transfer or bequeath an annuity to anyone but your spouse and you trigger recognition of the full appreciation as income.

About the only legitimate remaining use of a VA is for creditor protection. Many states, among them New York, Florida, and Texas, protect assets in VAs from creditors, to one degree or another. The laws, however, are complex. Therefore, before you purchase (or get talked into) an annuity for this specific purpose, you should consult your attorney. Doctors worried about malpractice suits, for example, might want to consider VAs. If this is the case, then you shouldn't pay a penny more than you have to in expenses.

Given that there are an estimated $1 trillion of annuities outstanding, there are lots of opportunities to both lower expenses and improve investment returns. If you are currently holding a high cost annuity, you should check out one of the low cost, no surrender charge annuities. If the applicable surrender charge period is over, or even nearly over, the decision to make the tax-free "Section 1035" exchange will be an easy one. Whatever you do, do not succumb to the sales pitch for the new "bonus" annuities. This is a new and highly aggressive tactic of the industry, to keep investors "imprisoned" in high cost product, and generate new and even larger commissions for the sales force. Annuity holders with a few years left in their surrender charge period are approached with the following "typical" story.

"I understand that you are unhappy with your current VA because of poor performance of the investment choices. I also understand that you have a 3% surrender charge left. We are going to "help" by giving you an up-front "bonus" of 3% to cover the surrender charge. It will not cost you anything to switch."

Unfortunately, the only "bonus" is to the salesperson. The new sale starts the surrender period all over again. And, with these new products the surrender period is often even longer and more expensive than on the original annuity. The surrender charge period may now be extended to as much as 10 years, and the prepayment penalty increased from 7% to as much as 9%. Given that the annuity holder will now be locked into another high cost (or even higher cost) product for a much longer time, you might ask: Where's the "bonus"? It is likely to be in the form of higher commissions to the sales force. It appears that the SEC is coming down hard on this practice. On June 5, 2000, they issued an "investor alert" and placed a brochure on its Website to help investors understand the benefits, costs, and risks of variable annuities, which combine features of mutual funds and insurance.[1]

The insurance industry has already been hit with a round of lawsuits on suitability of annuity sales and turnover. For example, since the only substantial benefit of VAs is their tax deferral feature, there is virtually no reason to hold them inside a tax deferral vehicle such as an IRA. Yet, many VAs were sold that way. Maybe the real "bonus" will be new business for the trial lawyers.

Library

The following books are highly recommended for those investors wishing to expand their knowledge of the subjects covered in this book. Gary Belsky and Thomas Gilovich, *Why Smart People Make Big Money Mistakes;* Peter Bernstein, *Capital Ideas* and *Against the Gods;* John Bogle, *Common Sense on Mutual Funds;* Charles Ellis, *Winning the Loser's Game;* Burton G. Malkiel, *A Random Walk Down Wall Street;* Jeremy Siegel, *Stocks for the Long Run;* and W. Scott Simon, *Index Mutual Funds.* I also recommend a little gem of a book called *The Coffeehouse Investor*, by Bill Schultheis.

For those investors interested in learning more about the history of financial follies, there are three excellent books. The first is Charles MacKay's *Extraordinary Popular Delusions and the Madness of Crowds.* MacKay noted: "Every age has its peculiar folly: some scheme, project, or fantasy into which it plunges, spurred on by the love of gain, the necessity of excitement or the force of imitation." His book is as relevant today as it was when it was first published almost 150 years ago. The others are *Devil Take the Hindmost*, by Edward Chancellor and *Irrational Exuberance* by Robert Shiller.

Glossary

Active management   The attempt to uncover securities the market has either under- or overvalued. It is also the attempt to time investment decisions in order to be more heavily invested when the market is rising and less so when the market is falling.

Arbitrage   The process by which investors exploit the price difference between two exactly alike securities by simultaneously buying one at a lower price and selling the other at a higher price (thereby avoiding risk). This action locks in a risk-free profit for the arbitrageur (arb) (person engaging in the arbitrage) and brings the prices back into equilibrium.

Asset allocation   The process of determining what percentage of assets should be dedicated to which specific asset classes.

Asset class   A group of assets with similar risk and reward characteristics. Cash, debt instruments, real estate, and equities are examples of asset classes. Within a general asset class, such as equities, there are more specific classes such as large and small companies and domestic and international companies.

Barra Indices   The Barra Indices divide the three major S&P indices

(400 for mid-cap, 500 for large-cap, and 600 for small-cap) into growth and value categories. The top 50% of stocks as ranked by book-to-market value are considered value stocks and the bottom 50% are considered growth stocks. This creates both value and growth indices for all three S&P indices.

Basis point One one-hundredth of 1%, or 0.0001.

Benchmark An appropriate standard against which actively managed funds can be judged. Actively managed large-cap growth funds should be judged against a large-cap growth index such as the S&P 500, while small-cap managers should be judged against a small-cap index such as the Russell 2000.

Bid-offer spread The bid is the price at which you can sell a security, and the offer is the price you must pay to buy a security. The spread is the difference between the two prices and represents the cost of a round-trip trade (purchase and sale), excluding commissions.

Book value An accounting term for the equity of a company. Equity is equal to assets less liabilities. It is often expressed in per share terms. Book value per share is equal to equity divided by the number of shares.

Book-value-to-market value (btm) The ratio of the book value per share to the market price per share, or book value divided by market capitalization.

Call An option contract that gives the holder the right, but not the obligation, to buy a security at a predetermined price on a specific date or during a specific period.

Coefficient of correlation A mathematical term describing how closely related the price movement of different securities or asset classes is. The higher the coefficient, the more prices move in the same direction and by similar amounts.

CRSP Center for Research in Security Pricing.

Data mining A technique for building predictive models of the real world by discerning patterns in masses of computer data.

Diamond: An exchange traded fund that replicates the Dow Jones Industrial Average.

Distressed stocks Stocks with high book-to-market values and/or low price-to-earnings ratios. Distressed stocks are generally considered to be value stocks.

DJIA Dow Jones Industrial Average.

EAFE Index The Europe, Australasia, and the Far East Index, similar to the S&P 500 Index in that it consists of the stocks of the large companies from the EAFE countries. The stocks within the index are weighted by market capitalization.

Efficient market A state in which trading systems fail to produce returns in excess of the market's overall rate of return because everything currently knowable about a company is already incorporated into the stock price. The next piece of available information will be random as to whether it will be better or worse than the market expects. An efficient market is also one in which the costs of trading are low.

Emerging markets The capital markets of less developed countries that are beginning to develop characteristics of developed countries, such as higher per capita income. Countries typically included in this category would be Brazil, Mexico, Thailand, and Korea.

EMT Efficient markets theory. See **efficient market**.

ETF Exchange traded funds, for all practical purposes, these act like open-ended, no-load mutual funds. Like mutual funds, they can be created to represent virtually any index or asset class. However, they are not actually mutual funds. Instead, these new vehicles represent a cross between an exchange-listed stock and an open-ended, no-load mutual fund. Like stocks (but unlike mutual funds) they trade throughout the day.

Ex-ante Before the fact.

Expense ratio The operating expenses of a fund expressed as a percentage of total assets. These expenses must be subtracted from the investment performance of a fund in order to determine the net return to shareholders.

Ex-post After the fact.

5%/25% rule   Numerical formula used to determine the need to re-balance a portfolio.

Fundamental security analysis   The attempt to uncover mispriced securities by focusing on predicting future earnings.

Futures contract   An agreement to purchase or sell a specific collection of securities or a physical commodity at a specified price and time in the future. For example, an S&P 500 futures contract represents ownership interest in the S&P 500 Index, at a specified price for delivery on a specific date on a particular exchange.

Growth stock   A stock trading, relative to the overall market, at a high price-to-earnings ratio (or at a relatively low book-to-market ratio) because the market anticipates, relative to the overall market, rapid earnings growth.

Hedge fund   A fund that generally has the ability to invest in a wide variety of asset classes. These funds also often use leverage in an attempt to increase returns.

I Bond   A bond that provides both a fixed rate of return and an inflation protection component. The principal value of the bond increases by the total of the fixed rate and the inflation component. The income is deferred for tax purposes until funds are withdrawn from the account holding the bond.

Index fund   A passively managed fund that seeks to replicate the performance of a particular index (such as the Wilshire 5000, the S&P 500, or the Russell 2000) by buying all the securities in that index, in direct proportion to their weight, by market capitalization, within that index, and holding them.

Institutional fund   A mutual fund that is not available to individual investors. Typical clients are pension and profit-sharing plans and endowment funds.

Institutional-style fund   A mutual fund that is available to individual investors, under certain conditions, such as through registered investment advisors. These advisors require their clients to commit to the same type of disciplined, long-term, buy-and-hold strategy that is typical of institutional investors.

Investment pandering Advice on market or securities values that is designed to titillate, stimulate, and excite you into action but has no basis in reality.

Investment pornography Extreme examples of investment pandering.

Leverage The use of debt to increase the amount of assets that can be acquired, for example, to buy stock. Leverage increases the riskiness of a portfolio.

Market capitalization The market price per share times the number of shares.

Modern portfolio theory A body of academic work founded on the following concepts. First, markets are too efficient to allow returns in excess of the market's overall rate of return to be achieved through trading systems. Active management is therefore counterproductive. Second, asset classes can be expected to achieve, over sustained periods, returns that are commensurate with their level of risk. Riskier asset classes, such as small companies and value companies, will produce higher returns as compensation for their higher risk. Third, diversification across asset classes can increase returns and reduce risk. For any given level of risk, a portfolio can be constructed that will produce the highest expected return. Finally, there is no right portfolio for every investor. Each investor must choose an asset allocation that results in a portfolio with an acceptable level of risk.

Mortgage-backed security (MBS) A financial instrument representing an interest in assets that are mortgage related (either commercial or residential).

MPT Modern portfolio theory.

NASDQ or NASDAQ The National Association of Securities (Automated) Quotations. An exchange on which securities are traded, frequently called the "over-the-counter market."

NAV Net asset value.

No-load A mutual fund that does not impose any charge for purchases or sales.

Nominal Returns   Returns that have not been adjusted for the negative impact of inflation.

NYSE   New York Stock Exchange.

Out of sample   Data from a study covering different time periods or different geographic regions from the original study.

P/E ratio   The ratio of stock price to earnings. Stocks with high P/E ratios are considered growth stocks; stocks with low P/E ratios are considered value stocks.

Passive asset class funds   Funds that buy and hold all securities within a particular asset class. The weighting of each security within the fund is equal to its weighting, by market capitalization, within the asset class.

Passive management   A buy-and-hold investment strategy, specifically contrary to active management. Typically, a passively managed portfolio purchases all securities that fit a desired asset class definition. The amount of each security purchased is in proportion to its capitalization relative to the total capitalization of all securities within the asset class. Each stock is then held until it no longer fits the definition of that asset class. For example, a small company can grow into a large company and would no longer fit within the small company asset class.

Prudent Investor Rule   A doctrine imbedded within the American legal code stating that a person responsible for the management of someone else's assets must manage those assets in a manner appropriate to the financial circumstance and tolerance for risk of the investor.

Put   An option contract that gives the holder the right, but not the obligation, to sell a security at a predetermined price on a specific date or during a specific period.

Qubes (QQQ)   An exchange traded fund that tracks the NASDAQ 100, the 100 largest capitalization stocks on that exchange.

Real returns   Returns that reflect purchasing power as they are adjusted for the negative impact of inflation.

Rebalancing   The process of restoring a portfolio to its original asset allocations. Rebalancing can be accomplished either through adding newly investable funds or by selling portions of the best performing asset classes and using the proceeds to purchase additional amounts of the underperforming asset classes.

Registered Investment Advisor A designation representing that a financial consultant is registered with the appropriate state regulators and has passed the required exams.

REIT Real Estate Investment Trust, a trust available to investors through the purchase of shares in it.

Russell 2000 The smallest 2,000 of the largest 3,000 stocks within the Russell index. Generally used as a benchmark for small-cap stocks.

Retail funds Mutual funds that are sold to the general public.

S&P 400 Index A market-cap weighted index of 400 mid-cap stocks.

S&P 500 Index A market-cap weighted index of 500 of the largest U.S. stocks designed to cover a broad and representative sampling of industries.

S&P 600 Index A market-cap weighted index of 600 small-cap stocks.

Short Borrowing a security for the purpose of immediately selling it. This is done with the expectation that the investor will be able to buy the security back at a later date, at a lower price.

Small companies, or small-cap stocks Companies that fall within the bottom 20% of all companies when ranked by market capitalization.

Spiders Exchange traded funds that replicate the various Standard and Poors indices.

Standard deviation A measure of volatility, or risk. For example, given a portfolio with a 12% annualized return and an 11% standard deviation, an investor can expect that in 13 out of 20 annual periods (about two-thirds of the time) the return on that portfolio will fall within one standard deviation, or between 1% (12% − 11%) and 23% (12% + 11%). The remaining one-third of the time an investor should expect that the annual return will fall outside the 1%–23% range. Two standard deviations (11% × 2) would account for 95% (19 out of 20) periods. The range of expected returns would be between − 10% (12% − 22%) and 34% (12% + 22%). The greater the standard deviation, the greater the volatility of a portfolio. Standard deviation can be measured for varying time periods. For example, you can have a monthly standard deviation or an annualized standard deviation measuring the volatility for a given time frame.

Style drift   The moving away from the original asset allocation of a portfolio, either by the purchasing of securities outside the particular asset class a fund represents or by significant differences in performance of the various asset classes within a portfolio.

TIPS   Treasury Inflation Protected Security: A bond that receives a fixed stated rate of return, but also increases its principal by the changes in the Consumer Price Index. Its fixed interest payment is calculated on the inflated principal, which is eventually repaid at maturity.

Turnover   The trading activity of a fund as it sells securities from a portfolio and replaces them with new ones. For example, assume that a fund began the year with a portfolio of $100 million in various securities. If the fund sold $50 million of the original securities and replaced them with $50 million of new securities, it would have a turnover rate of 50%.

Value stocks   Companies that have relatively low price-to-earnings ratios or relatively high book-to-market ratios. These are considered the opposite of growth stocks.

WEBS   Word Equity Benchmark Securities are exchange traded funds that track various foreign country indices such as the U.K., German, and French equivalents of the S&P 500 Index.

Acknowledgments

No book is ever the work of one individual. This book is no exception. I thank my partners at Buckingham Asset Management and BAM Advisor Services, Paul Forman, Steve Funk, Ed Goldberg, Joe Hempen, Mont Levy, Irv Rothenberg, Bert Schweizer, and Stuart Zimmerman, for their support and encouragement. Joe Hempen made major contributions to the material covering arbitrage and ETFs. A coworker, Bob Gellman, also made noteworthy contributions.

A very special note of thanks to Wendy Cook, who put in very long hours editing and making valuable suggestions on the text. Wendy also enlisted the aid of her mother, Sondra Ettlinger. Sondra provided valuable editing and structuring advice. Any errors are certainly mine. Finally, I thank the rest of the staff at BAM and BAM Advisor Services for their support and encouragement.

A special note of thanks to my good friend Larry Goldfarb, who not only provided editorial assistance but also contributed greatly to the organization and structure of both this and my first book. I would be remiss if I did not note the contributions of my agent, Sam Fleishman. I cannot imagine a better relationship between author and agent.

Acknowledgments

I also thank the people at DFA, especially Weston Wellington. I have learned much from DFA and Wes. He seems to always be able to explain difficult concepts in an easy and often humorous way.

I would also be remiss if I did not thank the many friends I have made on the Websites indexfunds.com and Vanguard Diehards. I have learned much from them through our long discussions. While it is impossible to list them all, I would like to especially thank Bill Bernstein (whose Website *www.efficient frontier.com* is an absolute must), Jeff Bolden, Steve Dunn, Mel Lindaner, Taylor Larimore, Darin Solk, and Jeff Troutner.

Finally, I thank my family. Jodi, Jennifer, and Jacquelyn, thanks for allowing me to monopolize our computer for over one year. I especially thank the love of my life, my wife, Mona. She showed tremendous patience in reading and rereading numerous drafts. I also thank her for her tremendous support and understanding for the lost weekends and the many nights I sat at the computer well into the early morning hours. She has always provided whatever support was needed, and then some. I also thank my mother for always believing in me, for always supporting me, and for being the best mother anyone could ask for.

Notes

Introduction

1. Mark M. Carhart, "On Persistence in Mutual Fund Performance," doctoral dissertation, University of Chicago, December 1994.
2. *Wall Street Journal*, January 15, 1998.
3. *Barron's* On-Line, June 2, 1997.
4. Peter Bernstein, *Against the Gods*.
5. *Business Week*, July 14, 1997.

Chapter 1

1. *Fortune*, March 15, 1999.
2. *Fortune*, October 11, 1999.
3. *Wall Street Journal*, April 29, 1997.
4. John C. Bogle, senior chairman, Vanguard Group, keynote speech at Intelligent Investor Conference, Philadelphia, October 3, 1998.
5. *Registered Investment Advisor*, September 22, 1997.
6. *Wall Street Journal*, December 22, 1998.
7. *Fortune*, October 11, 1999.
8. *InvestmentNews*, March 29, 1999.
9. *New York Times*, April 4, 1999.

10. *Investment Advisor*, September 1994.
11. *St. Louis Post-Dispatch*, December 12, 1997.
12. *Journal of Finance*, June 1995.
13. *New York Times*, April 4, 1999.
14. *San Francisco Chronicle*, November 24, 1996.
15. *Financial Analysts Journal*, July/August 1996.
16. *Financial Planning*, April 1998.
17. Gary Belsky and Thomas Gilovich, *Why Smart People Make Big Money Mistakes*.
18. AP Online, April 6, 1998.
19. *DFA Advisor Research Letter*, July 1998.

Chapter 2

1. Andrew Lo and A. Craig MacKinlay, *A Non-Random Walk down Wall Street*.
2. *Journal of Applied Economics*, Spring 1996.
3. *Business Week*, May 10, 1999.
4. *Wall Street Journal*, April 27, 1998.
5. *Journal of Applied Economics*, Spring 1996.
6. *Financial Management*, Spring 1996.
7. The Transaction-by-Transaction of Interest Rate and Equity Index Futures to Macroeconomic Announcements, *Journal of Derivatives*, Winter 1998.
8. *Journal of Portfolio Management*, Fall 1974.
9. *New York Times*, June 27, 1999.
10. Ibid.
11. Ibid.
12. "Efficient Markets: Fund Managers as Fruit Flies," *Investors Chronicle*, March 22, 1996.
13. Datastream.
14. "Untangling Emerging Markets," *N.Y. Times*, January 24, 1999.
15. *Wall Street Journal*, January 8, 1999.
16. Richard Evans, *The Index Fund Solution*.
17. *N.Y. Times*, January 24, 1999.
18. www.gsm.ucdavis.edu/~bmbarber/working.html
19. Bridge (March 2000).
20. Ibid.
21. D. Kiem and A. Madhaven 1998, The Cost of Institutional Equity Trades, *Financial Analysts Journal*, 54, 50–69.
22. *Bloomberg Personal Finance*, April 2000.

23. Morningstar.
24. Ibid.
25. Charles Ellis, *Winning the Loser's Game.*
26. *St. Louis Post-Dispatch*, August 12, 1997.
27. *NY Times*, July 11, 1999.
28. John Bogle, *Common Sense on Mutual Funds*, p. 286.
29. *New York Times*, October 10, 1999.
30. Ibid.
31. Ibid.
32. Mark M. Carhart, *"On Persistence in Mutual Fund Performance,"* doctoral dissertation, University of Chicago, December 1994.
33. Scott West & Mitch Anthony, *Storyselling for Financial Advisors.*
34. Blake, Elton, and Gruber, *Journal of Business* 66: 1993.
35. "Just How Bad Are Economists at Predicting Interest Rates?" *Journal of Investing*, Summer 1997.
36. "Yo: Bond Index Funds Wield Better Yields," *InvestmentNews*, January 25, 1999.
37. John Bogle, *Bogle on Mutual Funds.*
38. *Journal of Investing*, Winter 1999.
39. *The Financial Review*, May 1998.
40. *InvestmentNews*, January 25, 1999.

Chapter 3

1. *Wall Street Journal*, March 16, 1999.
2. *Wall Street Journal*, August 24, 1995.
3. *Business Week*, April 1, 1996.
4. W. Scott Simon, *Index Mutual Funds.*
5. Ibid.
6. *Wall Street Journal*, October 4, 1999.
7. *Business Week*, February 22, 1999.
8. *Wall Street Journal*, October 4, 1999.
9. *St. Louis Post-Dispatch*, April 6, 2000.
10. *Mutual Funds Café Website (www.mcafe.com)*, "Index Fund Initiative Paradox," April 5, 1999.
11. *Wall Street Journal*, December 8, 1997.
12. *Advisor's Network*, April 1997.
13. *Pension and Investments*, September 6, 1999.
14. *Journal of Finance*, March 1997.
15. *Wall Street Journal*, April 4, 1997.
16. *Dow Jones Asset Management*, January/February 1998.

17. Burton G. Malkiel, *A Random Walk down Wall Street.*
18. John Bogle, *Bogle on Mutual Funds.*
19. *Wall Street Journal*, May 10, 1999.
20. *Ranking Mutual Funds on an After-Tax Basis*, Stanford University Center for Economic Policy Research Discussion Paper 344.
21. Mark M. Carhart, "On Persistence in Mutual Fund Performance," doctoral dissertation. University of Chicago, December 1994.
22. Richard E. Evans and Burton G. Malkiel, *The Index Fund Solution*
23. *Wall Street Journal*, October 5, 1998.
24. *Business Week*, February 22, 1999.
25. *Wall Street Journal*, March 11, 1998.

Chapter 4

1. Peter Bernstein, *Against the Gods.*
2. Burton G. Malkiel, *A Random Walk down Wall Street.*
3. *Money*, February 1999.
4. *Business Week*, December 28, 1998.
5. *Business Week*, January 18, 1999.
6. Richard Evans, *The Index Fund Solution.*
7. John Bogle, *Common Sense on Mutual Funds.*
8. *Wall Street Journal*, May 16, 1997.
9. *Business Week*, May 25, 1998.
10. *Journal of Finance*, April 2000.
11. *Wall Street Journal*, October 20, 1998.
12. *Bloomberg Wealth Manager*, May/June 1999.
13. *St. Louis Post-Dispatch*, September 24, 1999.
14. *Journal of Finance*, April 2000.
15. Peter Lynch, *One Up on Wall Street.*
16. *Wall Street Journal*, December 31, 1996.
17. *InvestmentNews*, December 1, 1997.
18. *Forbes*, January 11, 1999.
19. *Journal of Finance*, "The Performance of Hedge Funds: Risk, Return and Incentives," June 1999.
20. *Business Week*, February 21, 2000.
21. *Financial Analysts Journal*, January/February 1997.
22. *Business Week*, May 26, 1997.
23. *Business Week*, June 1, 1998.
24. *Business Week*, May 31, 1999.
25. *St. Louis Post-Dispatch*, March 18, 1998.
26. *Wall Street Journal*, November 4, 1998.

27. Institutional Investor, April 1998. This section is based on an article in the St. Louis Post-Dispatch, November 3, 1998.
28. David G. Booth, January 1997, ''The Value Added of Active Management: International Country Funds.''

Chapter 5

1. Burton Malkiel, *A Random Walk down Wall Street*.
2. *Worth*, September 1995.
3. John Merrill, *Beyond Stocks*.
4. Tweedy Browne, *Semi-Annual Investment Manager's Report*, September 30, 1998.
5. Charles Ellis, *The Investor's Anthology*.
6. John Bogle, *Common Sense on Mutual Funds*.
7. John Merrill, *Beyond Stocks*.
8. *DFA Newsletter*, November 18. 1997.
9. *Business Week*, June 16, 1997.
10. National Bureau of Economic Research, Working Paper 4890, October 1994.
11. W. Scott Simon, *Index Mutual Funds*.
12. Andrew Metrick, ''Performance Evaluation with Transactional Data: The Stock Selection of Investment Newsletters,'' August 1998 (*Journal of Finance* Website).
13. *American Association of Individual Investors Journal*, September 1996.
14. *St. Louis Post-Dispatch*, October 4, 1997.
15. *Institutional Investor*, March 1998.
16. John Merrill, *Beyond Stocks*.
17. *St. Louis Post-Dispatch*, July 11, 1997.
18. Charles Ellis, *Winning the Loser's Game*.
19. Gary Smith, *How I Trade For A Living*.
20. *New York Times*, March 9, 1997
21. Charles Ellis, *Investment Policy*
22. Ibid.

Chapter 6

1. William Sharpe, *Portfolio Theory & Capital Markets*
2. Federal Reserve Bank of Chicago, *Economic Perspectives*, Third Quarter 1999, vol. 23, p. 36–78.
3. *Journal of Applied Corporate Finance*, Winter 2000

Notes

4. Annual Fama and French data as published by Dimensional Fund Advisors, Inc.

5. John Chisolm, "Quantitative Applications for Research Analysts," *Investing Worldwide II*, Association for Investment Management and Research, 1991.

6. *What Has Worked in Investing*, Tweedy Browne.

7. Angel Berges, John M.J. McConnell, and Gary G. Scharlbaum, "Turn-of-the-Year in Canada, *Journal of Finance*, March 1984.

8. Philip Brown, Donald B. Kiem, Allan W. Kleiden, and Terry A. Marsh, "Stock Return Seasonalities and Tax-Loss Selling Hypothesis," *Journal of Financial Economics*, 1983.

9. T. Nakamura and N. Terada, *The Size Effect and Seasonality in Japanese Stock Returns*, Nomura Research Institute, 1984.

10. "Cross-section of Expected Stock Returns," *Journal of Finance*, June 1992.

11. *Characteristics, Covariances and Average Returns: 1929–1997*, Social Science Research Network, working paper series, October 15, 1998.

12. "Value versus Growth. The International Evidence," *Journal of Finance*, December 1998.

13. *Financial Planning*, October 1997.

14. Ibid.

15. John Chisholm, Quantitative Applications for Research Analysts, *Investing Worldwide II, Association for Investment Management and Research 1991*.

16. Local Return Factors and Turnover in Emerging Stock Markets, *Journal of Finance*, August 1999.

17. Josef Lakonishok, Robert Vishny, and Andrei Shleifer, *Contrarian Investment, Extrapolation, and Risk*, National Bureau of Economic Research, working paper 4360, May 1993.

18. Baruch Lev and Theodore Sougiannis, "Penetrating the Book-to-Market Black Box," *Journal of Business Finance and Accounting*, April/May 1999.

19. *Barron's*, April 14, 1997.

20. *Forbes*, June 17, 1996.

21. *Fortune*, April 14, 1997.

22. Heartland Advisors, *Investor Letter*, Winter 1996.

23. Ibid.

24. Eugene F. Fama and Kenneth R. French, "Cross-section of Expected Stock Returns," *Journal of Finance*, June 1992.

25. *St. Louis Post-Dispatch*, April 14, 2000.

26. *St. Louis Dispatch*, March 2, 1998.

Chapter 7

1. Peter Bernstein, *Against the Gods.*
2. Jeremy Siegel, *Stocks for the Long Run.*
3. Peter Bernstein, *Against the Gods.*
4. Dimensional Fund Advisors, June 1999 client letter.
5. *Morningstar FundInvestor*, October 1998.
6. John Merrill, *Outperforming the Market.*
7. *Wall Street Journal*, December 18, 1997
8. As July 7, 2000 small value stocks, as represented by the DFA small value fund, had once again outperformed the S & P 500 Index by 5.9% to -0.4%.
9. *Fortune*, August 16, 1999.
10. Ibid.
11. Ibid.
12. David Plecha, *Fixed Income Investing*, DFA, working paper, March 1997.
13. *Business Week*, June 22, 1998.

Chapter 8

1. Robert Jeffrey and Robert Arnott, "Is Your Alpha Big Enough to Cover Its Taxes," *Journal of Portfolio Management*, Spring 1993.
2. *Ranking Mutual Funds on an After-Tax Basis*, Stanford University Center for Economic Policy Research Discussion Paper 344.
3. Richard Evans, *The Index Fund Solution.*
4. James Garland, "The Tax Attraction of Tax-Managed Index Funds," *Journal of Investing*, Spring 1997.
5. "Is Your Alpha Big Enough to Cover Your Taxes?" *Journal of Portfolio Management*, Spring 1993.
6. *Wall Street Journal*, June 10, 1997.
7. Schwab Center for Investment Research, *"How Tax Efficient Are Tax-Managed Funds?"* Volume I, Issue II, October 1998.
8. State Street Research, *Advisor News*, Fall 1998.
9. KPMG, *Tax-Managed Mutual Funds and the Taxable Investor.*
10. John Bogle, *Common Sense on Mutual Funds*. This section is based on an article in the *New York Times*, December 28, 1997.
11. *Wall Street Journal*, February 20, 1998, and October 2, 1998; www.mutualfundsinteractive.com.
12. *Barron's* April 6, 1998.
13. *Wall Street Journal*, April 24, 1998.

Chapter 9

1. *Wall Street Journal*, April 6, 1998.
2. *New York Times*, March 30, 1997.
3. *Institutional Investor*, January 1997.
4. *InvestmentNews*, November 17, 1997.
5. *AAII Journal*, July 1999.
6. Gary Belsky and Thomas Gilovich, Why Smart People Make Big Money Mistakes.
7. W. Scott Simon, *Index Mutual Funds*.
8. Dalbar
9. W. Scott Bauman, C. Mitchell Conover, and Robert E. Miller, "Investor Overreaction in International Stock Markets," *Journal of Portfolio Management*, Summer 1999.
10. Chancellor, *Devil Take the Hindmost*, p. 18.
11. Murphy, *Richard Cantillon*, p. 171.
12. Chancellor, *Devil Take the Hindmost*, p. 69.
13. Ibid., p. 170.
14. Ibid., p. 168.
15. Medberry, *Men and Mysteries*, p. 205.
16. Chancellor, *Devil Take the Hindmost*, p. 131.
17. *The Economist*, May 9, 1998, p. 5.
18. Mission Ventures, 2000 Annual Meeting.
19. *Wall Street Journal*, March 14, 2000. This section is based on an article in the *Wall Street Journal*, January 18, 2000.

Chapter 10

1. David Booth and Eugene F. Fama, "Diversification Returns and Asset Contributions," *Financial Analysts Journal*, May/June 1992.
2. Blake, Elton, and Gruber, *Journal of Business* 66: 193.
3. John Bogle, *Bogle on Mutual Funds*.
4. Domain, Maness, and Reichentstein, *Journal of Portfolio Management*, Spring 1998.
5. *Bloomberg Personal Finance*, April 2000.
6. Ibid.
7. Nick Murray, *Investment Advisor* magazine, April 1996.
8. Nick Murray, *The Craft of Advice*.
9. Ragnar D. Naess, *Readings in Financial Analysis and Investment Management*.
10. Phillip L. Cooley, Carl M. Hubbard, and Daniel T. Walz, using data

from Ibbotson Associates, ''Retirement Savings: Choosing a Withdrawal Rate that Is Substantial,'' AAII.com.

Summary

1. Scott West & Mitch Anthony, *Storyselling for Financial Advisors.*

Appendix C

1. *Journal of Finance*, March 1995.
2. *Wall Street Journal*, February 24, 1999.
3. *Fortune*, November 23, 1998.
4. *Wall Street Journal*, March 30, 1999.
5. *Journal of Finance*, June 1999.
6. *Wall Street Journal*, February 24, 1999.
7. *Business Week*, February 7, 2000.
8. *St. Louis Post-Dispatch*, April 6, 2000.

Appendix D

1. Thomas Friedman, *The Lexus and the Olive Tree: Understanding Globalization.*

Appendix F

1. June 6, 2000, www.cbsmarketwatch.com.